BUSHELL ON THE RAMPAGE

The Autobiography of Garry Bushell

BUSHELL ON THE RAMPAGE

The Autobiography of Garry Bushell

GARRY BUSHELL

FOREWORD BY BILLY MURRAY

APEX PUBLISHING LTD

First published in 2010, updated and reprinted in 2010 in hardback by
Apex Publishing Ltd
PO Box 7086, Clacton on Sea, Essex, CO15 5WN

www.apexpublishing.co.uk

Copyright © 2010 by Garry Bushell
The author has asserted his moral rights

**British Library Cataloguing-in-Publication Data
A catalogue record for this book
is available from the British Library**

**ISBN 1-906358-80-X
978-1-906358-80-8**

Typeset in 10.5pt Baskerville Win95BT

Production Manager: Chris Cowlin

Cover Design: Siobhan Smith
Front and back cover photographs: Kay Young

Printed and bound by
MPG Books Group in the UK

Publishers Note:
The views and opinions expressed in this publication are those of the author and are not necessarily those of Apex Publishing Ltd

Copyright:
Every attempt has been made to contact the relevant copyright holders, Apex Publishing Ltd would be grateful if the appropriate people contact us on: 01255 428500 or mail@apexpublishing.co.uk

This book is dedicated to the Wager family and Tania.

Contents

Acknowledgements

The author would like to thank Garry Johnson, Lol Pryor, Tom McCourt, Terry Bushell, Clyde Ward and Wilf Pine for their help in jogging his memory.

Foreword

I first met Garry Bushell at one of ITV's An Audience With shows nearly twenty years ago. I have met him since at boxing bouts, football matches, rock gigs and film sets. Wherever the place, be it a West End nightclub or the West Ham Working Man's Club, he has never been any different. He doesn't put on airs and graces. He doesn't toady to people. He is always down to earth and on the ball.

Garry is not like most journalists. To start with he's as straight as a dye. He doesn't set out to turn people over and when he interviews you, it's about you and not about him. I trust him, and I am not alone. Garry has a good name amongst many great actors, comedians and rock stars because they appreciate his honesty, intelligence and humour. When a performance is bad, he will rightly pan it but when it's good he sings its praises from the roof-tops.

Most television critics you suspect don't watch much telly. Many are happy to go for obvious jokes and weak puns. They slag off everything and everyone, and then they hide behind their column, rarely facing the people whose reputations they have besmirched. Garry Bushell is different. He cares about TV, as he cares about music and the British film industry. He has a passion for it. Garry was banging a drum for variety and talent shows long before Simon Cowell proved that television executives were wrong to ignore him. He does it with great humour too. No lesser authority than Bob Monkhouse said of Garry: "His gags are great and his writing style is so rich with observation, knowledge and wit that I marvel at how he can maintain the standard."

The Sun has never been the same since he left it.

If you ever watched Garry's late night Bushell On The Box show on

ITV you will have been amazed by the quality of guests he had – me, Bob, Barbara Windsor, Bradley Walsh, Ray Winstone, Paul O'Grady, William Roache, Dale Winton, Bobby Davro, Jim Davidson, Vic & Bob, Brian Conley, Penn & Teller. He had better bookings than Des O'Connor. You will be even more amazed to learn that we all did it for free.

Not only stars either. The likes of Roy 'Pretty Boy' Shaw and Lenny McLean were also made welcome on the Bushell sofa, along with Page 3 girls, Gladiators, footballers and the country's funniest comedians.

He had bands playing in his back garden – one week it would be the Drifters, the next punk rockers the Blood. Chas & Dave performed at his St George's Day party and Iron Maiden left messages on the show's answer machine.

That he still has close friends today that he made on Sounds thirty-odd years ago gives you an insight into the affection in which the man is held by the people he wrote about be they Mods, punks and hooligans or international rock stars.

There's an expression proper East Londoners have for people like Garry Bushell: he's one of yer own. There is no higher praise.

Best wishes
Billy Murray

Introduction

Few jobs pay you to hang out with living legends. I look back now at the time I spent on the road with Ozzy Osbourne, Debbie Harry, Paul Weller, Phil Lynott, Iron Maiden and Joe Strummer and realise I've had a charmed life. I just wish I could remember more of it. The prime reason for writing this book now is to get it all down on paper before the moths devour what little is left of my brain cells.

Quite how I went from managing the Cockney Rejects to lunching with the Prime Minister baffles me, but I know whose company I preferred, and it wasn't Mr Blair's.

The people who were my friends thirty years ago are still my friends today. I was just lucky also to have been befriended by comedy gods such as Benny Hill, Bob Monkhouse and Jimmy Jones, and led hopelessly astray by rock idol Pete Way.

I was never going to be liked by the Establishments – either the fading traditional one or the new liberal elite. I'm not keen on slippery politicians, snobs, or people who try to tell us what to think, feel and say. I distrust our government and loathe its attachment to the EU, bureaucracy and the cult of surveillance. Although I've stood for Parliament twice, I'm not a politician; more an awkward bugger. My message is a simple one: question everything, treat people how you'd like to be treated and run your own life. Live free; die free.

Inevitably I've changed over the years, but I think I've stayed true to the things that matter most: family, friends and flag; class and kin.

Making fortunes was never my motivation. I've never had a big career plan. I did what felt right and things seemed to fall into place. Even if that meant being strapped up by Freddie Starr or stitched up by Noel Edmonds. I don't claim to be a role model or a saint. I've done stupid things and made mistakes – haven't we all? But I hope that my stories will amuse you as much as remembering them has tickled me. If I were reviewing it, I'd say: "Garry's autobiography is painfully honest; unlike his singing, which is honestly painful."

Best wishes
Garry Bushell, May 2010

Chapter One
Early Doors

The kid sits quietly, slumped at a desk towards the back of the classroom, lost in his own thoughts.

The teacher, equally bored, has a way of looking both jaded and menacing at the same time. He peers out at his class of thirteen-year-olds and relishes the nervous fear on their faces. Impatiently, he drums a textbook with his fingers. Every eye is on him; they know what will happen next.

Pushing back his heavy black-framed glasses, the teacher points a bony finger at the boy.

"You!" he says, in a drawl that manages to sound both superior and disappointed. "Stand up and read from this." He waves the textbook at him.

The shy, slightly podgy child rises self-consciously, opens his own book and begins.

The teacher's face settles into a now familiar sneer. He interrupts the boy almost immediately.

"You're a little bit *fink* and *fort* it, aren't you, boy?" he says. "Or should I say, *ain't you?*" He pronounces the last two words as one: "ainchoo".

The class laughs. The teacher, Stanley Wolfson, goes on:

"You'd better get yourself a broom, lad. You'll need it to sweep up all those H's you've dropped on my lovely clean floor."

The boy reddens.

"We'll be calling you *Eliza* until you sort out that accent of yours. Come on, *Eliza*, repeat after me, 'In *'Artford*, *'Ereford* and *'Ampshire 'urricanes*

1

'*ardly ever 'appen.*"

The boy feels tears welling up inside and digs his right thumbnail into his index finger to hold his emotions in check. A friend, Peter Lunn, starts to speak. He thinks by asking Wolfson a question he'll distract him and spare his classmate from further public humiliation. There's one small problem: Lunn's voice is breaking.

Wolfson silences him with one quick, cruel sentence:

"Stop squeaking, Lunn."

Amused by his own dazzling wit, the teacher turns back to his original target and snaps, "Sit down, *Eliza*. Try again when you've mastered the English language."

The boy sinks into his seat and stares at his textbook until the colour leaves his face. He is hurt, confused and more than a little angry.

I know exactly how the kid was feeling, because that quiet child was me.

* * *

Garry Bushell – quiet? Shy? Sensitive? Are we talking about the same person?

Well, it was a while ago. I went to a school where anyone with a working-class accent was mocked for the way they spoke. Like any good grammar school, Colfe's was intrinsically conservative. The teachers were intelligent but for the most part sarcastic and cold. A broad streak of sadism ran through the establishment. Pupils were routinely brutalised and the values that the school tried to instil in us were thoroughly middle class. It was like being educated by the *Daily Mail*.

Like all the inmates, I was habitually abused both physically and mentally for minor misdemeanours; and I was one of the lucky ones. A boy in the year above me was suspended out of a first-floor window by his ankles. He couldn't complain to the Deputy Headmaster about it because it *was* the Deputy Head who did it. Mr Dacombe was his name. He was a strange man, slightly stooped and largely detestable. He wore a black cape and a permanent scowl. In his lighter moods, Dacombe liked to tie a tight knot in two boys' school ties. It made it easier to bang their heads together. We used to joke that he would have been drummed out of the Gestapo for sadism.

I came across quite a few people who were violent and emotionally disturbed while I was at Colfe's Grammar School. Largely, they were on the staff. Our Maths teacher, Dan Seary, spent most of his time in class during our 'O' level year typing out his column for a speedway magazine. His favourite trick was to hit you round the head with an eight-foot window pole; a welcome distraction from the pointless monotony of logarithms. Most fearsome of all was a Welsh geography teacher called Davies. He favoured the 'face-warmer' - a hard, open-handed slap. After dishing out punishment, Davies would frequently tell us, "I never repeat myself, I never repeat myself," and, apparently unaware of the irony, he would slap you again if you smiled.

The face-warmers stung, but the verbal bullying hurt more. Those of us with South London accents were picked out and ridiculed mercilessly. The 'Eliza Doolittle' scene wasn't an isolated incident. Every dropped 'h', every glottal stop, would be pounced on. In my first year at the school, my English teacher, Nicholson, asked me to stand up and spell the word 'chimney'.

I confidently rose and recited the letters: "c-h-i-m-l-e-y."

"That's the way *you* say it," thundered Nicholson, known as Old Nick because of his bald head and the satanic red glow of his cheeks. "And you say it like that because you come from a family of idiots!"

Fists clenched in impotent rage, I sank down into my chair. Spelling the word incorrectly was embarrassing; his public attack on my family was unforgivable. Although, looking back, the encounter was not without humour. Old Nick was Scottish, with an accent as thick as Highland

GARRY BUSHELL

bracken. Most of us found him largely incomprehensible. He attacked my diction when for the best part of his lessons he could have been speaking Martian. A couple of years later, Nicholson baffled us for weeks with news of what our next course book would be. It sounded like warning noises made by an irate Rottweiler. Confused, we would ask him repeatedly what the book was going to be. "Rrrrdrkkkkrrrrrndmmnn," Nick would growl. What? All of us were thrown. It was both a surprise and a relief when he finally distributed *The Adventures of Roderick Random* by Tobias Smollett. It was uttrrrrshhtttt.

What made my teachers try so zealously to eradicate our natural accents? I suppose the idea was to make us a better fit in the middle-class professions we were supposedly destined for; to sever our roots and make us look down our noses at our parents and grandparents with their normal jobs, small dreams and 'hideously common' voices.

It certainly made me think in terms of 'Us' and 'Them'. 'Us' were the close, loving family I adored. 'Them' were the sneering, psychotic snobs who ran the school.

I genuinely believe that every teacher we had at Colfe's was at best eccentric and at worst raving mad.

The strangest of all was the chemistry teacher, Mr Hussein, affectionately known as Abdul. He seemed to be permanently afflicted with dysentery and could never finish a lesson without running off to the bog. When his hands weren't clutching his backside, Abdul would wave his arms constantly as he spoke. On one occasion he was lecturing us about the danger of getting your arm too close to a lit Bunsen burner while waving his own arm right over the top of a blazing one. The sleeve of his lab coat caught alight. Our hands all shot up to speak.

"Sir! Sir!" we called.

"Why are all these hands up?" he asked in exasperation. "Are you at a bus stop? You, Bushell, speak boy."

"Your arm, Sir," I said. "It's on fire."

4

Abdul looked at me, looked at his coat, did a perfect double take and ran out of the room screaming.

Elsewhere there was Phil 'Rubber Nose' Edwards, a geography teacher who evacuated his nose with alarming alacrity; an American physics teacher who amusingly berated us for 'master baiting'; and the Latin teacher, Mr Wilkinson, who held his head at a 45-degree angle and said "all the while" all the while. At one stage we kept a log of the number of times he repeated the phrase during one lesson. The record, as I recall, was thirty-two.

Dacombe the Sadist was the most feared. He seemed to relish dishing out physical punishments. One year two ex-pupils returned to school and dragged him behind the gym to get their own back.

William 'Billy' Weir, the French teacher, kept a slipper which he called Excalibur solely for the purpose of dishing out beatings. I'd been on the receiving end of it more than once and Weir was my chief target when, six weeks before my fifteenth birthday, I masterminded a minor rebellion that became known as April Fish Day.

We'd planned a few pranks for April Fool's Day 1970, in between trying to flick peas into the pipes of the school organ at dinner time. These escalated into a morning of surreal silliness that our Monty Python heroes might have been proud of.

By chance, Billy Weir had to leave the class to take a phone call a couple of days before the big event. He'd forgotten to lock the stockroom cupboard where he kept Excalibur. I immediately ran in, grabbed it from its shelf and threw the slipper out of the window, retrieving it at break time. That evening, lined with fishing weights, I duly returned Excalibur to the Lady of the Lake ... or, to be more precise, I chucked it into the pond opposite the Princess of Wales pub on Blackheath. As it sank, my cronies and I saluted solemnly.

The theft gave me temporary hero status among my classmates, but Billy Weir took the loss badly, became grumpier than usual and vowed revenge on the perpetrator(s). For some reason (possibly months of cheek and backchat), I seemed to be prime suspect.

The April Fool's Day events were planned like a military campaign – the Iraq invasion to be precise. There was a lot of smoke, chaos and explosions, followed by a short-lived, misplaced feeling of triumph and a realisation that we'd actually achieved bugger all. Weeks before, I'd 'borrowed' various school keys, had them copied at the local shops and returned them with their absence unnoticed. On the big day, I led the gang into school early. Richard Cluer and Dave Pouncey were my chief henchmen.

Our form teacher was called Herring, so naturally we stuffed his desk full of dead fish. Less logically, we then swapped it with Billy Weir's desk, which we filled with stink bombs and onions – very Gaulish. On Weir's wall, I Sellotaped a home-made poster celebrating the French student uprising of 1968. Back in our form room, Andy Wood, a keen chemistry student, covered the floor with small home-made explosives, while I blitzed the blackboard with subversive, teacher-baiting slogans: 'Abolish Grammar Schools!', 'Beating Kids Is Weir-d!', '3 Rs: Riot, Rebel, Revolt', and the like. Then I smothered the duster with a heavy layer of chalk dust, leaving it perched on top of the board, before encouraging my classmates to conceal themselves behind the curtains and in the stock cupboard. We didn't have to wait long for a reaction.

Billy Weir had arrived in his classroom, caught the stench of day-old fish, opened 'his' desk and exploded in rage. Not surprisingly, he assumed that our class, Upper 4C, was to blame and thundered down the corridor to confront us. Where were the pupils? Weir stomped about in confusion, his every footstep causing a small bang. He was a short, overweight man and the explosions caused him to leap about like a toad on a hot plate. He ranted and he raved. Then he noticed the blackboard graffiti. Weir went to rub it out, reached for the duster and was covered in a shower of chalk, prompting another explosion – of laughter from those of us who could see. Infuriated, he demanded that the pupils responsible come to his room at 10 a.m. and stomped out.

It had been the funniest thing I'd ever seen, but now we had to pay the price. At 10 a.m., I trooped in behind Cluer and Pouncey. Weir seemed to have calmed down.

"You two," he said with half a smile.

"Three, Sir," said the oafish Cluer.

Billy Weir pushed the two of them apart and clapped eyes on his true tormentor. His mood changed instantly.

"BUSHELL!" he cried.

His face turned purple.

As he had no slipper to beat me with, he had to borrow a cane from Dacombe, who was happy to oblige. I got ten strokes on each hand, and it bloody hurt.

Any sense of triumph was short-lived, however. It didn't take Billy Weir long to buy another slipper: Excalibur 2! Coming soon to an arse near you.

* * *

Charlton is in the south east of London, in the historic borough of Greenwich, and at its heart is Charlton Village. Charlton is a contraction of 'churl town' – a settlement of churls, or free labourers. It has a reputation for raunchy revelry. In the 1720s, Daniel Defoe described Charlton as being famous for "the yearly collected rabble of mad people at Horn Fair." "The mob," Defoe wrote in his *A Tour Through Great Britain*, "take all kinds of liberties, and the women are especially impudent; their drunken behaviour immodest and indecent". So, clearly, little had changed in two-and-a-half centuries - except for the council housing that sprang up around the village.

Growing up here, we found history all around us. The royal

connection with Greenwich dates back to Henry VIII; the revolting peasants of fourteenth-century Kent had massed on the Heath. Our neighbour, and family friend, a softly spoken electrician called Cyril Best, would tell us how Shooters Hill had taken its name from the highwaymen and vicious footpads who operated out of the thick woodland at the top, including Dick Turpin, while villains were hanged at Gallow's Fields, to the east of the hill on the way to Eltham. There had been a Saxon settlement where Charlton Village stands since the eleventh century. To the north of the village, down Charlton Church Lane, was the south bank of the Thames, opposite Silvertown and Custom House – the arse end of the East End. To the south, leading down to Old Dover Road, were streets of 1920s-built council houses where every road name reflected the now-fading British Empire: Kashmir, Nigeria, Canberra, Grenada, Kenya and dear old Indus.

My earliest memory of Charlton is smog, the great thick blanket of filth that periodically descended over the streets like some alien menace in a science fiction B-movie. The power station and factories down by the river in Greenwich constantly belched out smoke and sulphur dioxide. Before the Clean Air Act of 1968 it was common to have to walk to Charlton Manor Primary School through a heavy soup of air pollution. You couldn't see more than a few feet in front of you. On smoggy days, Mum would wrap my scarf tightly round my face, and we'd warily cross the busy Shooters Hill Road with the aid of the friendly old lollipop man, who turned out to be a paedophile.

You wouldn't think it now, but Greenwich had been heavily industrialised with steelworks, mills, industrial chemicals, a gas works, a rope works, a dog food factory renowned for its 'pen and ink' and the Delta Bronze foundry. There was more crap in the air here than at a dung flinging contest in a monkey house run by coprophiliac clowns.

This external smog was matched by an ever-present internal fog caused by the enthusiastic chain-smoking of my nearest and dearest.

My widowed great-grandmother, May Mary Wager, lived in Indus Road. Nanny Wager had eight children. My Nan Annie, known as Nin, was the eldest. After her came my uncles Sam, Len, Arthur and John, then Aunt Mag (known as Auntie Gee – a contraction of Maggie) and finally the twins, Bern and Harry. They can't all have been in her tiny house at the same time; growing up it just seemed like it. The Wager family were like the *Shameless* clan on Channel 4, only with a work ethic. Nanny Wager had tattoos on her forearms, which she'd done herself with coal dust and a hot needle. Her sisters were known to fight bare-chested in Charlton Village. Well, they were from Poplar originally. Most of the local men were scared of them. All of the grown-ups smoked like laboratory beagles, and the blue haze never left that tiny living room. It's a wonder I don't have cousins called Benson and Hedges.

The other big health hazard I associate with Indus Road involved fireworks. Bangers were stuck through letter boxes, jumping jacks were casually tossed about and rockets were fired out of old bits of piping like bazookas. There was no concept of health and safety back then - as a few of us proved when riding a handmade go-kart down Charlton Heights. It was fashioned from lumps of wood and old pram wheels held together with part of a washing line. How it didn't disintegrate on use remains one of South London's greatest unsolved mysteries.

The Wagers liked to drink too – when Nin married my granddad, Johnny Barker, the party lasted from a week before Christmas right through to New Year's Day. The adults gambled most days. The men would trip to the betting shop and, on Sundays, the whole family would play card games like nap, rummy and three-card brag, stacking their stake money in uneven piles of silver and coppers. I played my first game and won my first kitty at six, only to be chased around the house by my cousins, Gill and Margaret. Not fully understanding the concept of gambling, they demanded their money back.

A few years later I played strip poker with the girl next door and we both wanted our money back.

To say the family were gambling mad would be under-egging the pudding. When cousin Gill got married, Uncle Arthur even opened a book on how long it would last. He gave 100-1 on them making their Crystal Wedding Anniversary, which was fair enough as it turned out. Gill always appreciated a change of jockey.

When I was ten and bored, I looked at the horses in Johnny Barker's *Daily Mirror* and casually picked out one of the runners: a 20-1 outsider that romped home like he was on a promise at the stud farm. Superstitious, like all gamblers, Granddad asked me to select another horse the following day. By pure coincidence, it won again. This happened for six races on the trot. Granddad was amazed! There was no doubt that he had begun to believe I had psychic powers. Solemnly, he presented me with his 'Spot the Ball' competition and told me to put my crosses on it. Not long after, a letter arrived from Littlewood's. We were rich! We had to be. Granddad eagerly tore it open. We'd won all right - a grand total of £1 for a 'near miss'.

* * *

My father, George, was a fireman. He was a big man, 6ft 4ins, and formidably strong. There weren't many tall blokes in our street, and at primary school the other kids thought he was a giant. Firemen worked unusual shift patterns then: two days, two nights, two days off. My mum, Eve, worried about him constantly.

Eight years old, waking from a bad dream, I climbed down from my top bunk, crept past my sleeping brother and walked along the hall to my parents' bedroom. Dad was out at work, the door was ajar, and through the crack I saw Mum propped up in bed, hugging her knees and crying. There was a major fire, a big 'shout', going on and she was listening to police communication on short-wave radio. I slipped into the room and cuddled her, trying to make her feel better, but Mum could never sleep when Dad was at a fire. She would stay awake fretting over him until it was all over.

For his part, Dad seemed indifferent to the danger. Like his workmates, Dad's sense of humour was as black as Newgate's knocker. Injured firemen would be told, "Your ears must have been burning last night." Sick? Maybe, but when you deal regularly with death and pain, laughing at it is the best way to stay sane.

George Frederick Henry Bushell would eventually receive a British Empire Medal for his services to the London Fire Brigade. He was never injured at work. In the end it was Mum who hurt him, by breaking his heart.

Family life in Charlton in the sixties was teeming with characters, like Unky Bunk, who was married to my nan's cousin, Aunt Kit. He was a jovial man, but strange looking. He had a swollen head caused by water on the brain, bow legs that couldn't stop a pig in a passage and a chest full of medals from World War I, which, like Uncle Albert in *Only Fools and Horses*, he always wore. Aunt Kit had a face like a corduroy cap. You could have grated cheese on her cheeks. Her daughter was Kitty Fluff and her granddaughter was called Kitten. Lord knows if they passed the name on and corrupted it any further. Nin and Aunt Kit had a barney about some long-forgotten slight and the two sides of the family drifted apart. If there's a woman in her thirties in Charlton called Kitty Hawk, Kitchenette or Kitty Litter, we could well be related.

* * *

Every other Saturday, the uncles would roll back to May's after football, beery and good-humoured. The family supported Charlton Athletic. Mum and Dad took me to my first match in 1963, Charlton v. Chelsea. I don't recall much about the game, but the sight, sound and feel of the home crowd were overwhelming. All that hustle and bustle and banter: a sea of flat caps peppered with good-natured songs, hoarse shouts of abuse and encouragement, and forbidden words I'd never heard at home. It was exciting and moving to be part of something so big and so united. That first impression of matey togetherness has never left me. Football was different then; less corporate, more local. Our streets were an extension of our homes, and in a way the Valley, Floyd Road, was an extension of our streets; a communal experience and occasionally a place of worship. More prayers were uttered in the Old Covered End than you ever heard in St Luke's Church.

None of the family was particularly religious. We were 'C of E' and that was the extent of it, although Nin always used to cook fish on Fridays, which suggests some Catholic element somewhere in the ancestry, probably on May's side. Her husband, Sam, Nin's dad, had been a craftsman. He was as bright as a button and, surprisingly, a teetotaller. Sam had been born Anglican but became an atheist. May's lot were acknowledged to be the rough side of the family. Oddly, no matter how hard up any of us were, we were bolstered by the conviction that we weren't as low as Deptford people. The good folk of SE7 might have been poor, but we had better morals than they did in SE8. Blimey, they had tramps in Deptford, proper crusty old Scottish vagrants who lurched about growling at you, with their possessions in sacks and the odd small dog on a piece of string.

We were brought up to look out for one another and, if you were male, to keep your emotions buttoned up. Nanny Wager died when I was eight. It was my first experience of death and I sobbed at her bedside. Uncle Bern came into the room, saw me and slapped me round the face. You didn't carry on like that, even as a kid. You were supposed to wipe your mouth and get on with things.

Certain matters were never talked about. Most of my great uncles had fought in World War II. Two of them, Uncle Len and Aunt Mag's husband, Reg Puttock, had been prisoners of war. They had both served in the RAF. Len had been caught behind enemy lines in civilian clothes and was tortured, but that was never discussed. Nor was my dad's time in prison. He'd been banged up in Italy during his national service for trading in contraband goods, earning him the nickname 'The Bilko of Blackheath'. Bern took part in the D-Day invasion, Arthur had been a Desert Rat, John was in Africa with the Royal Artillery and then Italy with the Royal Engineers, where he got evicted from an opera house for joining in, and Uncle Harry was in the Royal Navy. After the war Uncle Harry brought back a pot of caviar for Nin. When she opened it and saw it was black, my nan assumed that it was off and threw it away. Bread and dripping was her favourite snack. Mine too.

Nin was the hardest-working woman I've ever known. She'd been in service in her teens, working as a maid in one of the grand houses on the other side of the heath. Then she'd landed a job on the production line at the rope factory down at Greenwich, where she lost the fingers on her right hand in an industrial accident. This was in the thirties. The union fought for compensation and she received enough to buy a small semi-detached house: 56 Merriman Road, Blackheath, SE3. It was just a goal kick away from Indus Road, and after May died the centre of the family shifted there, along with the Sunday morning card games, the smoking and the back garden kick-abouts.

Like her dad, Nin didn't drink, and granddad Johnny Barker only indulged in a few sherries on Christmas Day - he'd be hanging off lamp posts all the way home from our local club in Charlton Church Lane. But Nin still hosted sozzled knees-ups on Old Year's Night. The parties were huge affairs. Up to sixty people crammed into two small 10ft by 12ft rooms. One year, the entire Charlton team turned up and gatecrashed. The set-up was always the same: women and children in the living room; men in the front room. Looking back, this seems odd, but the men would never swear in front of the women. It just wasn't done. I didn't hear my dad cuss until I was fifteen. He took a dim view of anyone who effed and blinded in front of women, even comics. Years later I tried to interest him in a Chubby Brown video. Dad turned his nose up, saying, "Anyone who has to swear to get a laugh is obviously a cunt."

* * *

It was said in the family that my nan loved a bare cock. This was true. Literally. Johnny Barker had actually been christened John Llewellyn Barecock. His name was his secret shame. John's dad had it changed by deed poll to the less saucy 'Barker' when my granddad was a boy, robbing him of a lifetime of ribbing. The 'Llewellyn' raised almost as many eyebrows, however, especially as John had been born in Charlton and sounded like it. His father and grandfather were also Londoners. The 'Llewellyn' came from his great-granddad who was from South Wales. This distant reminder of the valleys was passed down the family to me, and in turn to my son Robert. It means lion-heart. Stop sniggering at the back.

Nin and John had one child, my mum, Evelyn May Mary Barker. This was Nin's decision. She was definitely the boss in that marriage. Granddad's shoulders often seemed to slump from the pressure of her thumb. When they fell out, he'd escape to the ramshackle garden shed, which I later discovered housed the sort of magazines he could never have kept in the house, along with Bern's stash of home-brewed liquor – evil-tasting hooch that I learnt to my cost left you with a headache a yard wide.

Granddad was a painter and decorator. He never said much, but what he did say was worth hearing. In my teens an obnoxious French exchange student called Jean-Jacques came to stay with us.

"That kid will live forever," Johnny Barker observed.

"Why?" I asked.

"Cos Heaven won't want him, and Hell will be afraid he'll take over."

Mum, Dad, Nan, Granddad, me and later my younger brother, Terry, lived together at number 56 for the first eight years of my life: four adults, two kids and a dog called Cindy crammed into one small two-bedroom house. We didn't have a pot to piss in, but the house was always full of laughter.

It wasn't just the pace of life that was different back then; the sounds of life were too. Every Saturday evening, the *Evening Standard* sellers would be on the corners of our streets shouting, "Late results! Late Standard!" Rag-and-bone men would come down our road on their horse and cart too, with their own incomprehensible cries – and Johnny Barker would chase after them with a bucket to collect the horse shit for the back garden. We also had 'the knife man', who announced his presence with a horn. He came round to sharpen cutlery – a custom we should be thankful has faded away, considering how things are these days in South London.

I only have one rotten memory of those early years. I was five or six, it was sunny and I was playing in the back garden. Nin offered me an apple from the tree. I refused to take it. I told her I didn't want it because she was holding it in her bad hand. She tried not to react, but I could see the hurt in her eyes. I regretted saying it immediately. How must that have made her feel?

If I could change one thing about my early years, it would be that unthinking childish cruelty.

* * *

When I was eight, Mum and Dad bought the house next door, number 54, from the Cochrans, an Asian family who emigrated to Canada. The sweet but pungent smell of their curries lingered stubbornly for about eighteen months. Mum had decided we needed more space; Dad

15

worked part-time as a minicab driver and did shifts in a brewery to pay the mortgage. Mum started working for Barclay's Bank, which meant that Terry and I were effectively brought up by Nin, who had also taken in Uncle Bern, a milkman at the time.

We had a summer of worry in 1963. Terry got rheumatic fever and was in the Brook hospital for eight weeks. I thought he was never coming home. Three years later I put him back in there, by accidentally whacking him round the head with a metal golf club. I'm happy to report that the club was undamaged.

Nin was a whirlwind of activity for all of her life, with the energy of a thousand road-diggers. She'd get up early and keep busy, cooking, washing and cleaning until bedtime. She never complained. The only time she'd sit still was when we had company, and even then she'd be up every five minutes making fresh pots of tea. On Sundays there would be the traditional card school. But the aunts would congregate here on weekday afternoons: usually Mag and Eileen, who was married to Harry; sometimes joined by Sam's wife, Mavis, who was particularly warm-hearted and cherubic; John's wife, Violet; and Laura, a short, hard-faced Yorkshire woman who was married to Arthur and seemed to view him with constant disapproval. I would come home from school and sit in Nin's tiny backroom, in another family-generated cigarette haze, and listen to my aunts chattering away, gossiping and laughing. To this day, I love the sound of women laughing.

I felt a special bond with Nin's sister, Auntie Gee, who fussed over all of us like a mother hen. Mag had worked in a factory on the other side of the water before settling down with Reg on the laughably named Cherry Orchard council estate in Charlton. She was the most cockney of them all. One Saturday afternoon, when I was thirteen, Mag took me to Blackheath Village. It was crowded. I was pushed backwards in the crowd and accidentally trod on a woman's toe. Naturally, I apologised immediately - we'd all been brought up to be polite and treat women with respect. But this old bird was having none of it. She was every inch the Hyacinth Bucket - in her forties, heavily lacquered and ever so well spoken. She went into one, wagging her finger, shoving me and calling me a yob in her plummy voice.

Aunt Mag decked her.

* * *

June 1968, I'm at the Dreamland amusement park in Margate, Kent, with an older cousin and my friend Kevin from Charlton. There are gangs of leftover mods and rockers dotted about, along with a few mobs of skinheads. The mod girls look gorgeous with their bobbed hair and slacks or skirts that came just over their knees; but love is most definitely not in the air this day. The out-of-town mods eye the local rockers with contempt. Their displeasure is returned with a side order of venom. I'm thirteen, but the tension fascinates me. The mods are more numerous; the rockers – we called them 'grease' - are fewer but older and probably harder. The first fight kicks off. I'm not scared, it's exhilarating, but my cousin bundles me and Kev into an arcade. Opposite, a fella with Ted sideburns leaps over his hotdog counter to join the fray. An older kid sees a chance and seizes it. He vaults the counter, opens the till and helps himself to the contents, taking to his heels just seconds before the police arrive. Years later, the comedian Malcolm Hardee confessed to me that this opportunist tea leaf had been him.

I always loved Dreamland. It was a magical place, mixing fun and thrills, freedom and danger. Dreamland had a wall-of-death motorbike display, where you could look down as a lone rider roared around the wooden walls at breathtaking speed on his Norton. "The most fun you can have horizontally with your clothes on," my Uncle Albert called it. At times the biker was just inches from you, so noisy and in your face that you felt lucky to come away without a tyre track across one cheek and with ears that still functioned. Other attractions included a Roman Chariot ride, the water tubs, the big wheel, an ancient scenic railway, and the House That Turned Upside Down – an illusion, created by making the punters revolve in their seats. You could always tell what the previous riders had eaten by the colour of the vomit stains on the ceiling: pink for candyfloss, brown for hotdogs ...

Most of the Dreamland rides would probably be closed down now on health and safety grounds, but no harm ever came to us there. One sniff of frying onions is enough to bring the memories flooding back: screaming girls, dodgy stalls with their nobbled air rifles, and afternoons spent stealing kisses in the Sphinx Funhouse – and then trying to conceal the inevitable physical response. No wonder those Egyptians walked so strangely.

I spent a lot of time there, because my dad had family just seven miles away in Herne Bay - Uncle Albert and Auntie Ethel, who ran a sweet shop for the radio comedian Cheerful Charlie Chester, and their daughters Val and Tricia.

Herne Bay holidays were an annual event and I loved them. It was the seaside for a start. There were amusement arcades, shops full of saucy seaside postcards, a pier, live wrestling, and ice cream parlours selling Knickerbocker Glories. And Tricia was gorgeous. She was a couple of years older than me and had legs that could start fires. A well-reared girl, too. Her miniskirts certainly brightened up my adolescence.

Ethel, a former scullery maid, was a kind, cheerful woman, and Albert was a bricklayer with a saucy sense of humour. He was from Dorset – he'd been at Arnhem with the Dorsetshire Regiment in WWII – and when he got excited he needed subtitles; his accent shot off the scale. Dad was closer to his aunt and uncle than he was to his own father.

George's mum, Vera Estelle Bushell (formerly May), had died before I was born. He didn't speak to his dad, Fred, for years. Dartford-born Freddie had been a milkman and lived up to all the *Carry On* connotations of the job, pursuing a string of other women. George never forgave him for deserting his mum for one of them. The old man leaving had very different effects on my dad and his younger sister. George grew up valuing loyalty and family, whereas Margaret had three kids by different men and then abandoned them and disappeared to Canada, never to be heard of again; and all before I was ten. All I remember about Margaret are her eyes, which were large, melancholy and as dark as Fred West's heart. (George speculated that they may have had gypsy blood on the May side of the family, a claim dismissed as romantic nonsense by my Herne Bay relatives; later, Channel 4 were to find an alternative explanation, as we shall see.)

Fred eventually married Winnie, a cheery cockney, settled down in Walthamstow and became a beefeater at the Tower of London. He was a likeable rogue, with twinkling eyes. On the rare occasions we visited, it was hard not to warm to him - especially if he had never let you down.

George was born in nearby Whitstable. He met my mum when he was stationed at Woolwich barracks for the last few months of his national service and never went home. He'd been working in a garage when I was born and ended up a leading fireman – the equivalent of an NCO in the army. The tension between George and Fred, and Vera's early death, probably explain why my dad threw himself so enthusiastically into his new life in South London with the colourful Wager family. I never had the choice. I was born into it - on 13th May 1955, at the Memorial Hospital on Shooter's Hill. The war had ended a decade earlier, but the aftermath lingered on like a bad smell. Families still lived in prefabs down the road near Blackheath Standard, the black market flourished and food rationing had ended just a year before - Nin's cooking betrayed the years of make-do practicality, and she knocked up dishes like bubble 'n' squeak, pie and mash and bacon bones all her life.

* * *

I was born on the cusp of a great sea change, just as that old black-and-white *Passport to Pimlico* world was beginning to lighten up with the coming of rock 'n' roll and independent television.

As I arrived, so did a new kind of popular culture. The first TV show I ever saw was episode one of *Doctor Who* at Nanny Wager's. Nin got a telly soon after, and neighbours and friends would come round for events like *Quatermass and the Pit* and football matches. I was eleven when England won the World Cup. Nin's back room was heaving, beer and spirits flowed, and the atmosphere was electric, euphoric. Even Aunt Laura smiled. When the whistle blew I jumped on my bike and gleefully raced around the shops. The streets were deserted. Up by the off-licence there was a poster for a new horror movie called *Children of the Damned*: super-intelligent kids with big, staring eyes, out to take over the world. The image was spooky and slightly prophetic. England's World Cup victory marked a glorious end to one phase of my childhood. But *Children of the Damned* was a glimpse of a possible future. I could have ended up just like them if I hadn't become such a rebel.

I always questioned everything; I was that kind of kid.

At fourteen, during my stay in France with Jean-Jacques, I managed to upset his devoutly Catholic mother by telling her I didn't believe in God. She produced an expensive-looking hardback book full of beautiful, detailed religious art. "These are just drawings," I said, adding falteringly, "*Belles illustrations des rêves*. They don't prove anything." She didn't speak much to me after that. I made the same kind of faux pas when questioning US policy in Vietnam during a school trip to the USA. And my big gob almost got me busted in small-town Pennsylvania. A cop in a car pulled me up for jaywalking. "How would your folks like to come down to the station and pick you up?" he asked. "You'd have a ruddy long wait, mate," I retorted cockily. He asked where I was staying and advised me to get back there, pronto.

The highlight of that trip, for me, was meeting young black kids in New York who were selling the *Black Panther* newspaper on the streets of Manhattan. "I see you have the badge of England on your chest," said one youth, pointing to the metal Union Jack that we all wore on our lapels. "Do you wanna take the message home?" I was happy to oblige.

Most of our families were Labour voters; mine solidly so. My nan and granddad had been involved in the General Strike and had marched against Mosley. My dad liked to describe his politics as 'left of Left', although he was always against firemen's strikes as they meant putting the public at risk. My favourite uncle, Sam Wager, another fireman, was the only one who ever talked politics at home with me. He was genuinely far-Left. He even looked like Karl Marx with his whiskers and pipe and he filled my head with amazing stories of his adventures in the International Brigade during the Spanish Civil War, bullets whizzing by his head during the defence of Madrid. It wasn't until years later that I found out they were all lies. Sam had never been out of Britain in his life. He was the only one of my great-uncles who hadn't fought in the war. He'd joined the London Fire Brigade because he was a conscientious objector. But he was such engaging company that it was hard not to love him.

Most of my friends came from similar backgrounds to me. There was Mark Gladding, Peter Lunn, Alan Strawn, Paul Hale and Chris Culmer. We gradually came to think of ourselves as rebels and dissidents. We were fourteen when we started to get animated by politics. Almost inevitably, we became Marxists.

We started off educating ourselves about socialism, reading books in libraries at first, and then venturing up to a left-wing bookshop called Collet's in Charing Cross Road, where we bought papers, pamphlets and radical books – everything from Karl Marx to Jean-Paul Sartre via George Orwell, Jeff Nuttall, Paul Foot, Germaine Greer and Herbert Marcuse. In the wake of China's Cultural Revolution, a Maoist bookshop opened down the Old Kent Road. It was suitably austere. We got copies of *The Little Red Book* from there and distributed them at school. We weren't Maoists; we just liked the effect that the Chairman's thoughts had on the teachers. We drew up our own mini-manifestos, which we Xeroxed and pinned to school noticeboards, running a book on how long they'd stay on display before a red-faced master tore them up. We went on to circulate other subversive material, which Mao would never have approved of, such as the 'Schoolkids' issue of *Oz, Friends, International Times* and *The Little Red School Book*. We also started a branch of the National Union of School Students and connected with the Schools Action Union.

It was a great time to be young and revolutionary. The Left was on the rise, and our generation was in the forefront. For a while it was possible to believe that Che Guevara and James Dean were part of the same dream.

The uprisings in Paris and Prague had impacted on our teenage consciousnesses. The Vietnam Solidarity Campaign was often in the news, and I was aware of the big seamen's strike, largely because someone had painted 'Save The Seamen' on a wall in Lee. And someone else had painted out the 'a' in seamen.

By 1970 a few of us had started going to demonstrations and political meetings. The Vietnam ones were the largest and noisiest as protestors chanted: "Do-do-do-do do you remember/Gro-gro-gro-gro Grosvenor Square?" and posses of sectarian rivals glared at each other while they flogged their respective newspapers. There was *Keep Left, Socialist Worker, The Militant, Workers Press, The Black Dwarf* and the *Morning Star*.

The next logical step was to find a party that mirrored our views. The choice was as baffling as it was exciting. The sects seemed to hate each other as much as they despised the Tories. One of our peripheral mates, John Mitchell, was in the Young Communist League (YCL), although he was the most right wing of all of us. His father was a well-off university lecturer and a member of the Communist Party, who preached peaceful reform in public but would sing "We'll hang the rich from lamp posts high" unconvincingly to the tune of 'The Red Flag' at home.

Mark and I took against him, and I once wound him up spectacularly using Mark's sister Lisa's toy monkey in a phone stunt. You pulled a string and it would repeat ridiculous monkey phrases in a strange Spanish-sounding accent. Late one afternoon I called John's number from Mark's house. His dad answered the phone and proceeded to have a five-minute argument with the toy primate, who repeatedly called him "a verrry funny monkey" and implored him to "geeve me nuts" and "geeve me love". Mitchell senior, who may have been tipsy, lost his rag and demanded to know the ape's identity. When he accused it of being a "capitalist running dog" I had to hang up. It was not physically possible to laugh any more.

Unaware of these shenanigans, John invited us to a YCL meeting in Lewisham. There were about eight of us in a hired room, and the speaker was an earnest middle-class man in his twenties with long hair and drab clothes. I asked the speaker how he could call the repressive Eastern Bloc regimes socialist. He replied that I'd been brainwashed by the press and that they weren't at all repressive, as he'd been to East Berlin and met other young people with long hair. Not the weakest political argument you'd ever heard, but up there jockeying for a place in the top three.

The miners' strike of 1972 strengthened my political views. All of my immediate family despised the Heath government, and when the strikes led to power cuts we had candlelit tea parties in their honour. The miners were 'like us' in a way that the hippies and yippies we saw on the TV news were not.

After the first strike I resolved to join a political party - but which? A few of us went to a Labour Party meeting down at Greenwich, which was as dull as cold tea. We then tried out the Socialist Labour League (SLL) (now the Workers' Revolutionary Party [WRP]) in Eltham. They were the most determinedly proletarian but also undoubtedly the maddest, with their insistence that the Revolution was months if not weeks away and the constant unrealistic 'demands' they issued. Mark and I thought they were nuts, the Seventh Day Adventists of Trotskyism, but his younger brother Si was won over. He joined their youth branch, the Young Socialists, and shot through the ranks. He ended up addressing their conference later that same year. He didn't stay with them long though. No one did. The SLL burnt up people quicker than medieval witch-finders. After a few months Si found a different solution in booze and drugs.

Mark and I were far more impressed by the International Socialists (IS). For a start, their political analysis had moved on from the 1930s. They didn't pretend that the Eastern Bloc countries were 'deformed workers' states'. They saw these oppressive regimes as state-capitalist. Even at that age we could see that there was nothing 'progressive' about the austere, repressive USSR. The uprising in Czechoslovakia, like Hungary before it, couldn't be swept under the carpet. Trotskyism made more sense, especially to Mark Gladding and me, because it offered an explanation for the failure of the Revolution. The IS also had a coherent theory – the permanent war economy - to explain the post-war boom in the West, which confounded organisations singing from the standard Trot hymnbook.

IS activists seemed less intense and more forward-looking than their ideological rivals, and more human too. They aspired to fill 'the vacuum on the Left' caused by the bankruptcy of the Communist Party (CP) and their leader, Tony Cliff, insisted that "the emancipation of the working class is the act of the working class". They also had a neat slogan: "Neither Washington nor Moscow, but international socialism."

The IS were growing, with more than 2,000 members in 1972, their numbers swelled chiefly by the Vietnam Solidarity Campaign in the late sixties. Their weekly paper, the *Socialist Worker*, was easy to read and free of jargon. We went to a couple of their meetings in Charlton House and took papers to sell from a member, a teacher who lived locally.

* * *

My family weren't at all racist. Nan always said, rightly, that there was good and bad in all races. It was just unlucky for her that two of the West Indian bad ones robbed her in the sweet shop post office at the bottom of Shooter's Hill, knocking her to the floor in the process. The closest the family got to any kind of bigotry was the way they reacted when Mag's son, Mel, married a German girl. He had to – he'd knocked her up. Gunda was beautiful if somewhat sullen, but the family never took to her. Memories of the war were too fresh for them. After all, a German bomb had blown off Nin's roof. Granddad called her 'Girder' and claimed that she had legs of steel. He certainly stole enough looks at them.

The first racism I encountered was at school. Our headmaster, Herbert Beardwood, apologised to us before our America trip, because we had to take some of the children of the school trustees with us, and they were – shock, horror - Jewish. We had a few black and Asian kids in our year. One of the black boys was the son of an African diplomat. When I was seventeen he approached me in the Lord Northbrook pub and sneered.

"Why are you drinking in the saloon bar? You're a Communist. You should be in the public bar."

By then I'd read enough Lenin to know the answer. "After the revolution, comrade, all bars will be saloon bars."

"With free beer for all the workers," piped up Al Strawn.

Almost inevitably, my politics eventually caused problems in the family. A CND (Campaign for Nuclear Disarmament) march was the catalyst. I was sixteen and had decided to march to Aldermaston. Uncle Reg exploded. He loathed the CND, deeming them "anti-British". But I couldn't be talked out of it. Mum and Dad thought that I should go if I believed in the cause that strongly. But the truth was, I didn't. My real reason for going on that march was a brunette Bolshevik from Catford called Shelley, whose lecturer parents were CP members. I forget how many mind-numbing CP meetings I attended, listening to dreary geeks drone on about the wonders of tractor production in the Soviet Union, simply because I was besotted with this girl.

So I marched, not to ban the bomb, but under the banner of unrequited love. My fellow demonstrators were a strange mix: young and old, Commies and peaceniks, Methodists and hippies dropping 'Mandies' (Mandrax, a downer); not my kind of drug or my kind of people, but it felt grown-up to take part.

One game old girl with a megaphone kept up a continual barrage of slogans, imploring bemused commuters to "Get off the bus and march with us" in a voice more suited to Radio 4's *Woman's Hour.* On day two Shelley made it clear that she liked me just as a comrade, so I took solace in under-age drinking and a fumble with Mary, a podgy Christian socialist from Newham - an incident I later turned into a sketch called 'The Kiss of the Cider Woman'. It wasn't so much love at first sight as lust at last orders.

Looking back, the best thing about that CND experience was seeing Hawkwind play at the end - with Stacia, a heavy-breasted, 6ft tall beauty, who performed wearing nothing but luminous paint.

When people complained that political meetings were like watching paint dry, they had clearly never seen it dry on a very bouncy, naked woman.

* * *

At school our gang took over the Christian charity Task Force. We'd do odd jobs and gardening for pensioners living on Eltham's Middle Park

Estate. Some of them were dirt poor. It wasn't living, just existing. Instead of giving them religious literature on the way out, we'd hand them copies of the *Socialist Worker*. Not much practical use, I suppose, although they probably burned better on the fire.

I got close to one old dear, Doris, a widow whose late husband had been decorated during the war. She was a lovely woman, but she couldn't even afford a TV set. Kev's older brother, Bill, managed to procure a knocked-off telly, which we gave her. I told her we'd won it in a raffle.

Other charity work outside of school was more politically motivated. Through the YCL we got involved in collecting door-to-door around the private roads at the top of Blackheath Village. We said we were collecting for Vietnam refugees, but if you read the small print of our leaflets, as only a few householders bothered to do, the money was all going to the Communist north – but we were always told to deny this on the door.

The only person, besides my teachers, who ever tried to talk me out of my political convictions was Uncle Mac, who was married to my mum's best friend, Joan. He was from Southern Ireland and thoughtfully Conservative. Mac lived on a council estate over in Chelsea and used to take us to Battersea Funfair until a fatal accident shut it down. (Another of my mum's close friends, Pat, was married to Eddie Firmani, the Charlton manager, whose presence at my 18th birthday party impressed all my mates. They wouldn't have been left more open-mouthed if Ho Chi Minh had decided to drop by and cook us a stir-fry.)

Outside of politics, my chief interests were music, American comics and comedy. I used to walk down to Greenwich from Blackheath just to buy the latest copies of DC and Marvel comics, and get the bus to Lewisham to buy ska imports. Dad and his Uncle Albert had always enjoyed British war comics, but I preferred Superman, the Fantastic Four, Deadman, whose supernatural adventures were hidden away at the back of Aquaman comics, The Mighty Thor, the X-Men and the Silver Surfer. Nerdish conversations about Aquaman's lung capacity were, I'm afraid to say, commonplace. I also had a fine collection of Donald McGill seaside postcards. We followed boxing and football, but not slavishly. I didn't start going down the Valley regularly till the mid-seventies. At school we played rugby, and I was a second row prop.

There was always a lot of music played at home. Mum was into soundtracks from the musicals. Dad went for Johnny Cash, Marty Robbins and The Dubliners. Nan and Granddad loved Music Hall and had various old discs featuring the likes of Charles Coburn and Harry Lauder. Johnny Barker taught me all the classic comic songs like 'If It Wasn't for the 'Ouses In Between' and 'A Mother's Lament'. He was a huge Max Miller fan and filled my head with stories about the great Music Hall performers, as well as lesser-known turns like Mutton Eye, who was a local one-eyed busker. My elder cousins liked the Beatles. The first pop star I tried to emulate was Lonnie Donegan, the king of skiffle; strumming along on the family banjo at four. But the first music that was mine alone was Tamla Motown: The Supremes, Smokey Robinson, The Four Tops - the most perfect, purest pop music ever written.

1969 was the summer of skinhead reggae. The charts rang out with the joyous sounds of Desmond Dekker, Jimmy Cliff, Bob & Marcia, Cats and the rest, and I blew my pocket money on them and more obscure singles by The Upsetters, King Stitt and Laurel Aitken. At fifteen, I fancied myself as a suedehead. Kev and I had the Ben Sherman and Brutus check shirts and Sta-Prest trousers. There was a factory at the bottom of Victoria Way, Charlton, which put on an after-work skinhead reggae disco for local kids in the canteen, but the best place to dance and flirt was a club above the Co-op Halls in Catford. In the October of 1970, however, I had a change of heart. Black Sabbath and Deep Purple both appeared on *Top of the Pops* with 'Paranoid' and 'Black Night' respectively. I was converted on the spot and started to learn to play guitar. Jimi Hendrix and Ritchie Blackmore were my idols. My old record collection includes everything from the credible – Rod Stewart, the Faces,

Hawkwind and Captain Beefheart's *Trout Mask Replica* – to Neil Diamond and Cat Stevens' *Tea for the Tillerman*; all of which I'd still play. It also betrays a strong glam rock, too: Gary Glitter, T. Rex, Alice Cooper, David Bowie, Sweet, Mott the Hoople, and the mighty Slade - four skinhead yobs with mutton chop sideburns who exploded into my heart playing 'Get Down and Get With It' on an ITV teatime show in 1971. Later, they developed a look that crossed old bovver boy sartorial style with bold Music Hall checks and ludicrous platform boots. Slade knocked out amazing rock anthems that were as joyous as they were rowdy. We weren't supposed to like them. Other kids looked down their noses at Noddy Holder and co., preferring the more cerebral, po-faced outpourings of Yes, Genesis and Emerson, Lake & Palmer, but for me, Nod was God.

From that moment of hard rock satori, I lost the Harrington jacket and acquired an ugly greatcoat from an army surplus store down in Lewisham. I grew my hair, too, getting sent home for the dubious honour of having "the longest hair in school" by Beardwood, who also carpeted Chris Culmer for refusing to pray in Assembly. "You're here to learn, not to think," he said. The man was a complete hypocrite. As well as being a magistrate and a closet anti-Semite, he was also bedding one of my friend's mothers (she slept with him to 'help' her son, she said. She really didn't need to - he was one of the smartest boys in our year).

* * *

Our school was single sex. We had no sex education at all, and my dad never gave me the 'birds and bees' talk. I don't think any of our dads did. So we had to piece together the sexual jigsaw from playground whispers. The closest thing to mildly pornographic material available was the *Health & Efficiency magazine*, which used to airbrush out the women's private parts. This left us even more confused. What the hell was down there? I was quite shy around girls, but that didn't stop me dreaming about them. My teenage pin-ups included Lt Uhura from *Star Trek*, Elizabeth Montgomery – Samantha in *Bewitched* – and, bizarrely, Angela Davis, the political agitator. Barbara Windsor in her Carry On incarnation also loomed large in my fantasies. Many's the time I splashed out on her pictures. I was first aware of being aroused while reading a book of rugby songs at thirteen. This may account for the kind of humour that later flourished in my column. And why 'Ivan Skavinsky Skavar' was my spectacularly unsuccessful seduction music of choice. That was a joke, of course. It was actually 'Three German Officers'.

I was seventeen when I lost my virginity to a friend of Paul Hale's sister at a party in Middle Park Avenue. She dragged me upstairs and seduced me in a bedroom on top of a pile of coats, while Desmond Dekker's 'You Can Get It If You Really Want' provided a perfect soundtrack. Her name was Sue, a nineteen-year-old biker with a ready supply of cannabis, who unfortunately lived on the south coast. Not exactly a meaningful rela-tionship.

We tried dope for the first time at fifteen. All the gang sat on the floor in John Mitchell's big house in Micheldever Road and passed around a joint. The effects were disappointing. The newspapers had built pot up as some huge, mind-bending experience and not a lot happened. We giggled a bit, but that was it. Working on the theory that the papers might be lying about LSD too, I tried acid tabs a bit later at a friend's house on the Middle Park Estate in Eltham. Nothing much occurred for the first couple of hours and I left to get the bus home. It was autumn, and as I started to walk up the hill to the high street every leaf I trod on turned into a small bird that died screaming under my feet. Horrible. I only dropped acid a couple of times and didn't rate it. It wasn't what the underground papers said it was. They claimed that acid "opened the doors of perception". Well, I knocked and no one was in. I wasn't keen on dope either. Drugs weren't the answer; they were a sideshow. Speed became my drug of choice, because you could work on it and drink more on it. It gave you energy and confidence and made you feel euphoric. Shame about the comedowns.

* * *

Comedy and rock were as important to us as politics. I'd listened to radio comedy for as long as I could remember: golden oldie shows such as *Round the Horne*, *The Clitheroe Kid* and *I'm Sorry I'll Read That Again*. All of the gang at school were fans of Spike Milligan, John Lennon and Monty Python (our standard of Python scholarship was way ahead of our Latin and divinity); but also *Steptoe* and *The Comedians*. We produced our own handmade comedy magazine called *Pink Tent*, full of sketches, gags, fake adverts and cartoons. Pink Tent became the name of our schoolboy band too. We played basic twelve-bar blues songs at parties with tortuous lead breaks. We called ourselves Groucho-Marxists long before that was an old joke and put on 'street events' down at Lee Green. In retrospect, these seem hideously embarrassing, involving a ferret stole, dubious political slogans and comic skits. I have a memory, which sadly refuses to be suppressed, of Al Strawn dressed in a flat cap and army greatcoat, John Lennon glasses, a metal Chairman Mao badge and an armband reading 'IRA', reciting a nonsense poem to bemused shoppers. It's just a mercy that no home movie footage exists.

Pink Tent was also the title of the first song I ever wrote. It was an adolescent love song to the female sex organs – something of which at the time none of us had any practical knowledge. My finest composition at the time was the thirty-second-long Surrealist Blues:

"Woke up this morning, I'd turned into a fish/Iguanas ate my codpiece and my neighbour is a quiche/I got the surrealist blues/Oh yeah the surrealist blues/Come stroke my wombat, baby/And pay your union dues ... pole vault!"

Yeah, I know. Don't call us.

31

After Aldermaston we started going further afield to see bands. In rapid succession I saw Cockney Rebel up at Waterloo with Harley looking pained, before they were signed, Slade, Quo, Mott and Wishbone Ash. All of us bundled into Pete Lunn's Cortina to see Chuck Berry, Gary Glitter, Bo Diddley, Little Richard and Jerry Lee Lewis on a rock 'n' roll bill up at Wembley Stadium in August 1972. Incredibly, MC5 were on the bill too but got forced off-stage after about twenty minutes by howls of derision from the purist/moronic elements of the crowd.

Pubs, parties, football matches and 'the pictures' were our regular haunts. *If*, a film about public school rebels taking out violent revenge on their masters, had a huge impact. So did *A Clockwork Orange*, about an ultra-violent street gang turned on by rape and Beethoven and with their own secret language - me and Kev used rhyming slang and back slang when we didn't want anyone else to know what we were on about. All of these teenage interests were reflected on the wall of the box-room bedroom I now had sole use of. The walls and ceilings were plastered with images and graffiti: pictures of Marx, Lennon, Che, Angela Davis, Bowie and Malcolm McDowell as Alex the Droog competing with Dali prints, political slogans, a Bronco Bullfrog advert, cartoons and pin-ups. I could escape up there, undisturbed for periods of teenage angst accompanied by bursts of 'Manic Depression' or the parent-baiting, foul-mouthed racket of Grand Funk Railroad. Nirvana.

* * *

During my early teens something happened that shattered the domestic bliss. Mum and Dad were having more and more rows. There was a tension at home that I'd never experienced before. One day I got in at teatime and found my dad crying his eyes out. It was the first and last time I ever saw him weep. The big man who'd carried me on his shoulders seemed smaller from that day on. But he never let on why he was in such a state.

Years later, when my first wife had an affair, my mum told me everything, and all the anger and tears made sense. She'd been seduced into a fling by a smooth-talking bank executive where she worked in Northumberland Avenue, she said. He'd seemed charming, and he promised her everything, although he turned out to be a serial cad. She had even taken me to meet him once. I was about thirteen, and I remember her introducing me to a smarmy bloke uptown. I had no idea what was going on until years later, but I knew I didn't like him much.

Some of George's firemen mates in Essex had spotted the slippery creep driving Mum about in his sports car and tipped off Dad. The affair hadn't lasted long and Mum ended it. George was devastated but he wouldn't leave her. Then Mum became ill with back and lung problems and seemed to waste away agonisingly slowly before our eyes. Dad nursed her throughout. She died in April 1987. As soon as her funeral was over, George packed his bags and took off with Hélène, the French woman who lived over the road. Nin never forgave him for that, but Terry and I did. Dad had done his duty; he'd done the right thing. Surely he was entitled to a new shot at happiness?

* * *

Our local pub had been the Fox Under the Hill at the bottom of Shooters Hill, but by the time I started drinking the uncles had regrouped at Charlton Conservative Club, with cronies like Freddie Brown and Johnny Castle, a comical tree-feller. Despite being mostly Labour, my uncles pretty much ran the place. It was a busy social club just round the corner from Charlton's ground, with pictures of Churchill and the detestable Ted Heath on the wall. (I once took Kelvin MacKenzie there and he likened it to the Winchester Club in *Minder*. Just as well he never came to the Blackheath & Newbridge Working

Men's Club – that made the CCC look like White's.) The club had bingo nights and turns, and the men always put suits on to go there. This wasn't unusual. Back then, men would put on a shirt and tie even to go the doctor's.

Many of the club's clientele were Labour voters, except for Sid the Lip, a communist who worked in the print. But, from the age of sixteen, I refused to go there, except for Christmas Day, as a matter of principle. I didn't want to give my money to the 'bloody Tories'. This went down about as well as the CND march. But I caused more upset two years later.

Uncle Bern had given up his milk round and now operated a crane at the power station down at Greenwich. We'd gone down to his works' dinner and dance. At the end of the evening, they played the national anthem. Everyone stood up except me. "Stand up," said Bern. I shook my head. "Stand up," he said again. Again I refused. Bern slapped me hard round the face. I got up and walked out. I was seventeen. I thought I was an adult and yet Bern had treated me like a kid. I felt humiliated. Now I understand why he did that, of course. I was in his company; I was his guest. By dishonouring the Queen, I'd let him down. And for what? To make a point? To show off? To feel good about myself? At the time I was genuine in my dislike of the royal family, but what had my little protest achieved, apart from hurting my uncle? Bern took it in a way I'd never intended, as a personal snub. Yet Bern's loyalty never wavered. He continued to buy two copies of the *Socialist Worker* off me every week, one for him and one for a workmate; more, I suspect, out of loyalty than conviction. I should have learnt more from Uncle Bern. He was like a lot of working-class Labour voters. He backed left-wing union leaders, but loved Queen and country. He drank at the Conservative Club, but thought that Churchill had been a 'warmonger'. He wasn't a racist, but he was concerned about immigration. Bern loved his class and his country. His politics didn't fit into any neat box. There are millions like him. Millions like us.

I was nursing a secret when that incident happened. I was in love. I'd met a woman in the saloon bar of the Lord Northbrook. Her name was Joy. She was 23, married and lived quite near the school in Manor Road. Joy wore long hippy skirts and tops that emphasised her heavy breasts. She had red hair and green eyes and smiled a lot. There were only six years between us, but in terms of life experience we were worlds apart. To me, she was sophistication personified. We'd got chatting about politics one day in the pub after school, and we started to meet up regularly. I made her laugh. She made me excited. Joy sympathised with the International Marxist Group. One afternoon she bought a copy of the *Socialist Worker* from me, put her hand on my wrist and said, "Come back to my house and I'll show you my Red Mole." She said it deadpan, with no apparent hint of an intentional innuendo, but her hand lingered slightly too long, arousing more than my hopes. Joy pretended not to notice … until we got back to her house. As soon as she had closed the front door she pushed me against the wall and gave me a long, passionate kiss. We made love right there in the hallway.

Afterwards she told me that her husband, David, was infertile and had a low sex drive. She also told me she had gone on the pill for me. Dave worked up town, so we could sleep together at lunchtimes and after school. Red mole, pink pole, open goal, never dull …

This carried on for a couple of months, until Joy announced that she and Dave were going to South Africa for his work. I begged her not to go. "Silly boy," she said. "It's just for a couple of months."

I never saw her again. When I finally went looking for her, the house had been sold. She'd left no forwarding address. Sometime later I was standing at the bar drinking with Kev and heard one of the barmaids say she'd heard that Joy was pregnant.

What? How? Trying not to let my voice betray my emotions, I asked if she had a number for her. She claimed she hadn't.

I have no reason not to believe that I have another son or daughter out there somewhere whom I have never seen.

The realisation that I'd been used hit me like a kick in the guts.

That was the second time I cried over a woman, but this time I didn't let Uncle Bern see the tracks of my tears.

Chapter Two
Carry On Comrade - The Rebel Years

1977 and I'm up in Leicester with an East London docker called Eddie Prevost. Turning a corner, we come across a whole batch of freshly plastered National Front (NF) posters. Deep joy. Eagerly, we set about tearing them all down. Nine posters in, I spot a woman waving her arms frantically in our direction, as if she were trying to re-enact D-Day against the clock in a game of charades. What the …? Suddenly we hear a bellow of "You SCUM!" above the traffic. We spin around and see John Tyndall, the Nazi Party's fuehrer and around fifteen of his self-styled 'Honour Guard' – hulking great blokes who constitute the Front's fighting elite – on the other side of the main road. Oh shit. Tyndall might be the Captain Mainwaring of British fascism, but his heavies are more like the Waffen SS. Out of condition maybe, but brick wall hard with leg of mutton forearms …

And now the whole lot of them are red-faced, foaming at the mouth, hollering obscenities and coming our way. A bus had obscured our view of the building opposite, which turned out to be the NF election HQ. Doh. We thought we were the left-wing answer to Regan and Carter. Turned out we were closer to Laurel and Hardy or a pair of cartoon clowns. Our legs become a whirl. I've never run so fast in my life. All we're missing is a 'skedaddle' sound effect. We make it round the corner to where Eddie's old banger is parked. If that car hadn't started first time I'd be dictating this book through a medium.

I had joined the International Socialists three years earlier at the age of eighteen and was plunged full-on into a world of demos, fly-posting, paper-selling and street fights. Wherever there was trouble, from Red Lion Square to Grunwick's, I was there in the thick of it as an enthusiastic participant. Before long I was working alongside the party leadership and had attracted the attention of the British security services. But that's to jump ahead.

My memories of this period are about as clear as a pint of Pete Doherty's urine, but I'm fairly sure that Eddie and I were up in the East Midlands for an election campaign – the NF were doing well at the polls in the area. The IS had just become the Socialist Workers Party and we were fielding a Scottish electrician as our very first parliamentary candidate. A local Asian businessman let us stay in one of his properties. It must have been winter, because the place was unheated and it was nine degrees below Tilda Swinton.

For warmth I shared a single bed with a nice, chunky comrade from East London called Elaine Delay, but there was no funny business. At those temperatures she would've had to play Hunt The Thimble.

The heaviest fighting I was involved in was the battle of Lewisham in 1977, where in true *Carry On Comrade* style I ended up getting knocked to the floor by half a house brick lobbed by one of my own side. Not for the first time, I wondered: how the hell did I get into this?

* * *

In the summer of '73, I left school and started working up in the post room at the Shell building on the Embankment. An old fella called Ron used to sort the post, and I'd deliver it round the departments on a trolley. Ron was an East Ender, an ex-docker, who wore a permanent neck collar after getting crushed between a ship and a jetty. His stories were captivating and his opinions of politicians, bosses and union officials chimed with mine, which strengthened my resolve to get things done. People were more radical back then and mass working-class action was growing, much of it spontaneous and unofficial. We'd had the miners' strike, the Shrewsbury 24 and the Pentonville Five – workers were getting slung in jail. New generations had been radicalised by Vietnam and the student movement, and after Paris and the Czechoslovakian uprising of 1968 the Old Left could no longer cut it as a genuine alternative. Labour and the Tories were converging, the old-hat Communist Party were permanently tainted by the crimes of Stalinism, and the sell-out trade union bureaucrats were another enemy.

I was young, angry and hungry for change. The IS ticked all the boxes. I decided to join.

It's hard to convey the sense of wonder I felt at my first IS meetings. I was still at school, where the teachers told me that my views were "extreme" and "ridiculous", and yet here were people who thought the same extreme and ridiculous things as I did but who were grown-up. The Woolwich branch met at Charlton House, a well-preserved Jacobean mansion in between the village and the top end of Indus Road. A lecturer called Fred from the Poly was the branch chairman, and a teacher called Ted, who had served in the RAF, was his wingman. They had around thirty-five regulars, including a middle-aged pipe-smoking Ulsterman who was a shop steward in one of the factories in Greenwich.

The core belief of the IS was that the working class had to be the engine of the coming socialist revolution. Unfortunately, most of the members were either white-collar workers or students. So the 'turn to the class' translated into regular early morning sales outside the factories down by the Blackwall Tunnel. We'd stand there for an hour or two, often in a light drizzle of rain and a heavy bombardment of exhaust fumes and occasional abuse, and feel delighted if we flogged six papers.

I ended up doing my journalist training on the *Socialist Worker*, with many unexpected consequences.

As soon as my byline started appearing in print, strange things began to happen. Men would park up in cars and watch the comings and goings at both houses. A ferret-like bloke in a raincoat once followed me to the pictures (not the lollypop man). And on two occasions I got stopped and searched by uniformed police officers, once on apparent "suspicion of being a cat burglar", although nothing about me suggested agility. Back then, I didn't even have the whiskers.

I didn't twig what was going on until David Shayler, a former high-ranking MI5 operative, broke ranks in 1997 and revealed that I had been under surveillance by the spooks, along with such notables as John Lennon, the reggae band UB40 and folk singer Ewan MacColl – father of Kirsty. I had visions of some poor sod having to decipher the lyrics to songs by my punk band The Gonads, such as the impenetrable 'Got Any Wrigley's John', and decoding my mum's phone calls.

"What's the latest, Bond?" M would ask.

"Apparently the woman next door is liaising secretly with a character called 'the butcher', sir, who is supplying 'sausage'."

"Careful, 007, careless pork costs lives."

Talk about Walls have ears.

Many shady-looking characters would have been spotted coming in and out of number 56, all of them Bern's card school cronies.

According to Shayler, I was spied on for having extreme left-wing beliefs from 1976 to 1977, and again in 1981 when I was suspected of being Bushellini, the sinister right-wing puppet master behind the Southall riots (and I wasn't even there.)

When the story broke, *The Sun* was furious and wrote a leader condemning the secret service for wasting taxpayers' money and ordering MI5 to "leave Comrade Bushell, the Che Guevara of Eltham, alone".

I typically made light of it, accusing MI5 boss Stella Rimmington of being "the spy who loved me" and warning my wife that, should the phone transcripts become public, references to 'Melinda', 'Fleur' and 'massage oils' were all code words for revolution, ending my piece with the stirring battle cry: "Freedom for Charlton!" And yet, looking back, it was probably sensible for MI5 to have kept tabs on anyone working for the *Socialist Worker*. We were, after all, openly preaching revolution, and Lennon did give large sums of money to the WRP – and the IRA.

A close friend of mine, an undercover detective, was under investigation by the police 'Rubber Heelers' at the time, so the two of us used the story as an excuse to go on the missing list for a long weekend, calling ourselves Bent Cop and The Comrade, frisking barmaids for listening devices and scanning the skies for imaginary choppers between rounds.

Shortly afterwards another family friend, then attached to the SAS, looked up my name on a military computer and "set the alarm bells ringing like a bank raid".

* * *

I married my first wife, Carol Cousins, in July 1976. I trust MI5 got a good shot of Paul Foot at the wedding.

I'd met Carol in the late summer of 1973 at a party on the Coldharbour Estate in Eltham – she lived in Leverholme Gardens, the same road as Mark Gladding. Carol was a sixteen-year-old former skinhead whose best friend was an Afro Girl called Diane Campbell. One of the things we had in common was a love of ska, but her mum, June, didn't share it. When June heard us playing Max Romeo's Wet Dream in the front room she furiously yanked it off of the Pioneer and threw it on the fire. I kept my Judge Dread singles well away from her.

The Cousins family were extraordinary. Dad Frank was a bus driver who barely said a word when he was sober; he just slumped in his chair watching sport on the telly. Former Teddy boy Frank made Harpo Marx look like Ben Elton. He didn't talk, he just grunted at people. June – real name Eunice – was as bright as a button. Carol was the eldest. Then came John, her epileptic brother, who got involved in street fights and socialism with me, and the ICF through me. Sister Shirley would date and marry Sean, a plasterer, who became the leader of the Young National Front in Kent, which led to some lively differences of opinion around the kitchen table, couched in the kind of language that you rarely hear on *Question Time*. Then came Alan and Sandra.

The iron law of the Cousins clan was that no three of them could ever be in a room together without an argument breaking out. They made the warring Costanza family on *Seinfeld* seem like the Waltons.

Looking back, I suppose Carol was a bit like Nin; she was the same height, stoic and the eldest child of a large family who ended up a surrogate mum to her siblings. A psychologist might have fun with that. When Carol inevitably fell out with her mum, she moved in with Nin next door to me. We were engaged soon after.

I wasn't much of a prospect when I first met Carol, being a long-haired layabout on the verge of starting college. As soon as I began attending IS meetings, Fred encouraged me to apply for a sociology course at the North East London Poly – not because I had any burning ambition to be a social worker but because the sociology department was run by the IS. The department was housed in Livingstone House, a converted cigarette factory in Stratford, East London. Half of the lecturers there were card-carrying members, and most of the others were fellow travellers. The members included fast-talking Lionel Sims – last seen hosting a Channel Five TV show about Stonehenge, Sabby Sagal, Joan Smith and Joyce Rosser, whom I would have been encouraged not to describe as a smart, sexy blonde. There was no better way for young party cadre to get schooled in Marxism at the taxpayers' expense.

The downside of this was that I was plunged head first into a maelstrom of student activism, with all the attendant marches and sit-ins, thus depriving myself of the bog-standard student's right to spend three years getting legless, experimenting with drugs, sleeping through lectures and getting laid. The plus side was that the third year of the course included a block release section – two weeks on a journalism course at the London College of Printing followed by a couple of months working on the *Socialist Worker*. The comrades fiddled me a National Union of Journalists membership card and I found myself stationed at the party's Bethnal Green printing plant.

Soon I was off covering striking miners in South Wales. I loved every minute of it. On one occasion I was sent to try and infiltrate an organisation called GB75, which had been set up by Colonel Sir David Sterling, the Scottish laird who founded the SAS. One meeting that I attended was held in a plush West End hotel and was addressed by General Sir Walter Walker, who was convinced that Harold Wilson was "a proven communist" and claimed to have the backing of an assortment of high-ranking military figures, along with Michael Bentine of The Goons.

The IS were convinced that GB75 were planning a coup. My problem was clothes. I couldn't go along to their meeting in my leather jacket, so I had to borrow one of Frank's old sports coats. He was a good four inches shorter than me, however, and the sleeves were so tight that I could barely lift my arms. It looked as though I'd been dressed by Michael Bentine. The jacket fitted me about as well as Oliver Hardy's did him. It was so loud that it's a miracle that Walker could be heard above it.

So were they a threat to democracy? Potentially, but no more than we were. Walker did say that he thought the country might prefer "rule by the gun" in preference to anarchy – views that were extremely reactionary to us, but probably commonplace, if not liberal, in the crustier private gentlemen's clubs of the West End. And frustrated top brass had been associated with far-right pressure groups for half a century. GB75, and other groups like them, did have close links to British security. But nothing came of them and Sterling is now remembered more for his military achievements than his civilian plotting.

One story of mine that made a double-page spread in the *Socialist Worker* was our struggle for a council flat. Carol and I wanted to set up home together but couldn't get anywhere in Greenwich. One alternative was a Peabody estate - Carol was working as a legal audio secretary for Bruce Douglas-Mann, the Labour MP, who offered to pull strings. Luckily, Hammersmith Council were running a scheme whereby a few properties would be released periodically on a first come, first served basis, which is how we ended up queuing overnight in temperatures that would've made a brass monkey weep. The families rallied round, bringing up blankets and thermos flasks. Bern sent a hip flask. June excelled herself by cooking huge bowls of stew, which Frank ferried up from Eltham wrapped in towels to keep them hot. We had so much that we were doling it out to the other poor sods in the queue. We were sixth in line and we got our flat: 86 MacKay House on the White City Estate, just off Loftus Road. Our first place together. Home, sweet home.

The magic was shattered on the first night – as were some of our ornaments. The family beneath us were Irish and had a party so loud that they fell off the wall and smashed. Jesus. Or should I say bejesus? It wasn't even St Paddy's Day. Worse was to come. A week later a geezer hanged himself. One morning I was woken up at 6 a.m. by someone knocking on the door. It was my dad, desperate to make sure that we were all right. A guy on the landing below had run amok with a carving knife, tried to stab his wife and ended up slicing a cop instead. Bern had heard it all on police short-band radio – this passed for entertainment back in the days before Sky Plus. Everyone on our block had watched it happen, except us. We'd slept through it.

Drugs, gang fights and racial hatred were rife on the estate, but it was never anything as simple as black vs white. The Africans hated the West Indians, who despised the Asians, who didn't like the Turks, who looked down on the Africans … It wasn't a world I recognised from the pages of the *Socialist Worker*. It was more like a war zone.

I'm not going to slag off my old comrades. My political views may have shifted, but my impressions of the people involved remain unchanged. One of the great strengths of the IS compared with rival revolutionary sects was the decency, humility and humanity of the leading members. I had, and still have, enormous respect for some of the people I worked and campaigned alongside. Especially Paul Foot, dockers Bob Light and Eddie Prevost, doctor David Widgery, print worker Roger Huddle - the ex-mod who co-founded Rock Against Racism, investigative reporter Laurie Flynn and our glorious leader Tony Cliff.

Some of the comrades were distinctly odd. Chris Harman, the leading intellectual, had trained with the PLO yet was so absent-minded that he once managed to leave his own baby in a bag under a table. Not exactly a suspect device, but that nappy could've done some damage. Harman also managed to nod off during conferences. Not hard. But once you got past his awkwardness, Chris was a funny guy and quite fearless. In 1976 he went to Spain, which was still under Franco's rule, to hook up with the OIC (Left Communist Organisation), whose first congress took place secretly in a monastery. To avert suspicion, the assembled revolutionaries had to make frequent stops to sing hymns. One false move and it could literally have been a case of 'Nearer My God to Thee'.

On the whole, the comrades were good-humoured and enthusiastic. They liked a drink and were open to debate. I only ever fell out with Roger Huddle over music. A Stones fanatic, he was horrified that I liked Queen and compared the sentiment of Jagger's 'Street-fighting Man' to the "pretentious" lyrics of 'Bohemian Rhapsody'. Well, it was pretentious of course - overblown ham playfully masquerading as rock opera - but it was also a bloody great song. And besides, Roger's argument suggested that he'd never listened to the words of 'Street-fighting Man', let alone 'Brown Sugar', which gleefully celebrated slave owners whipping hot black women. But what did I know? I was just a poor boy, from a poor family, sparing my ears from such monstrosity.

Rock and pop were often on the comrades' minds. The charts even influenced the leader. Tony Cliff had been born Ygael Gluckstein in Palestine and took his new name from Cliff Richard. However, unlike pop's biggest fifties star, Cliff was short, tubby, scruffy and largely bald. Paul Foot described him as looking and sounding like a rag doll. He looked to me more like a mad professor. He was hugely intelligent and articulate, and almost theatrically Jewish. He was a tremendous orator, generous and likeable. Like Paul, he was also funny. The party supported Labour "like a rope supports a hanging man," he'd say, quoting Lenin. If a Labour MP ever got something right, Cliff would quip, "Even a stopped clock is right twice a day," or "Even a blind hen can occasionally pick up a grain of corn." Once in the *Socialist Worker* office he announced, "There can be no women's liberation until after the revolution, so put the kettle on Joanna." It might not have gone down well at Greenham Common, but it made me laugh, and Joanna, a rather posh girl, didn't seem to mind.

Of course, the new politics that were carried into the mainstream Left by middle-class radicals would soon put an end to that kind of harmless joking.

Foot himself was fired by a burning belief in justice. He was a force of nature with a pudding basin haircut, campaigning tirelessly on behalf of the four men falsely convicted of killing Carl Bridgewater, who were eventually freed as the result of his relentless exposure of the flaws in the prosecution case. Paul was proved wrong about James Hanratty though – DNA evidence later confirmed that he was the A6 murderer, although Paul stubbornly insisted, "If the science is saying he did commit the murder, I say well that clashes with my belief that he didn't commit the murder and there must be something wrong with the science."

That doesn't strike me as being much different from someone like Sarah Palin saying, "If science proves the Earth is 5,000 years old, there must be something wrong with the science."

Paul was seen as being on the right of the IS, and Cliff always joked that he was soft. Not as soft as the party's theories, as it turned out. Those disinterested in Marxism might be advised to skip the next couple of pages.

The IS took off at a time when left-wing politics were changing. The radical seeds planted in 1968 had blossomed into a hundred flowers and a multitude of weeds: women's lib, greens, vegans, gay liberation, black sections, and so on, many of which were a sure bet to alienate most working-class people, especially blokes. Female workers fighting for equal pay was one thing, but not the rest of the man-bashing, family-hating crap that came with the largely middle-class Wimmin's Movement.

The leadership resisted this in much the same way as Canute resisted the tide. They also tried and failed to suppress an IS Gay Group. By 1976, however, activists were being told to turn out to protect the Paedophile Information Exchange. This disgusted me, and it was one of the key reasons why I fell out of love with the IS. There we were, the self-appointed vanguard of the working class, helping to keep angry East London parents – real working-class people - away from revolting, child-molesting creeps. My sympathies were entirely with the parents.

Our attitude to the IRA was another insurmountable stumbling block. In 1974 they'd planted a bomb in the Kings Arm pub in Woolwich, killing two men: a sales clerk and an army gunner. Selling the *Socialist Worker* in Woolwich that Saturday morning, I was approached by a middle-aged woman who sneered, "Still support the IRA now, do ya?" I had nothing to say to her, because I never did support them. I didn't believe that terrorism was ever justified in a democracy. That same month four people were murdered and fifty injured by bombs in Guildford, and twenty-one youngsters were slaughtered in two Birmingham pubs.

These were not military targets. The IRA were targeting the English working class. The IS position of supporting the bombers 'critically but unconditionally' was clearly ludicrous. What do you say to some teenage car mechanic with half of his leg blown off? "We're critical of how this happened, mate, but we still support the bastards who did it unconditionally. Come and join us on the next Troops Out march. Bring your wheelchair, I'll push"?

The hitherto rapid growth of the IS slipped into reverse over this period. Between 1974 and 1976 membership plummeted, many factory branches went belly-up and most of the rank-and-file movements shrivelled up like a dwarf's balls in an ice-cold bath. The leadership did more flips than an Olympic gymnast and more zigzags than a champion skier. Suddenly the Right to Work Campaign became the be-all and end-all of party activity. Student politics, once sneered at, were enthusiastically embraced with the formation of the NOISS (National Organisation of International Socialist Students). Then there was an attempt to create an organisation for *Socialist Worker* supporters – people who bought the paper but wouldn't join the IS. It didn't work and was quickly abandoned, to be replaced with a new emphasis: fighting fascism.

As the NF prospered, we issued leaflets with the slogan 'They're welcome here'. This didn't go down well with the white working class, but quite a few Asian youngsters joined up. I took part in an anti-racist demo in Barking, the only white face in the protest. The NF marchers looked like the participants had walked straight off the Upton Park terraces. We were failing spectacularly to connect with the young working class.

In the context of fighting the Front, a decision was taken to become the Socialist Workers Party (SWP). This occurred on 1 January 1977, and by 2 January I'd heard the first person quip that we were so called because we weren't socialist, weren't workers and had no idea how to throw a party. Sean made his verdict readily available: "SWP," he said. "Shit, wind and piss."

Other IS veterans declared the move to be "a journey into cloud cuckoo land without a map."

The IS always wanted to build themselves into the revolutionary party, but if you'd asked Tony Cliff in 1968 if this could be done with 3,000 mostly middle-class members he would've laughed you out of the room - especially if the change meant neglecting shop-floor work to 'build the Party'.

The SWP became more deluded and less democratic. It had always been Cliff's baby – "an orchestra only needs one conductor," he would say. But now debate was stifled, opposition was demonised and persistent dissidents were expelled. The flexibility that had marked the early IS had been replaced by cynical political opportunism. He changed horses like a jockey on piece rate. Cliff's other slogan, "tactics contradict principles", came into play. Tony Blair would have taken his hat off to him, provided the receipt could be claimed as a legitimate expense.

The members still did good things, however. In 1976 Huddle set up the entirely admirable Rock Against Racism (RAR) with another former mod, Red Saunders. I was happy and proud to contribute to their paper *Temporary Hoarding*. RAR were a roots-up movement, which the party quickly tried to co-opt into their top-down creation, the Anti-Nazi League (ANL).

Both organisations were passionate, popular and responsible for major events and great music. RAR created gig opportunities for terrific bands such as The Ruts and Steel Pulse. The ANL's two London festivals both attracted more than 100,000 people. I took John to the first one, in Victoria Park, Hackney. X-Ray Spex were excellent, and when The Clash played, Sham 69 frontman Jimmy Pursey jumped on stage with them to holler along to 'White Riot', blokes were embracing each other and punching the air – not quite the reaction that greeted Tom Robinson singing 'Glad to Be Gay', when thousands of straight men edged away from each other in embarrassment, hoping the ground beneath them would open up and swallow them. Sing if you're glad to be gay; cringe if you're not.

More toe-curling moments came at the 'Evening of Comedy and Music Against Racism' at Wembley Conference Centre in June. The great Dave Allen, a brilliant comedian who sent up political hypocrisy, bigotry and religious cant, was the star turn. His act was heckled and interrupted by a succession of middle-class whingers who stood up repeatedly to moan: "Mr Allen, as a gay man I object to that joke"... "Mr Allen, as a feminist I find that gag sexist and offensive" ... "Mr Allen, I am a full-time sanctimonious pain in the arse who will ruin the flow of your rueful, rib-tickling routine to draw attention to how woefully right-on I am" ... Shut the fuck up!

By the time of the second ANL fest in Brockwell Park, Stockwell, I was writing for *Sounds* and the SWP were locked further into a downward spiral of unprincipled alignments that ended with them in bed with the ultra-reactionary, gay-hating, women-hating, union-bashing Muslims of the Noughties (whom they had previously and correctly written off as clerical fascists). The catastrophic defeat of the miners in 1985 meant that the class war had been lost for a generation and sped up the SWP's degeneration. The comrades would brook no criticism of Arthur Scargill, the megalomaniac NUM leader who called the strike in spring, after a mild winter, ignoring the old miners' adage "Never come out when the sun's on your back", and refused to ballot his members. Bernard Manning got it right when he claimed that Scargill's surgeon had been unable to circumcise him as "there's no end to this prick".

The SWP would go on to defend the indefensible, describing suicide bombers as the "resistance of the oppressed" – in other words, apologising for terrorism. It was moral and intellectual cowardice. IS Marxism had morphed into a new ideology - radical middle-class liberalism that, although dressed up in the language of socialism, had as much to do with working-class lives as a polo match or a grouse shoot.

Another huge gap between theory and reality was their attitude to patriotism. Many on the far left wrongly confused it with nationalism, which led to my great uncle Albert, who had actually fought real Nazis, being called one by moronic students simply because he wore a Union Jack pin badge on his lapel while working as a caretaker at Canterbury University. George Orwell attacked this wrong-headed tendency long before I was born. Shrewd socialists know that a people's natural love of their country is a healthy, positive emotion. The rootless global elite are the real antisocial class.

Of course, once you start to question one thing, you often question everything – even the fundamentals. The theory of the permanent arms economy (which claimed that arms sector spending had put paid to boom and bust) seems laughable now and had started to go tits-up in the '70s. Those of us who went back and read Karl Marx found other flaws, not least that the basic thrust of Bolshevism completely stood Marxism on its head. The scales began to fall from my eyes even about dear old Footy. His defence of Lenin amounted pretty much to Paul saying that Lenin can't have been a tyrant because in his book *The State* and *Revolution* he repeats that socialism and democracy are indivisible. That's like saying that the Kray Twins can't have killed anyone because they once promised a magistrate they'd go straight.

His book on Shelley was equally nuts, with Paul manipulating Percy to make him fit his own revolutionary politics – something that the poet explicitly opposed. But it was easy to kid ourselves back then. For all our noise and anger, our little world was hermetically sealed against reality. We may have been bright – in the Livingstone House canteen I was considered an intellectual because I understood the theory of dialectical materialism - but we were astoundingly naive.

One of the things we were told was that everyone could be a genius given the right opportunities, because we only use ten per cent of our brains. It was a fallacy based on scientific misunderstanding. I wonder

51

how much 'progressive' educational policy was informed by this kind of thinking. We were also taught to see black people through rose-tinted glasses. Because they were 'the oppressed' they were incapable of racism, we were assured. This is something that was easy to believe in a college seminar and harder to accept when you lived on the White City Estate.

Our heads full of this kind of well-meaning dogma, on the August Bank Holiday 1977 Carol, John, Debbie and I went down to the Notting Hill Carnival. The girls, both heavily pregnant, were walking ahead of us when they were encircled by a gang of black youths. John and I ran forward and pushed the women out of the way, effectively taking their places as the intended victims. One of the six black kids produced a knife. There wasn't much we could do. At that moment a police meat wagon careered round the corner, sirens blaring, and the gang legged it. A full-scale riot was developing. Other cops on foot patrol suggested that we'd be safer taking shelter in a pub than walking the streets - advice we took enthusiastically.

A few years later my brother Terry and I had popped in to the chip shop in Charlton Church Lane to pick up fish 'n' chips for the family. A gang of four black guys, about Terry's age, came in being lairy and aggressive. They followed us outside. One of them pulled a knife and demanded our wallets. Terry picked up a milk bottle, smashed it against the brick wall and said, "Come on then." The guy with the knife was outraged. "Don't you know who I am?" he said. We didn't, and neither did we care. He gave us a load of verbal but backed off. My Granada was parked round the corner and, as luck would have it, by the time I'd started it up and turned it round the knife-man was standing on his tod in the middle of the Delafield Road mouthing off at a terrified old lady. I drove straight at him, beeping just in time. He went one way and his bag of chips went the other. When the chips were down, he was halfway to Charlton station.

As Nin always said, there are good and bad in all races. The comrades, although right to confront bigotry, were wrong to pretend that non-whites were always in the right and white people always in the wrong.

In the mid-1990s I was having pie and mash in Shadwell when an old cockney lady recognised me and told me that whenever the white locals had any disagreement with local Muslims the Labour Party would always take the side of the immigrants. The old dear had tears in her eyes. She'd voted Labour all her life, and now the party no longer stood for her. Worse, it no longer respected or even liked her.

* * *

Back in 1976 I also found myself drifting back into the old London world of pubs, gigs, films, football, betting shops and cockney comedians up the Old Kent Road – Jimmy Jones and later Jim Davidson, who would both become friends. We boxed a bit and drank a lot. It might be true, as the IS had said, that the emancipation of the proletariat was the task of the proletariat itself. But most of the actual working class were having too good a time to bother about it.

As my doubts about the party grew a new, a wildly different kind of protest kicked its way into my life: punk rock.

I've written about the birth of punk at length in my last book, *Hoolies*. Rock music had become bloated and complacent. Stadium rockers ruled the roost, and according to the music papers jazz fusion was the wave of the future. The likes of Chick Corea, Al Di Meola and 'Mahavishnu' John McLoughlin were certainly incredible musicians, but they couldn't have been further away from rock 'n' roll if they'd worn perfumed wigs and waltzed to Strauss. The only live rock excitement in the mid-1970s was coming from bands like Dr Feelgood. Consequently, I took to punk like a tramp to cider, buying The Damned's 'New Rose' down at Shepherd's Bush market on the day it was released and catching bands like The Clash, Gen X, the Buzzcocks and later Sham 69 before they broke big.

The older comrades weren't impressed. Paul Holborrow, whose brother Jonathan later edited the *Mail On Sunday*, advised me sternly that punk was a juvenile distraction. Several older comrades distrusted punk because of Malcolm McLaren's provocative use of swastikas. *The Socialist Worker* ran a debate with someone – it may even have been Widgery – condemning punk as proto-fascist, and me using Clash lyrics to defend the scene. (Of course, I didn't know then just how manufactured and faked The Clash's image and working-class credentials were. I was such a believer that when I met Joe Strummer for the first time I was tongue-tied; I thought of him as a guru.)

Looking back with 20/20 hindsight, I think we were both wrong. The true spirit of punk was neither communist nor fascist – although the swastikas were always dumb. Punk was about individuals and free thinkers. "Free yourself from this," Jimmy Pursey sang in 'Red London', "individuals rule." Its true essence was DIY: form your own band, write your own 'zine, design your own clothes, form your own label, tear up the rule book, kick over the statues, think for yourself.

Punk happened under a Labour government. *Labour* councils tried to ban it. Of course, Tory politicians hated it too, but the soul of punk, its spirit, was libertarian through and through. It was vibrant, radical and non-conformist - the polar opposite of bureaucracy and stifling state control, which had come to equal socialism in practice.

This didn't prevent the Left from attempting to hijack the movement. The first issue of *Temporary Hoarding*, largely put together by Roger Huddle, was full of the words to Clash songs like 'London Burning'. RAR put on gigs across the country. I re-formed my band (see Chapter 9, 'Go Mad with The Gonads') and brought out a couple of issues of a fanzine called *Napalm*, featuring interviews with Marian Said from Bromley, Kent, better known as the wonderful Poly Styrene from X-Ray Spex and Sham's gobby hooligan general Jimmy Pursey. These - and, I suspect, my tattoos - helped land me a job on *Sounds* in the summer of

1978.

1977 was a heady year. I spent it rocketing between gigs, college and political activities. I was on the crest of a wave. To be young and punk in '77 was to be part of a world pregnant with possibilities - as pregnant as Carol turned out to be. I was walking on air for most of the year.

The euphoria did not last. Our baby was born at Hammersmith Hospital on 23 December … only he wasn't. The pregnancy had been straightforward, but Steven was stillborn, strangled by his own umbilical cord.

I can still see the face of the junior doctor, who broke down in tears as he told me the worst news an expectant parent could ever hear. I was paralysed with grief. Everything seemed to drain out of me. In a trance, a nurse took me to see the lifeless body of my first child. Steven was the mirror image of me, from his black hair down. By the time I left him, Dad had arrived at the hospital and I broke down in his arms; a kid again. We didn't sue the hospital or demand an inquiry. What would have been the point? It wouldn't have brought Steven back. But from that day, I changed. I grew up overnight and started making plans.

We couldn't stay on the White City Estate, so I got in touch with the council and arranged a transfer back home to South London – to the Ferrier Estate in Kidbrooke, SE3; 21 Clegg House, Pinto Way, to be precise. We decided to try for another baby as soon as possible. Carol was four months pregnant when I landed my *Sounds* job. I took driving lessons and passed my test in time to buy my first car (a motorised hairdryer known as a Singer Chamois) and pick up mother and baby from St Alfege's in Greenwich when our daughter Julie was born on 23 November. I was reviewing the singles that week, and such was my joy that I made four different records 'Single of the Week', including Ian Dury's 'Hit Me With Your Rhythm Stick'.

My reasons to be cheerful were abundantly obvious.

Chapter Three
Runnin' Free - The Rock 'n' Roll Years

I wasn't expecting a visit from the police, so when two gents from Essex CID turned up at the door of my South Ockendon semi flashing their warrant cards I was mystified. I was also disorientated, as I'd been writing my Iron Maiden book all day and self-medicating with single malt. Being two drinks ahead of reality may oil the creative wheels but it isn't much help when your drum suddenly becomes a potential crime scene. They didn't have a search warrant, but asked if they could take a look around.

I had nothing to hide. "Sure." I shrugged. "Come in. What are you looking for?"

"We can't tell you that, sir," the senior detective said, the words coming with an unspoken side order of "like you don't know, son".

He was softly spoken and amiable; his sidekick shorter and surly. They could have been auditioning for a 'good cop, bad cop' part in a mediocre TV drama.

They proceeded to look behind the settee, in the cupboard under the stairs and in every kitchen cabinet. I made tea and tried again.

"What are you looking for?"

"Can't tell you, sir," they replied.

Up the stairs they went. They looked in the airing cupboard, in the children's toy box and under my bed.

"What are you looking for?" I said again, a note of exasperation in my voice. "Maybe I can help …"

Eventually, the taller one broke his silence. It seemed that rock band

Motorhead's stage bomber had been stolen and someone had tipped off the Old Bill that I'd had it. Come again?

For those who don't know, Motorhead's famous stage prop was an impressive scale model of a Lancaster bomber, which was suspended over them while they performed. It weighed more than half a ton and had a twenty-foot wing span - and these muppets were looking for it under my bed!

"You could have dismantled it," they said.

"Yeah," I replied. "And the bed would have been eight foot off the ground."

They asked if I had an outbuilding. I said I had a garage. And you could see it in their faces: "We've got him. It's in the garage." I took them out to it. It was a double-door garage and one stood on either side of it, still clearly thinking, "We've got him. It's in the garage. We've got him. It's in the garage ..." And then they pulled open the doors, expecting to see a replica of a mighty World War II bomber, and all that was there was my little girl's tricycle. Their disappointment was tangible.

"Thank you, sir," the taller cop said. "We'll get back to you in due course."

I never heard from them again.

The stage bomber's theft in 1984 had been reported in the papers and someone had anonymously grassed me up for a laugh. I never did find out who. I suspected Motorhead's manager, Doug Smith, but he has always denied it. This kind of wind-up happened a lot back then, over a wild, seven- year period that probably qualifies as the happiest time of my working life: The Rock 'n' Roll Years.

If you can call it work, that is. Being paid to hang out with your heroes, interview bands, travel the world, ingest large quantities of beer and other stimulants, and discover the joy of mescaline.

This wasn't work - it was winning the lottery of life.

I joined the staff of rock weekly *Sounds* in July 1978. My first review, published in the 8 July issue, was of The Specials' first ever gig supporting The Clash at Aylesbury Friars Club. I also reviewed the U.K. Subs and The Tickets. Within weeks I'd interviewed The Rezillos, The Members, Bob Geldof and Steel Pulse. By September I'd talked my wise and witty editor, Alan Lewis, into running my feature on the Right to Work March.

Back then, I was punk rock and socialist to the point of being puritanical.

Initially, I resisted many of the opportunities that working for the music press in one of its most exciting ever periods presented. Dave Angry (Dave McCullough, another former fanzine writer who came along slightly later) and I set ourselves firmly against the music business. Foreign trips, tour jackets and freebie meals weren't for us, and we sneered at those who enjoyed them as corporate whores and sell-outs, slaves to The Man.

What berks we were.

With that in mind, it seems odd that the first time I went properly off the rails was on tour with someone who was even more puritanical than I was: Jerry Dammers. The Specials had invited me to New York to see their first US shows in January 1980. I loved the band and jumped at the chance.

I wasn't expecting Deborah Harry to take me there.

I'd interviewed Debbie in Newcastle the previous year. She'd been pleasant but suspicious and a little stand-offish, after being stitched up by some arsehole from the NME (New Musical Express). She was delighted by my piece in Sounds, however, and being a Specials fan she insisted on coming along with Chris Stein to ferry me and my photographer, Ross Halfin (a man with revolting personal habits, known and loathed as Gross Halfwit), to the gig at Speaks Club, Long Island.

I was too punk to be star-struck, but I will admit that as I was being driven in a huge black stretch limo over the Brooklyn Bridge at sunset, with Debbie Harry, the most beautiful woman in pop, sitting opposite me, her eyes so blue they made the Med seem murky, Chris Stein chopping out lines of cocaine, and a magnum bottle of champagne on ice sitting in the corner, there was a fair bit of pinching myself going on, along with the recurring thought: wait till I tell 'em about this in the Swan in Charlton Village.

It gets better/worse though. At the gig, Ross and I were chatted up by two Brooklyn punkettes with accents broader than Central Park, and we ended up inviting them back to the hotel. Debbie was disgusted and I was shunted up the front with the chauffeur, with both of the girls on my lap. This was when Claudia whispered in my ear, "My friend doesn't like your friend ..." Back in Manhattan, we lost Ross, found a dealer, drained the minibar and ... let's just say that I enjoyed the kind of night that had so far eluded me after they called last orders at the Blackheath & Newbridge Working Men's Club.

Things changed after that. I was true to my principles in that I never took a bribe or a jaunt with a band I didn't like just for the travel opportunity, but equally I never turned down a trip with a band that excited me again. I went on to traverse the globe with everyone from Ozzy Osbourne to The Selecter. Japan, Germany, the USA, India, France, Scandinavia ... a world of opportunity opened up and I readily partook of it. At times it was Animal House with rock 'n' roll beat. Not that I ever stopped banging my drum for socialism – I urged readers to vote Labour at the general elections of 1979 and 1983, and I interviewed Labour leader Neil Kinnock for the paper. (It got picked up by the nationals, because he slagged off Arthur Scargill.) Pete Way, from rock gods UFO, used to call me 'The Leader', which was short for 'The Leader of the Revolution'.

In 1984, I was approached by a rock manager who was also a prominent member of the Labour Party in Darlington East, who asked me whether I would consider standing as a Labour MP.

It wasn't the only strange offer I declined. A record company exec spent far too long admiring my tattoos one night in The Ship in Wardour Street, then held my wrist and blatantly suggested that if I let him lick my tatts, and various other body parts, he'd be happy to sign up my band. In other words, my gonads for my Gonads. The band remained unsigned.

Sexual favours were often on offer but more usually from women, and because I was married I generally declined. Call me old-fashioned. but going to bed with someone you'd just met because she wanted to get close to a band you happened to be with was scarcely less empty than paying for a hooker. At least with a brass you'd know what the deal was. Although the stunning Lolitas who stalked Def Leppard in the States – see next book - were a damn sight more appealing than the average female Dumpy's Rusty Nut enthusiast. Sometimes meaningless sex is enough, of course, but it never really floated my boat.

Looking back, I'm amazed at the sheer volume of bands I saw, reviewed and interviewed. Because, unlike many rock writers, I would happily go out of the West End to see new bands, I was there to witness the birth of 2-Tone, New Mod and Oi. As well as The Specials, I wrote the first ever reviews of bands like Conflict, Twisted Sister and U2, who used to come to the pub with McCullough and I just to watch us drink.

The fun came with a price tag, of course. I've lost most of the hearing in my right ear as a result of prolonged exposure to the likes of Motorhead and Maiden. My memory has been scrambled by substance abuse. I was beaten up by neo-Nazis at a London gig, and threatened by two others at knifepoint on a train. And as a result of the Southall Riot, which I wasn't even at, I have spent the last thirty years being called a fascist by media liberals and a communist by the far right. In August 1983 the Young National Front printed my home address in their hate-rag *Bulldog*, branding me a race traitor, resulting in abusive mail and threats so graphic I had to move my family from our maisonette, 100

Ebdon Way on the Ferrier Estate, to another. For a while I felt like a walking bullseye. And yet I still think of the *Sounds* years, 1978–84, as the happiest times of my working life. The golden years.

Later on I would work and film with the likes of Freddie Starr, Michael Barrymore, Al Murray and Jim Davidson. But none of the antics of these notorious comic legends were as shocking as the time I interviewed Judge Dread in the restaurant of a Hamburg brothel while an obliging female dwarf gobbled him off under the table.

You didn't get that on *Come Dine With Me*. Except probably in Gillingham. And I never had to step over sleeping groupies to interview Ronnie Corbett as I did the late great Phil Lynott …

These were my Rock 'n' Roll Years …

My Pal Ozzy

November 1981, I'm on the road with Ozzy Osbourne. He's due to play Leicester tonight, only he's doubled up in pain in the foyer of the Holiday Inn. "I ate a dodgy hamburger," he moans.

"It was cordon bleu," manager/girlfriend Sharon Arden – the future Mrs O - tells him.

"It should be fuckin' cordoned off!" Ozzy retorts. "It was made of rancid cat meat. I can't go on, Sharon. I've got food poisoning. I'm in agony."

Reluctantly, Sharon cancels the gig. Ozzy requests a 'medicinal' brandy, we hit the bar for a large one and his stomach ache is rapidly forgotten. But not by the promoter, who is Sharon's father, Don Arden, otherwise known as rock's answer to Don Corleone – a man who was much feared in music press circles after he responded to a bad review of ELO by sending two of his heavies to hang an *NME* hack out of a third-storey window by his ankles. I don't think either of them was Mr. Dacombe. You felt with Don that he might rip off a head as casually as he ripped off his acts. (The only rock manager with a heavier reputation was the great but ruthless South Londoner Peter Grant, whom Arden had originally hired to work for him as a tour manager.)

Within minutes of the show being pulled, Don starts to page the pair of them. But we're all having too much of a good time to take his call. Around 8 p.m. we realise that the paging has stopped and assume that the old man has given up. Result! Unfortunately, we're wrong. Don has only stopped calling because he has made his son David drive him up from London.

Shortly after 9.30 p.m. I go to order a round just as a squat raging bull of a man in a state somewhat beyond apoplexy materialises in the hotel bar. The crowd of nervous drinkers part before him like the Red Sea parting for Moses. Shaking with rage, Don roars up to our table, jabs a stubby finger at an unfortunate lighting man and tells him, "You – fuck off!" He complies. I stay at the bar and witness a masterclass of insults and invective couched in language that would have made Gordon Ramsay blush. Don rants, he raves, he seethes; he practically emits steam. Sharon and Ozzy return the tirade. For a good twenty minutes the air is as blue as Dot Cotton's varicose veins, and then Sharon says something that changes her father's mood in an instant.

"Dad," she says, in that 'little girl lost' voice. "We're getting married."

And that was it. The swearing and threats stop immediately. They're hugging and kissing, and Don's ordering champagne. I get called over from the bar. Don hugs and kisses me. We have a right old time. But to this day I'm unsure whether the Osbournes' marriage was actually planned, or whether it was an inspired spur of the moment invention to deflect Don's not inconsiderable wrath.

At around 10.30 p.m. the now teary-eyed promoter decides it's bedtime, leaving Ozzy to go back on the brandies. The rock star's eyes fill with mischief. There are Japanese businessmen at the next table, and bread rolls within the rock star's reach. The pelting commences. Sharon and I manage to restrain him.

"Come on, Oz," I say. "Let's hit the sack. You've got an early start."

He rises unsteadily to his feet, and glances out towards the hotel lobby.

Suddenly his mood changes.

"What the f...," Ozzy says.

"What?" asks Sharon.

"Fucking filth!" Ozzy roars.

We look over. Two uniformed policemen are in the lobby.

Ozzy is outraged. "I'm going to do the bastards," he says, and he starts to stagger towards them.

Sharon looks at me. "Stop him, Garry," she pleads.

Gulp. I'll try.

I run after Ozzy and grab him by the shoulders. He's stronger than I am. The cops are leaving but are still in the hotel. If Oz reaches them, or they see the commotion they've inadvertently caused, he will be nicked. Sharon runs to join me. I have one arm and she has the other. Together we manage to keep Oz in the bar until the police have gone.

"Bye cunt-stables," Ozzy slurs as Sharon steers him towards the lift. "Bye orifacers."

It was, we agree over breakfast the next morning, a relatively uneventful night …

* * *

Birmingham-born Ozzy was always one of my favourite rock stars. I've known him since 1979 and he's always been as funny as he is crazy. Once he casually let slip that he'd bedded ALL of his first wife Thelma's girlfriends. When I asked if his missus had minded, Oz replied, "Why should she? I fuck her as well."

But Sharon is most definitely the power behind the throne. She may seem like sweetness and light on TV, but the former Sharon Arden is every bit as tough and shrewd as her notorious father.

63

Back in 1981 we arrived at a concert in the USA. Ozzy was supposed to be topping the bill but wasn't. Sharon asked the Yank promoter why

He started to reply, saying, "Listen, little lady ..."

He was a big guy, about 6ft 5ins and at least 16 stone, but he didn't get any further.

She knocked him out with one punch. "Patronising git," she said.

When Sharon threatened that she would cut off someone's dick and ram it down his throat, nobody doubted that she was capable of doing it. I always laugh whenever I see her on TV these days, putting on that 'ickle girl' voice and claiming to love even the naffest wannabe singer, because inside she's as soft as an iron bar.

It was Sharon who saved Ozzy from drug-raddled obscurity after he was sacked by Black Sabbath. She lured him away from Don, who promptly sent her to Coventry for nineteen years, uttering such paternal pleasantries as, "When my daughter dies I'll be at the funeral, pissing on her grave." Sharon mortgaged their home to put Oz back on the road and give him the space and the support he needed to make it all over again in the USA. I was lucky enough to be there at the very start of that comeback. Between 1980 and '85 I toured the world with Ozzy. We were so close that he even asked me to ghostwrite his autobiography. (As did Don.) Why didn't it happen? Consider our first day of interviews for the book and the consequences:

> *12 noon.* We meet in a West End pub, drink beer and brandy for two hours.

> *2.30 p.m.* Back to their rented gaff near Grosvenor Square. Ozzy supplies two bottles of wine, I chop out two fat lines of sulphate. An interview of sorts takes place.

> *7 p.m.* Back to the pub.

> *8 p.m.* Chinese meal, more beer, brandy and banter.

> *10 p.m.* Back to the pub for last orders and Ozzy's favourite tipple: a pint glass filled with a shot from every spirit on the optic, ordered with

a cheery, "Once round the wall of death, please guv'nor."

> *10.30 p.m.* Back to his place. More beer, more shorts.

> *12 midnight.* The telly's on and I pass out.

> *12.08 a.m.* I wake up. There's a stab of pain over my right eye. I assume that Ozzy has thrown an empty can at me. I growl at him and stagger up to bed.

> *Thirty-two hours later.* I take my kids to primary school. I think the mums are looking at me strangely, but I put it down to post-speed paranoia.

> *10.30 a.m.* Steve Kent, the guitarist in my band, knocks at my front door. He takes one look at me and says, "Gal, where's yer eyebrow?" Ozzy has shaved it off.

I'm not sure what disturbs me most about this story – that Ozzy had been that close to my eye with a razor blade in the state he was in, or that I'd been so out of it the following day I hadn't even noticed that my eyebrow was missing.

I was lucky. Oz once shaved off his keyboard player's entire head of hair. He has been known to set fire to roadies, or pass around a hip flask full of aftershave. I once saw him piss in the jacket pocket of unsuspecting rock photographer Ross Halfin, which absolutely shocked me. I wouldn't have pissed on Ross if he were on fire.

Careless urination was always a feature of Ozzy's lifestyle. He got arrested for it in Texas, when he pissed on the ruins of the Alamo. But this wasn't a mark of disrespect to the people of Texas - he'd had a skinful and it was just a handy wall for a leak. He'd previously been arrested for peeing on the hood of a parked car in Memphis. The police report said he was "staggeringly drunk". No change there then. He also fell out with Don, who caught him piddling in the sink of the bar in his living room.

And it gets worse. We were checking into a Marriott Hotel in Florida once when Ozzy felt the need for a crap. Anyone else would have asked for the restroom. Ozzy merely dropped his trousers and defecated in an ashtray in the lobby. We were understandably asked to leave.

Strangely, Ozzy's road crew looked on him as a kind of tattooed agony aunt. One poor dim-witted Scottish roadie contracted a sexual disease a week before they were due to come home from that same tour. Distraught, he came and found Ozzy and asked the rock god for advice.

Ozzy thought about it for a moment and then, straight-faced, advised the poor wretch to bathe his diseased bits in Domestos.

"Really, Oz?" said the roadie.

"Yes," Ozzy replied sagely. "Because Domestos kills 99 per cent of all known germs."

The roadie went away happy, and we all knew that he did what Ozzy had advised because about half an hour later we heard the screams from two floors below.

That tour was exhilarating and life-threatening in equal measure, so very much typical of the Ozzy Osbourne experience.

It ended with a sell-out show at Daytona Beach. Afterwards we all partied recklessly. Lightweight that I am, I turned in at around 2 a.m. Two hours later I awoke to what sounded like a guerrilla attack on the plush hotel masonry. Was that machine gun fire? What the f...? Gingerly, I crawled to the window and looked out, expecting to see an invading Cuban army. Instead, I saw Oz celebrating the end of ninety-three gruelling dates by showering the hotel exterior with stage firecrackers. Two squad cars full of angry, armed cops drew up outside and Oz led his entourage inside. Like a *Carry On* farce, lights went on and off all over the hotel as they moved from room to room, avoiding their pursuers long enough to let off a round of firecrackers before escaping to the next safe haven. Eventually, Ozzy led his party onto the tour bus, which of course was private property, and told the cops to bugger off till they could come back with a warrant ...

Ozzy was never one for unwinding by sunbathing or reading a good book. One time in Seattle, to combat the boredom, Oz dropped a fishing line out of his hotel window and landed four baby sharks. He gutted two and laid them out in his bed like the horse's head in *The Godfather*, and left the other two swimming in his bath. Then he called room service and left for the night's show.

MTV didn't show things like that on *The Osbournes* ...

Of course, the funniest Oz story was when he was on tour in Japan. Steaming drunk, Oz pulled a geisha girl and took her back to his hotel room, completely forgetting that Sharon was on tour with him. Sharon took one look at the girl, snatched a painting off the wall and smashed it right over her head. Sayonara slapper.

Halfin found Ozzy the next morning lying prostrate in the hotel corridor.

He wasn't much for groupies when I knew him, although he was nearly at the centre of a sex scandal when his new bass player started choking while they were in the shower after a gig. The naked Ozzy started the Heimlich manoeuvre on him, at which point the bass player's girlfriend walked in and got entirely the wrong impression.

Booze was Ozzy's mistress back then. He thought nothing of breakfasting on an entire hotel minibar – and yet he'd still perform in the evening. At his worst, he would consume FOUR litre bottles of brandy a day. One night drinking with him after a show in Sheffield, Ozzy asked what I wanted as a short to finish off the night. I said a Hennessy brandy. Oz replied, "Great idea," and ordered us a bottle each.

He told me that he'd got drunk for the first time at the age of 14 and in the next 22 years was hardly ever sober. Sharon initially tried to stop him boozing by hiding all his clothes. Famously, Ozzy just dressed up in her clothes and went down the pub anyway.

He freely admits that if it wasn't for Sharon, he'd be dead. Yet even before he tried to kill her, Ozzy and Sharon would row constantly. We nearly ploughed into the central reservation when they started screaming at each other, with Sharon at the wheel, on the road in the Midlands. And half an hour later, it was all forgotten.

* * *

Ozzy was always open about his drug consumption. As long ago as 1982 he asked me to warn kids that heroin was "shit", and that LSD was "crap, not worth taking".

I asked how often he'd dropped acid when he was in Black Sabbath. Ozzy replied, "Only about 900 times. I used to swallow handfuls at a time. The worst trip I ever had was after I took four tabs of acid and two tabs of mescaline. I wandered into this field totally out of it and started talking to a horse. I talked to this bloody horse for hours and in the end the horse told me to fuck off – that's when I knew things were getting out of hand."

He was always great copy, and I naturally loved provoking him into saying something outrageous.

I was with him shortly after he'd bit the head off a dove while being introduced to CBS executives in Los Angeles. Ozzy was amazed by the outcry, and then outraged by it.

"What's the difference between a dove and a chicken?" he protested to me. "No one gives Colonel Sanders the stick I've had and he murders about nine million chickens a day."

What did it taste like? I asked innocently.

"Warm," he said. "Like tomato sauce."

So have you got a taste for uncooked fowl?

"Oh yes," he said. And to prove it he bit the wings off a pigeon.

I was with Ozzy in New York in 1981 when someone threw a live bat at him on stage. Thinking it was a toy, Ozzy bit its head off too – but not before the bat bit him. "What a horrible dumb animal," said the bat.

Oz was rushed to hospital for rabies injections. When he arrived he told shocked nurses, "I've got rabies," and started barking. He howled at the moon when the mood took him for days on end. Later he said that the bat reminded him of Sharon's cooking and claimed that it was rushed to hospital "to get Ozzy Osbourne shots".

An anti-Ozzy backlash kicked off, as Christian campaigners understandably objected to his unholy presence on their shores. The crazies in his audience responded by bringing dead animal 'tributes' to his shows. The macabre menagerie that got past security included: a dead dog carcass, white rats, a snake, a severed cow's heads, pigs' heads, an ox's head and, in Des Moines, a skinned 18in Louisiana bullfrog.

One kid killed a cat outside a gig and tried to get in with it tied round his waist like a belt. At another show, someone threw a dildo onto the stage with a live bullet attached to it and a note saying, "Now bite the head off that."

I was in Providence with Oz when some nutcase hurled a cherry bomb on stage just as the band were about to come on. It exploded, knocking Sharon unconscious. She was rushed to hospital but wasn't seriously hurt. I pity that kid if she ever finds him. I fell out with Sharon, briefly, when I was half-writing Ozzy's book. It wasn't a pleasant experience. But she is capable of much kindness too. When I wasted a day of my holiday in 2001 due to a misunderstanding, Sharon flew my wife and kids from Vegas to LA and treated them to a great day out at Universal Studios.

In all the years I've known Ozzy, he has never failed to make me laugh. He never minds being the butt of the story himself and, although he loves to play up to his satanic image, he has no time for the black arts. When an earnest US fan once asked Ozzy about black magic he replied, deadpan, "I prefer Milk Tray." But, just to wind people up, Sabbath did record a backwards message that when deciphered said, "Your mother sells whelks in Hull."

The only band ever to outdo him were the Cockney Rejects, who while recording at Rockfield studios, South Wales, decided to pay Oz a visit at the mansion he was renting a few miles away. Tanked up on lager and Bob Hope, they turned up at his place with 12-bore shotguns. Wearing sheets over their heads, they started chanting odes. Vince, the bassist, fired off a round and the top window flew open. It was Ozzy, looking as if they'd interrupted him in the middle of a bad acid trip. Clearly freaked out by the robed figures in the front garden, he insulted them in pure Anglo-Saxon and then started to intone Latin church verses as if trying to exorcise evil spirits. The lads fired off a couple more rounds and legged it before the police turned up. Jeff said it might even be their fault that Ozzy started shaking.

When he discovered his tormentors' identity (from Halfin) Oz was initially outraged, but after a while he congratulated them on the wind-up, branding the band "men after my own heart".

* * *

I met up with Ozzy again in New York in 1999, a year before The *Osbournes* TV show propelled him to a whole new level of global fame. Proudly, Ozzy boasted that he hadn't touched a drop for seven years. And yet, when I caught up with him in LA three years later, he admitted that he'd been burying vodka in his back garden and sneaking out to "walk the dog" behind Sharon's back.

He told me: "Remember I got in trouble with the council for installing floodlights in the garden of our place in Buckinghamshire? I said I wanted them for late night gardening, but I was really digging holes to hide the vodka."

He doesn't do hard drugs anymore though – just tranquillisers and painkillers. And he isn't unfaithful to Sharon anymore either – it's far too risky. The woman is madder than a wet hen.

So what's my take on Ozzy? That he is one of the real people in rock 'n' roll. What you see is what you get with him. The Ozzy you see on screen is the Ozzy I've known for half my life.

His only weakness is hypochondria and his most endearing quality is his constant air of wounded innocence. No matter what befalls him, Ozzy believes it is never his fault.

I'll end with my favourite Ozzy story. Back in the late '70s, before the dove incident, Ozzy got back from touring with Black Sabbath to discover that his first wife, Thelma, had bought some chickens.

Within a day the noise from the clucking was driving him nuts, so Ozzy took his shotgun and started blasting them.

"The last one wouldn't die," he told me. "So I took a sword and started chasing it. Suddenly, I was stopped by the sight of my very respectable neighbour looking at me over the fence.

"Unwinding again, John?" she said.

Classic.

* * *

Ozzy Tour Notes

June 1981, New York's Plaza Hotel is so posh you wouldn't be at all surprised to turn round and catch the Queen Mum sliding down the banisters between courses, or James Cagney in a top hat and tails tap dancing down the stairs singing 'Yankee Doodle Dandy' at any given moment.

Myself, I enjoy being here immensely, not least because I know the likes of me shouldn't be here, and *they* know the likes of me shouldn't be here, but there's sod all they can do about it.

Ozzy Osbourne doesn't seem anywhere near as chuffed. In front of him is a month-old copy of *Sounds* open at a Letters Page criminally stuffed with anti-Osbourne propaganda viciously asserting that recently published pictures of him sensitively biting off a dove's head amounted to 'an over the top macho display', 'a sickening obscene act', 'a vile abuse of publicity', and, most outrageously, 'a has-been engaged in a cheap publicity stunt'.

To say Oz is a little miffed would be like comparing a leg amputation to a neatly clipped toenail. "They're all hypocrites," the Brummie rock god snarls. "Anyone who complains, just ask the arseholes do they eat meat, and if they do they're worse than me cos they're lazy bastards. They're so dumb they believe in the system, they believe it's alright to go to the butchers and see a dead cow hanging up as long as they don't have to kill it."

"Y'know what I'd like to do?" he demands rhetorically, tattooed pinkies closing menacingly round the neck of Sharon's pet pooch. "I'd like to open up a restaurant and every time someone ordered a steak I'd bring a live cow in and slaughter it in front of them. Every time people eat meat they should think of me. I'm a great advert for the vegetarian society."

He should know what he's on about – Ozzy started work at 16 as a slaughter-man in an abattoir, shooting 200 head of cattle a day for a meagre 17 notes a week.

Tell us how the dove incident came about, Oz.

He shakes his shaggy head and sighs. "If people would only look at the situation ... I've been in this business 15 years and if they realised the shit I have to go through for my name to be remembered ... I was at a CBS Convention, right. All the old codgers are there and they don't give a fuck about you, it's just a sham. They play your album while you're there, then forget you. Well, I wanted to make a real impression. The scam is the bird was dead. We were planning to release it there, but it died beforehand. So rather than waste it I bit its head off. You should have seen their faces. They all went white. They were speechless. That girl in the pictures was screaming. Eventually a bloke came up and said, 'You better go'."

What did it taste like?

"It tasted warm, like tomato sauce. Next time it'll be a piranha fish."

I heard you bit a pigeon's head off the next day too.

"No, no, no ... yes. That was dead too. I bit the wings off it. I'm not really sick, I'm just deranged."

I mention an old rat-catcher in Custom House who for the price of a pint would bung a hankie over a rat's head and bite it off, to much general amusement. Oz grunts in acknowledgement of a kindred spirit, but he is preoccupied with his lily-livered critics.

"What's the difference between a dove and a chicken anyway? One poxy bird. They wanna see me when I start on cats. I shot a cat once for shitting on my car. The cat cost 35p and the car cost six grand – no contest. I had to shoot it seven times. The bastard wouldn't die. It haunted me. This cat was wild living in my garage and it kept having kittens and shitting everywhere. So I said to my old lady, it's either me or the cat. So after many attempts to kick it out me bed I shot it. I shot it in the eye first with a 22 bullet. Next morning it came crawling back to eat our food, and it shat on the car again. So I loaded up and shot it straight through the neck. Three days later it hobbled back and shat on the bonnet with its one eye all white and glazed like something out of that film *Zombies*. So I shot it again. A couple of weeks later I came back from Australia and there was this cat back – it had so much lead in it I could've sold it for scrap metal. I took a double barrel and shot it clean over the fence. God's honest truth, three days later it was back again, so it had to be the water treatment. But y'know, live and let die."

It'd be no exaggeration to say that Oz has had me in stitches for five whole days. It isn't that he cracks gags, it's more the way he is and the way he tells 'em. Y'see, the Ozzy experience is total, an exercise lesson in complete over-the-toposity. For the sensitive, to know him is to loathe him.

Example: first thing we have to do is visit a quack's, Oz, a notorious hypochondriac, having apparently cracked his ribs the night before.

Had he been hauled into the audience, I wondered?

"Nah, I fell over while I was pissing on Lyndsay on the bus."

That's offstage organ player Lyndsay 'Gladys' Bridgewater from Ipswich, who's the butt of some cruel practical jokes. The night before Oz had shaved off his eyebrows and cut off half his hair Phil Oakey-style while Gladys was steamed out of his box. In the morning he convinced him he'd done it himself. The next night the roadies told him there was an electrical fault so that he couldn't put both feet on the floor at the same time while he was playing. The poor sod spent the whole gig hopping from one foot to the other.

But pissing on people is a fave Oz preoccupation, and he's truly outraged to recall how a few nights back the bus driver had pulled up and come back yelling at him for pissing over some unfortunate. "Of course I sacked him there and then," Oz froths, fully indignant. "The cheek of the bastard."

The quack reckons Oz has just got some bad bruises, so we have a beer and shoot off to tonight's gig at the Palladium.

Up in the dressing room Oz strips off with gay abandon, revealing more tattoos, a dagger on his leg and two smiling faces on his knees. Like a lot of his arm tats these are homemade, done while he was doing time in Brum's Winson Green Prison.

"My job was to scour corridor floors with graphite," he says. "So I used a pin to prick designs on my skin, then I rubbed graphite in to make them tattoos. I was in for burglary. I used to work with this Irish guy called Pascal Donegal. He used to go and clock houses, find out when people went to work, and then we'd burgle them. This time the idiot didn't realise the house he was watching was a boarding house. People had gone to work but the owner was on night shift and he was still in bed. When we broke in he beat seven shades of shit out of us. I got three months – it was burglary, larceny, assault, ABH and possessing dope all in one thing. Mind you, I quite liked the nick – free food, free tobacco.

It was heaven to me cos I'd had no dough. I shared a cell with a murderer. He used to tell me about all the ways he'd killed people. I quite got into it at the time."

Out in the Palladium, the crowd are going apeshit like I've never seen yanks go apeshit before. Chants of "Uz-zy, Uz-zy" fill the air where space is vied for between homemade banners, makeshift crosses and placards that proudly proclaim "Ozzy rules, Dio drools". The atmosphere is like a Cup final. Suddenly it's show time. Evil smoke billows everywhere. The crowd temperature rises 200 degrees. And the Vampire Son of Brum stands stage centre, peace signs puncturing the mists. "I'm back with a fuckin' vengeance," he roars. "Are you ready to rock 'n' roll? It's been a long time, but I'm back!"

Powerful operatic build-up music – Carl Orff's *Carmina Burana*, long before it became a TV cliché - brings the atmosphere to fever pitch: '*O Fortuna, velut luna statu variabilis, semper crescis aut decrescis …*'

"Oh shit," a kid behind me says in rapture. 'Crazy Train' powers out of the sinister mix of mist and classics, and Oz catapults into the air, his silly frilly shirt swirling like ten plates of spaghetti tossed at the ceiling in an Eyetie nosherie. This is the first time I've clocked the new line-up of Blizzard of Ozz – it was only finalised five weeks ago. New drummer, Tommy Aldridge, is a huge-conked half-Native American from Littlerock, Arkansas, with an emaciated frame and a face more weathered than a North Sea oil rig. He's a mighty meaty beat-keeper. Drum solos as a rule bore me shitless, but this former Black Oak human rhythm machine workout is hypnotic. Drumsticks twirl with the grace of a trained juggler whirling skittles, and when he carries on the solo with his hands … All I can do is reiterate Oz's definitive "flash American bastard".

Frail Randy Rhoads, ex-Quiet Riot, is an exceptional rock guitarist, fluid and versatile. He makes his Gibson soar and roar, producing screams more gruesome than the squeals of a thousand chickens getting their legs broken simultaneously. Bassist Rudy Sarzo, also from Quiet Riot, plays his instrument at a weird and wonderful array of angles – a predilection he acquired to relieve the boredom of playing the same set seven nights a week in a Florida bar band. While fifth man Gladys stands in the wings, out of sight but in full stage make-up (?!?!), supplying competent keyboard frills.

Master showman Ozzy leads his motley crew through a procession of crowd-pleasers, his voice ranging from a cacophonic cackle to a blood-curdling scream. The set features the best of the first Blizz disc, two tantalising tasters from the newly completed second album (to be called *Diary of a Madman*, oh trembling unbelievers) and naturally the set-ending/encore succession of Sabbath faithfuls, 'Iron Man', 'Children of the Grave' and 'Paranoid', that timeless tasty sounding as magnificently mindless as the first time I heard it on *Top of the Pops* way back when, and was instantly plunged into teenage HMery (see also Dick Emery).

Jet lag kicks in, so I cab it back to the hotel; Ozzy doesn't get any kip at all, however, getting outrageously rat-arsed instead. The next morning I'm up early, soaking up the grandeur of this great city, the huge triumphant buildings standing proud against the heraldic blue of the sky. When it's cold in New York, like it is now, the air is as sharp as a guillotine blade. I'm about to risk a stroll through Central Park when I spot Ozzy coming out of it. He's been up all night drinking and had hit the park at the crack of dawn, doubtless looking for stray sparrows and other helpless examples of edible wildlife. "Oi Garry," he shouts. "Breakfast!" Outside the Plaza we chance upon three young hairy fans who'd spent the night in the brass-monkeys cold just to glimpse their hero in the morning. Ozzy invites them in with us only to discover to his disgust that the Plaza won't serve alcohol at the breakfast table. Oz leaves the kids to tuck in on him, and retires to his room for a proper beery brekkers on room service. Preferring sight-seeing to fright-seeing, I make like a *News of the Screws* hack in a brothel; I make my excuses and go.

Early that afternoon we leave town on the luxury tour bus, and Oz immediately begins to amuse himself by insulting passers-by (along "Is your face hurting you, cos it's killing me" lines) and bemoaning his stupidity at getting just two hours' sleep.

"I've got a head like a bag full of toss," he announces. "Still, there's [singing] NO BUSINESS like SHOWBUSINESS!"

"Can we go up the top of the World Trade Centre for some pictures?" whines my blob-like sidekick, fatso Ratso Halfin.

"Fuck off," yells Oz. "I get vertigo when I put platform boots on."

The good humour of the trip is defused as the bus passes a demonstration of New York IRA supporters marching for Bobby Sands. Oz explodes.

"What the fuck to these bastards know about it? Look at them, having a lovely stroll through New York on a Sunday afternoon. What do they know about kids getting blown up and mutilated? Where were these bastards when the IRA blew up that pub in Birmingham and killed 22 innocent people?"

No one has an answer. Half an hour later the bus runs out of beer. Oz instantly orders the driver to stop, unaware that we're in the heart of Harlem. Within minutes a huge, largely hostile crowd has gathered round us, but Oz just doesn't give a toss, casually pushing past mobs of glowering locals to stroll back with an armful of goodies, seemingly unaware that the atmosphere is heavier than Buster Bloodvessel in concrete Doc Martens.

A couple of miles further down the road and we're, ahem, cruising past the decaying dockland area with its street-corner mobs of Village People fanciers trying to out-pose each other in the muscle and moustache stakes. Ross is getting far too excited for his own good, so I slip up the back with Oz for a semi-civilised interview. Starting with the subject of his nuttier fans ...

"This geezer came at me with a sword on stage once, but me road manager bashed him with a mike stand. Another time there was this bird I thought I'd pulled. I thought she was a bit funny cos she didn't smoke or drink. When she got back to the hotel room she started on about being a redeemer and how I was polluted and how she was gonna save my soul ... She learnt how to fly in less than a minute."

He rates the US:

"I love the American way of life. Let's be honest, what's Britain got now? English people are just paying for the politicians' fuck-ups. They should have a Maggie Thatcher Burning Night instead of Guy Fawkes. Her head's full of shit. And to think I voted for her just to give a woman a chance ... Politicians are scumbags. They're all fucked. What about the people? The mass unemployment? I'll tell ya, I predict a bloody revolution over there. People say I've got power over people, I should make a stand, but that's not up to me ... Don't get me wrong, I'm not a communist, far from it, there's just got to be a better way of living. We can't even educate people about the dangers of nuclear war. Over here there's fallout shelters everywhere. Who's got 'em in Britain? The politicians and the very few. What about us? It's about time people started to question the government. All we'll get is an HM Government Warning – this bomb may seriously damage your health."

Oz had little time for fashionable pop fads like futurism, which he described as being ...

"... like having diarrhoea on a hot day. It's like think-music; shove a pen in yer earhole and an album will fall out yer arse. It's like androids on stage. It's nowhere music. When I started there were all these cosmic bands just like today's lot. They didn't last. But rock 'n' roll will never die, cos it makes you move, it makes you jump. I respect disco more than I respect fuckin' sputnik music. It's all intellectual crap, but if brains were dynamite they wouldn't have enough to blow their hats off."

What about you, Oz, what ambitions have you got left?

"Seriously, my only ambition in the world is to go to Egypt, stand on top of the Central Pyramid and piss all over it. I'll never stop touring. I love it. I'm a rock 'n' roll gypsy, I'll never give up. The only time I stopped was after the Sabbath split. It took me a long time to get over it - after all, it was eleven years of my life, and I got really ripped off. I lost six million pounds' revenue through fuck-ups and rip-offs. After the split I just sat and got pissed and stoned for six weeks. But this band's given me reason to go on."

Poughkeepsie is the next gig I spend entirely with Oz and 2,500 kids in the middle of nowhere. The kids are even crazier than the day before, hurling firecrackers at the stage, shrieking and hollering. How mad would they be for Tony McPhee and The Groundhogs? (Poughkeepsie, Groundhog Day. No? Please yourselves).

The next night is Springfield in front of a frenzied five thousand faithful. Then, with work behind us, we hit some bars and get totally arseholed. Most of our conversation survives only in a hazy netherworld. But the bits I do remember include his account of a visit to a strip club in Rochester, New York, when he held his cross up at the stripper, yelling, "Get thee behind me Satan," only to have the poor girl come up and whine, "What's the problem here? Are you harassing me?" in a broad Noo Joisey accent. Naturally, this became tour saying of the day.

You could tell he was sloshed cos he was coming out with nonsense like: "Geoff Barton deserves a medal for his services to HM." And after threatening to blow the Cockney Rejects' bollocks off if they ever tried to spook him out again – see I Am Der Management - he came round to admitting they were men after his own heart.

My last memories of the trip concern us crashing out of a lift and me leaving Ozzy sprawled out in the hotel corridor with his trousers round his ankles and his finger up his arse, muttering something about going to get a cab to the New York Zoo.

Whale meat again? Don't know where. Don't know when …

VIVA LAS WHISKERS: ZZ TOP IN VEGAS

June 1983, Las Vegas, Nevada: hot, superficial and shallow. I'm going to fit right in. But how will a roughneck boogie band like ZZ Top go down in the city of sin, Sinatra and Bugsy Siegel? Would their gritty Texan street cred survive the experience? Would mine? It's my first time, Vegas. Be gentle.

We fly in at night. It's pitch black. There's nothing to see in any direction. Then the pilot tells us to look to our left. There's an audible gasp from first-time tourists as we catch sight of what appears to be a huge neon mirage rising out of Nevada desert. Vegas is like a beautiful whore, tempting and beguiling but loaded with danger. You know you shouldn't be taken in by her, but you also know you will be. She'll take your money and screw you hard but you'll only remember the good bits.

I spend most of my first week with my mouth open, catching flies.

A taped greeting from sparkling git Liberace greets me and my loathsome sidekick Ross Halfin as we enter the airport building.

It's starting with some kitsch ...

Liberace's voice is pure treacle, oozing showbiz insincerity. And the tack attack has only just begun. A bank of one-arm bandits lines the moving walkway; it's a first fence that the desperate lemmings among the disembarking holidaymakers happily fall at. Quarters are disappearing into slots as rapidly as sex-starved roadies at a bikers' orgy.

We clear Customs, grab a taxi and wonder at the sights. Hoardings hustle for the attention, with promises of big-legged dancers and big-gutted comedians punctuated by the smarmy smiles of yesteryear's cabaret legends.

At night the place explodes in neon like Blackpool on a cocktail of acid and angel dust. It's like being trapped in a giant pinball machine, a great flashing monument to the capitalist Babylon, placed with comic surrealism worthy of Dali or Cleese, just a dice throw away from the breathtaking natural beauty of the Grand Canyon.

I loved it – with reservations … which were in the Desert Inn, the hotel built by the Cleveland Mob and the first one bought by Howard Hughes. The biggest names in the variety firmament have played the Desert Inn: the Rat Pack, Tony Bennett, Bobby Darin, Barry Manilow, Jerry Lewis, Don Rickles, Dionne Warwick. But like all the hotels here, it's basically a casino with guest rooms. And what rooms! Mine is bigger than the place I was born in. Seriously. The hotel is 'comping' the entire ZZ Top party, so we all get suites – with our own hot tub. Dave McCullough would be furious. It'd be "J'accuse" all day long. Or at least "Jacuzzi".

Down in the lobby and across the gaming floor there is no natural light, and no clocks. Nothing to distract the mug punters from the tables, except the 24-hour bar and the long, stocking-clad legs of discreetly available hookers, as high class as Vegas can manage, for the few lucky winners …

These big-haired, double-fronted women would get you stiffer than a mob rat in a shallow desert grave. And if that sounds superficial, well what other word does Vegas justice? Everywhere there's the loaded bait of A Better Life and A Better Lay just a wager away. More shirts have been lost pursuing that dream than have been lifted by every gay man in Frisco combined.

Guys in cowboy hats are playing poker when I go to bed, and are still playing the next morning when I come down for breakfast. (And our chosen breakfast here – a Bloody Mary 'eye-opener' – raises no eyebrows.)

Later, Dusty Hill, wearing a beret, will teach me how to play Texas Hold 'Em on that very table – an image that sounds like something I might have dreamt after chewing on a Tequila worm but, like everything I do during these wild few days, is Actually Happening.

This isn't just my first trip to Nevada, it's also my first encounter with the self-styled "little ol' boogie band from Texas". Both are mind-blowing, but Top are a revelation. I always thought there was something wonderful about them. For starters, two of them have got whiskers that make Captain Birdseye look clean-shaven, while the one who's called Beard hasn't got a beard at all. Dusty Hill looks like a hirsute Popeye on steroids. They've got a manager called Ham and accents that you could have scraped off the wall at the Alamo ...

Billy Gibbons is so cool you could store frozen chickens underneath that beard for months. He talks excitedly, not of groupies, drugs and the usual rock band agenda, but of meeting Bob Marley, checking out the Roxy in '79 and at his surprise and joy at running into Annabella from Bow Wow Wow while wandering through some tiny New Mexican township with a taco in his hand. The guy is as enquiring as a Marlowe on piece rate. Pretty much as soon as I meet him, he's asking me about happening bands like Big Country, Hanoi Rocks and the Bad Brains, savouring the flavour of anything new and different.

Back at the hotel after their show, we drink and chat into the early hours. The Desert Inn must have broken a lot of dreams but it sure as hell doesn't break Dusty Hill, who scoops a nice couple of grand on Blackjack and even tutors Halfin, who as usual was guilty of drinking on an empty head, into winning 200 bucks, which delights him like hooking a duck from a fairground side-stall might thrill a small, backward child.

Ross has readily succumbed to that old gamblers' adage: in this life the dice are loaded, so why not get loaded too?

Billy is surprisingly tall, six foot two (eyes of blue), and he speaks in a gentle, measured drawl, which, much to everyone's amusement, will be rubbing vowels with Liberace and J.R. Ewing star Larry Hagman at Vegas airport shortly. Only, natch, the Gibbons welcome will have more cool (sample: "Hi, this is Billy Gibbons of ZZ Top. All you slower folk please stand on the right so all the faster folk wishing to boogie may do so on the left," or "Have mercy! Watch those chilluns carefully ..." or even "When approaching the end of the moving walkway keep an eye on your boogie shoes ...").

Gibbons is an incredible character. In his early days, to supplement his income, Billy passed himself off as a preacher selling 'Bible balls' and rubber 'prayer balls'. The Rev. G guaranteed that if you threw 'em against the wall as you were praying your prayers would be answered. By Arthur and Daley ... He also subverted a religious radio show by appearing as the Reverend and playing the dirtiest blues tracks known to Southern man: "real, low, nasty stuff".

And yet Billy was also an artist and spent three months back in 1973 living in bohemian Paris and Florence soaking up the vibe. Not every band's interests run from titty joints to art galleries.

He was six years old when he first saw Little Richard live in concert and thirteen when he passed his driving test.

Dusty is shorter and stockier with big, powerful arms and a buffalo tattooed on his right bicep. He had it done while blotto on tequila, getting banned from the tattooist's in the process (no mean feat) and ending up almost getting lynched by Mexicans (for shouting, "Remember the Alamo," in a bar), rucking drunkenly with a taxi driver in the middle of a road, and pulling a bird who turned out to have a lesbian lover as well. "Two days later this bull dagger" – dyke - "came after me with a hunting knife," he chortles. "I had no idea ..."

Finally, there's beardless Frank Beard in his *Face* magazine-approved Fila gear, looking dapper from his napper to his feet. He speaks in such a lazy drawl that it sounds as though he might wake up any minute.

"Frank was the inspiration for 'Sharp Dressed Man'," Billy tells me. "He's Rod Stewart by the way of the *American Gigolo*."

"Yeah," laughs Frank, "the movie. I freaked out over Georgio's stuff, and by the time everyone else was into it I'd got the Fila kit, shirts and tennis outfits ..."

It's all very Casual, I tell them, very modern Mod. Billy grins. "ZZ Top can make the scene, even though we're late."

I don't see much of Frank outside the interview, as he was either golfing or with his wife (who has sadly reformed him from his wild brawling days). But Dusty is just as captivating a character as Billy, again managing to combine pride in his own culture and heritage (he had two relatives die at the Alamo) with being open-minded about other people's. Rhyming slang is his big interest and, being a good South London boy (which is where it originated, stuff the East End), I was able to keep him well supplied with essential phrases; such as Bob Hope (dope), Jack and Danny (fanny) and Iron Hoof (Ross Halfin).

Amazingly, Dusty got his pro grounding playing with Freddie King at the tender age of fourteen. The only white kid in a band who would often be joined for onstage jams by legends like B.B. King, he had no choice but to, in his own words, "get good quick". He adds, "It doesn't take much to be good, but it takes a lot to be *real* good."

How good is Dusty? Well, he wrote 'Tush' in ten minutes during a soundtrack. Oh, and he cites Richard Pryor as one of his influences.

ZZ Top's history is longer than their beards and more colourful than their stage lights. Though, as it's been related at length in nearly every Top feature I've ever read, I won't dwell on it here. You probably know how Houston boy Gibbons from a band called Moving Sidewalk and Dallas band American Blues members Dusty and Frank got together to form the Top in February 1969 and toured their way into the US nation's heart, releasing such killers albums along the way as *Tres Hombres* and *Fandango*! The climax of their early success was their legendary worldwide Taking Texas to the People Tour in 1976, which played to over a million people, grossing over ten million bucks, and only never made Britain because our quarantine laws prevented the band bringing the 'props' into the county – namely longhorn cattle, buzzards, snakes and buffalos and, according to Dusty, "us three animals".

ZZ Top are as working class as the Cockney Rejects, although both their set and their conversation are less reliant on the alleged glories of West Ham United. I am still dazed by the Vegas experience when I reach the gig, and am slightly surprised to find that a standard blue-collar rock audience has turned out for them – just a bunch of crazy kids keen to disassociate themselves from the Caesar's Palace cabaret world that's all around them.

The band's seventeen-number set is hot enough to thaw the most cynical critic, with the Texan trio negotiating a rich variety of southern-fried formats. Highlights include the trotting blues of 'Jesus Just Left Chicago', the anthemic 'I'm Bad, I'm Nationwide' and the terminally demented '(I Wouldn't Touch It With) A Ten Foot Pole', which has barely audible growled vocals and a rhythm so dirty you feel like you need a shower halfway through. Dusty and Billy execute a neat synchronised walk midway into the number, looking like a cross between Flanagan and Allen and Rip Van Winkle.

These guys are the ultimate barbecued blues and boogie band, and yet on occasions they can be more off the wall that a vandalised fag machine. Some of their songs are shot with madness worthy of Beefheart, which can only be A Good Thing. No wonder their numbers have been covered by talents as diverse as Motorhead and Hank Williams Junior. Watching – no, make that *experiencing* - ZZ Top live is the only way to appreciate how much their music means to them. Their sheer pleasure in playing is matched only by their near-telepathic precision and onstage camaraderie. They're immortal, immaculate and indivisible; at once superbly forceful, joyously tuneful and tighter than 30in jeans on a 34in belly.

It's easy to see why both Hendrix and Ted Nugent rated Gibbons so highly. He's a real craftsman, despite his "lumberjack fingers". Spurning the wanking into the wind five-minute guitar solo, Gibbons makes every note count, sometimes to blinding effect. Why unleash a hundred ill-conceived notes when ten on-target ones will do the job even better? He also plays guitar with a Mexican peso rather than a pick.

A brief respite of serious blues appears to follow soon after, with Billy wringing out a soulful solo and singing in a voice dripping with grief ... and then you realise that this is actually the intro to 'A Fool For Your Stockings', a rampant toast to the ultimate ladies' leg wear, which would go down at Greenham Common like the ghost of Trotsky running amok with an ice-pick plucked from his own bloody head at the Tory Party conference. The equally rudely evocative 'Pearl Necklace' comes next, pun fully intended, with Francis supplying some tasty Syn-drum rolls and Dusty's bass driving the whole shebang as big and fat as a Tex-Mex breakfast. 'Cheap Sunglasses' and the supercharged rock 'n' rolling 'Party on the Patio' brings the set to a close.

"ZZ TUP, ZZ TUP," thunder the punters, and they're back with a promise to "tear this house down right now". Much whooping and ten-gallon hat throwing ensues as Billy coaxes the crowd into some good-natured community singing: 'I know a girl who lives on the hill/She won't do it but her sister will ...' Ahh. 'Tube Shake Boogie', but it could be the Max Miller Shuffle.

So entrenched in matters carnal have things become that the boys have no option but to round things off in grand saucy style with 'La Grange', a growlin' howlin' hymn to the legendary 'best little whorehouse in Texas' carried along on the 'On the Road Again' riff, followed by the wholesome filth of 'Tush'.

What was that about sex, style and subversion again?

After all this stimulation at least one of the band goes off to get his tube shaken by a professional lady who looks a lot like Sue Ellen from Dallas. I can't reveal his identity. Or dust off his nickname.

I meanwhile manage to shake off the attentions of a woman from San Diego, higher than Elvis's old penthouse apartment in the Hilton, who had seen me with the band and was offering a number of neighbourly inducements in return for an introduction. "Does your wife blow you?" was the opening gambit of her small talk.

Blow me? She'd have sucked my heart out with a Hoover down the throat had I succumbed to a suck-cum.

Early the next evening we converge on the hotel room of genial tour manager JW, who, with typical Texas hospitality, orders up a lorry load of lager and we chat for hours. I ask 'em to recall the peaks of their career. Billy smiles and says, "The one Dusty had last night had some righteous peaks".

Frank recalls their first big headline gig at the University of Texas stadium in Austen in front of 80,000 fans. The hooligans carved 'ZZ Top' in big letters in the Astroturf with blades.

On bad experiences, they're more forthcoming. Dusty recalls "a place in Michigan we played. We had three days off there and when we got there it was terrible. It had one movie house, no nightlife, and the water smelt like sulphur. We pulled into town and said, 'What's happening?' They said 'ZZ Top are here in two days' … that was it! We were the only excitement. Never again."

"How about that time in Lubbock when the equipment didn't show up?" says Billy. "We were in a hotel opposite the venue, sharing one room – one had the bed, one had the mattress, one had the pillow and blanket. We had to sneak out the hotel. We were hanging out the window on a rope!"

The Top have reinvented themselves with their new *Eliminator*. It's a modern rock album that successfully marries synthesisers and electro effects with their finger-lickin boogie without watering down their drive one iota. It's an obvious front runner for rock album of the year, and it's doing mighty fine business stateside. It's clocked up 610,000 sales at the interview time and went on to make the Billboard Top Twenty.

"It sold 70,000 in LA the week we were there," says Frank.

"We're a band who know our figures," adds Billy.

"Yeah," drawls Dusty, "38-24-36."

(It ended up going quadruple platinum; and if you're wondering, the Eliminator itself is a cherry red 1933 Ford Coupe hot rod.)

"We vary the set somewhat," Frank volunteers, attempting to raise the tone. "Sometimes we might leave out the slower songs altogether – sometimes all they want is the big monkey beat right up their ass."

"Right up the khyber," corrects Dusty in mock-cockney.

"We just hit on these heavy sounds," says Billy. "The heavier it got the better we liked it."

Gibbons tells me about the time he walked into Jimi Hendrix's room to find the maestro lying on the floor with his head shaved bald at the back with a peroxide stripe going through the remainder.

"He was just lying there playing this unbelievable undying string of riffs," Billy says. "And he said, 'What d'you think?' I said, 'I've never heard that song before.' He said, 'No, what do you think of the haircut!"

Talking hair, Frank, Dusty and his brother Rocky dyed theirs blue in 1968, which must have been pretty radical at the time ("Well, we got some strange service," Dusty laughs). And it turns out that the Dolly Parton *Best Little Whorehouse* movie was inspired by 'La Grange', which extolled the virtues of the legendary Texas brothel of a 100 years standing (or should that be laying?). Seems the place was only shut down after it was "exposed by an overzealous reporter after a touch of notoriety".

"The real sheriff was seventy," reveals Frank. "He didn't look like Burt Reynolds. The reporter didn't look like a real reporter either. I play golf with him."

Do you ever talk to him about it?

"No. Mostly I talk to him about cheating on the golf course ..."

On the way out of JW's room I notice a sign, saying: 'To conserve energy please turn out your lights'. Outside there wasn't a single bloody building that wasn't swimming in neon!

Crazy town, crazy time, crazy guys ...

* * *

I didn't come back to Las Vegas until 1995 when, as well as celebrating my fortieth, I spent a strange couple of days with showbiz legend Engelbert Humperdinck – of which, more in book two. I've been back six times since. In 2000 I got married there (See Chapter Eight, The Great Escape) and I've seen the likes of Rodney Dangerfield, Jay Leno, George Carlin and Andrew Dice Clay perform. The city has never looked the same. Vegas expands like killer vegetation in an old B movie and, try as I might, I never tire of it.

Back Passage To India

Hanoi Rocks, India, February 1983. I took heroin once, by accident. Yes, I know that sounds ridiculous, but it's true and the circumstances were extraordinary. I was in India with Hanoi Rocks, the wasted brat kings of 1980s glam-punk, and a photographer called Justin Thomas, or, as I knew him, Justin Focus. It was February 1983, back when the capital of the state of Maharashtra was still known as Bombay. The city was renamed Mumbai in 1995 in honour of the goddess Mumba. (No, not Samantha Mumba.) Here is my diary entry for the trip:

The first thing you notice is the heat. Even at 3.30 a.m. it's closer than kissing cousins and clammy enough to make us jostled refugees from the European winter feel about as comfortable as rhinos on stilts. Then the smell hits you, the all-pervading stench that hangs over Bombay like the LA smog, a cross between month-old eggs and a schoolboy's stink bomb. Finally you notice the eyeballs. Row after row of Indian faces survey the weary arrivals struggling through baggage claim with the keen interest of vultures circling close of play on a battlefield. All are suitably bewitched by the sauntering satin and tat intro of Hanoi Rocks, the notorious Finns fatale. In particular their eyes are drawn to the lithe, louche and aloof figure of vocalist Michael Monroe, a dyed blond Adonis who pouts his way past the dapper airport officials wearing skin-tight leather strides and a drape jacket.

Monroe would turn heads in Carnaby Street; but in Bombay, which up to this time has only ever been host to four other rock bands (The Police, The Boomtown Rats, Classix Nouveaux and Wishbone Ash), Mike gets the kind of looks you'd expect to greet a flashing succubus in a nunnery - a mixture of shock, revulsion and fascination.

He is from Helsinki, but Monroe is so different from everything these people have ever seen he might as well be from Alpha Centauri.

Hanoi Rocks look exactly like they sound – they're degenerate brats exuding sleazy decadence, teenage arrogance and anarchic sexuality. From their speed-freak skinny frames, unkempt barnets, mutant rockabilly drapes and bootlace ties to their extravagant earrings and fedora titfers the sick bastards just ooze rock 'n' roll. Monroe – born Matti Fagerholm some 23 summers ago - is the most perfect, the prettiest star, sexually ambiguous enough to have once fooled even hard-nosed Scottish he-man Wattie Buchan from The Exploited into making passes. And I never had him down as a kilt-lifter.

Fag-paper-thin bassist Sami Yaffa is having similar problems. In London town his effete, oriental features are enough to make the Old Bill, who habitually pull him up on drunk and disorderly suspicions, insist he's Japanese; here the Indian officials are convinced he's a woman in disguise. "People keep thinking I'm female – what's wrong with me?" he hollers with mock indignation, flexing a feeble bicep like Popeye before the spinach.

No such trouble for surly guitarist, the nicely named Nasty Suicide (Jan Stenfors), or lone Englishman drummer Nick 'Razzle' Dingley in his peculiar Andy Pandy pyjamas, who respectively glower and wisecrack their way through Immigration Control.

It takes an hour and a half to clear Customs. Every piece of electrical equipment has to be logged, and if there's any missing on the way out of the country they'll have to pay a hefty surtax of 360 per cent. The long process isn't helped by the near nick-nicking of my over-keen photographer Justin for reckless snapping.

Thankfully, Indian promoter Yusuf Ghandi (no relation) is waiting to take us into town. He's instantly cornered by Hanoi's main guitar star and chief Keef lookalike Andy McCoy (born Antti Hulkko). This guy talks like an AWOL Trappist monk, is as affable as a drunken Labrador and has the cheek of Arfur Daley on speed.

"But Yusuf," Andy grins, helping himself to his first India King fag, "are the women here any good?"

This is entirely in keeping. After the obligatory "Can you buy us a pint?" Andy's first words to me were, "You won't find another band who shags as much as us," and he went on to reel off figures of carnal conquests on their first Finnish tour that put Giacomo Casanova to shame.

Is India ready for this? Am I? Certainly not at this ungodly hour. It's 5 a.m. now, and there are queues outside the airport terminal like a Harrods sale day, but the faces aren't here for the band. The only fans are ventilating the dilapidated minibus that drives us at about 30mph through the dirty pre-dawn streets to our hotel. We need ventilation, too, because Bombay has open sewers and everywhere stinks like Cyril Smith's khazi after 18 pints of Guinness and a vindaloo.

"I don't believe it, us a *punk* band and we're here," Andy says. (He keeps saying they're a punk band to get on my good side.)

McCoy's amazement is echoed by Razzle. "Just think." he says, "We must be the first herberts in India. It's great, but ..." He looks at the promoter. "What about the smell?"

"Don't worry," he replies. "We'll soon get used to you."

Yeah. I think I'm going to like Yusuf.

Razzle too. He's the funniest and least up-himself member of this extraordinary band, who are somewhere between glam rock and glam metal, with serious lashings of attitude. They're Finland's answer to the New York Dolls, with a tendency to mouth off and run away from the consequences – they recently bottled out of an open-air fist fight with my good pals from Twisted Fucken Sister in Covent Garden. But their natural arrogance has convinced them that India will fall for them like it did for Robert Clive. It would, they'd assured me, be the ultimate rock 'n' roll adventure. And besides, it's on the way to Japan, where they're even more confident of wooing the punters.

The first real seeds of doubt about what we've let ourselves in for are sown quickly. As we travel into town, it's hard not to notice the hundreds of citizens who have been reduced to sleeping in bags on the streets. Then there's the hotel. The Bombay International Hotel is a four-star job that ranks in the city's Top Ten. We decide on a kip, but when I get to my room and pull back the bed sheets you can see the bugs jumping. It's the same for everyone else too. So we can either play squash or chat, and we go for the yapping option, discovering masses of shared musical memories – Slade, Sweet, MC5, Alice Cooper, Desmond Dekker and most reggae of the '69 kind.

"How come everyone thinks we're heavy metal?" Andy rounds on me in his half-Finnish, half London yobbo accent. "That's the last thing we are. We're a bloody punk band! We're punk on stage and R&B on record. We're like a mixture of punk, fifties rock 'n' roll, seventies glam and the Shangri-Las."

So what brings you here?

"Everyone's got to be somewhere," he smiles, quoting Spike Milligan.

I thought this might be an over-reaction to that Twisted Sister challenge. I know they're big boys, but this is ridiculous …

"Twisted Sister …" Andy shakes his head in contempt. "They're not even worth talking about. They're old and they're ugly and they ain't even a good heavy metal band."

"Girlschool are the best heavy metal band," observes Nasty.

"And they're harder than Twisted Sister," adds Andy.

"Only girls should play HM," sniffs Mike, bringing this segment of scintillating conversation to a decisive close.

Years later Hanoi Rocks would support Twisted Sister on tour and none of these opinions would be repeated. Not in front of them, anyway.

By 7 a.m. we're sitting on the quayside, knocking back vodka and coke and enjoying the view of uptown Bombay, which looks like some toy-town Manhattan over the bay. Within five minutes of getting there, we become a sideshow ourselves, surrounded by curious passers-by and a motley crew of shoeless and limbless beggars. There are big-eyed, dirt-encrusted urchins, a wild-eyed and literally legless geezer propelling himself along on a trolley and, *would-ya-believe*, a bona fide snake charmer who thrusts his coiling cobra into my own sweating palms. It looks about as friendly as a feminist on Father's Day, brandishing a castrating knife.

"Charmed, I'm sure," I say. "At least I hope it is." I'm not ashamed to say my bottle started to go.

McCoy is less taken aback. He hugs the snake like it's a long lost fiancée and merrily blows away on the charming pipe.

"Didn't you want a *feather* boa?" asks Razzle.

"It's an Indian civil serpent," jokes Justin.

Pleased by this cheerful reception, the snake's owner pushes his luck and produces a scorpion in a box and a particularly evil-looking porcupine.

It's too much for Razzle. "Ain't you got any proper food?" he snorts hilariously before temporarily shooing away our new-found pals with a masterly Pythonesque outburst of "Fuck off, I'm not the Messiah."

The adults and their menagerie don't faze me half as much as the little kids do. Many of them have been cruelly deformed by their own parents to make them all the more pitiable/profitable. In their belief system, everyone is reincarnated umpteen times, so one life as a beggar ain't so bad. Call me old-fashioned, but I'd want some kind of proof.

Andy ends up dishing out fags, toast and beer left, right and centre.

"I can't help it," he shrugs. "I know I can get it all back in London – they need it more."

Things get more nightmarish in direct proportion to the heat. By noon I reckon I could fry an egg on Razzle's forehead. Outside our hotel balconies the beggars assemble, and at any signs of life from the funny-looking Westerners they launch into their bizarre repartees. One bloke balances his baby on a 15ft pole from his forehead. Kids do gymnastics that'd put Olga Korbut to shame, leaping through knife-lined hoops. And one grubby-looking gent brings out monkeys that he's trained to fight each other with pointed sticks.

Half to escape and half to see what fresh insanity this city could possibly bombard us with, we jump into cabs for some sightseeing. Except for Mike Monroe, that is. He's scarcely able to move outside the hotel without causing a riot of lust, outrage and/or amazement. The crowd's reaction to this exotic being is genuinely surprising. It's as if Elvis had turned up in Peckham at the height of his fame and started twirling his dick around in the middle of the high street while shouting, "How about this for a Good Luck Charm?"

Monroe is certainly all shook up.

Like everything here, except the alcohol, the taxicabs are ridiculously cheap – the cabbies think they're ripping you off smartly if they charge you 70p for a 50 pence ride. But they drive like they're in *Death Race 2000* and if they're held up at lights for more than 30 seconds it's odds-on a beggar will be poking his sorry stump through the window. One poor sod had a stump for a right arm and his left arm had been shorn off cleanly at the shoulder. "Don't worry, he's 'armless," Razzle wisecracks, but no one is laughing.

Inevitably we end up at the 'The Cages', a street where the world's least appetising prostitutes, aged from eight to eighty, are jam-packed into iron-bar-lined cells from where they leer and beckon passers-by like Bizarro World sirens. It's no coincidence that the street is book-ended by 'modern VD and skin problem' clinics that look as though they were built about the time of the East India Company.

On the corners lurk mobs of 'billy-boys', hideously made-up transvestite fag-whores whose main man looks amazingly like a brown-skinned burlesque edition of David Johansen. Fittingly, as we shall see, it's these who ambush Andy McCoy's cab, hammering on the roof and demanding to supply their services. But the only thing he wants to buy is cocaine, and plenty of it.

Back in the hotel room we drink lager and smoke the dirt-cheap hash. Andy passes round some opium cake, and I finally manage to stop muttering "unbelievable" long enough to ask the inevitable question – doesn't all this poverty and degradation make you realise just how absolutely trivial rock 'n' roll is, especially for a band like Hanoi Rocks who are totally dedicated to getting wrecked, getting laid and getting famous? (Two out of three ain't bad …)

Everyone agrees. "It's a real eye-opener," Andy says. "The only good things here are the drugs and it ain't worth it for that. I feel sorry for them, but what can I do? I'm not a hero; I'm a rock 'n' roller."

At this stage his soliloquy gets interrupted by a knock on the door. I open it to find a small Indian who shows me a note in what appears to me to be Hindustan. "Sorry pal," I say. "I don't speak your language." He hands me another note, this time in English. It reads: "I cannot speak, I have no tongue, it was cut off when I was a baby, please give me money."

I look from the paper to the man and he flings his mouth wide open to prove, horrendously, that he's not telling porkies. The shock of seeing the inside of his big tongue-less gob freaks me out and I slam the door shut on him, but then feel bad for doing it. What was I supposed to feel? Remorse? Sick? Guilt?

Living in such circumstances, any sane person would either have to become a thief or a revolutionary. But us, we're here on a tourist ticket.

I felt like a voyeur on a snuff film set.

Naturally, these initial confused feelings are shortly rationalised. Realising our complete inability to change the way things are here, the band rapidly adapts to them. Even the beggars begin to seem normal.

Andy wastes no time mobbing up with some local dealers, and by the second afternoon Justin is cheerfully addressing the masses from our balcony in holy double-Dutch with British Airways eyeshades over his eyes and a walking stick in his hand.

Encouraged by Razzle, everything begins to seem like a Monty Python sketch, while the Indian promoters and punters are a friendly reminder that there's life beyond the beggars. Mostly we start looking forward to the challenge of the first gig.

On the second morning I am awaken by a tapping on my window. As I'm on the first floor this surprises me. It turns out to be another baby on a pole. "Thanks, pal," I mutter, "but I think I'll skip breakfast." (I don't risk eating until we reach New Dehli.)

Outside the hotel we find that the promoters have provided a horse and cart festooned with a large Hanoi Rocks banner. It's for the band to tour the local universities and drum up an audience for today's show. This puts paid to the rumour that the band would have to change their name because of its supposed 'communist' connections (and that tells you clearly that Mrs Ghandi's 'socialism' isn't quite the same as the Redskins', or even Mitterrand's brand).

"Shame, we could have called ourselves The Turban Dogs," cracks Nasty. Or indeed Bengal & The Jets. This painful flash of pun-full genius sets me off on a horrendous sidetrack. Would our heroes curry favour with the chaps and chapattis, or would they end up with tears on their pilau? Could Hanoi Rocks make *Top of the Popadoms*? Or if I were an Indian punter would I prefer to hang mahatma on Sari Secombe serenading me on *Singh Something Simple*? Who can Patel ... Sorry, sorry, you could have had two pages of these rotten puns, but I reckon it'd make you think I was a right Ravi Shankar, so let's explain instead why so few Western rock bands play here.

Unable to break India out of the stranglehold of the world economy, or even guarantee the first freedom - freedom from hunger - Ghandi's government had fallen back on those old stalwarts, repression and protectionism. The latter is enforced so stringently that foreigners aren't allowed to take money out of the country – i.e., the band won't get paid.

Instead, groups play India for expenses, the gigs are charity benefits, the promoters foot the hotel bills and the weirdo Westerners keep the beggars in chapatti butties for a week or two.

To complicate matters, the 360 per cent surtax mentioned before applies to all gear being imported into the country. In other words, amps cost a small fortune and you won't find a 3K rig this side of Japan. Consequently, soundman Mick Staplehurst is left cursing an amateurish (but in retrospect half-decent) set-up all afternoon at the Rang Bhavan, an open-air arena previously pioneered by The Police.

We learn that Indian exposure to Western rock is limited to imported records and only about a half-hour of radio broadcast a week.

Overhead, ominous-looking kites are circling as the punters arrive for the seven o'clock kick-off. Most of the crowd are young students, although a few families have turned up as well, making the numbers up to well over 2,000 – and that's not including the hundreds perched on walls and up trees around the perimeter.

Amazingly, they're treated to a warm-up tape including 'Holiday In Cambodia' by the Dead Kennedys, 'Stranglehold' by the U.K. Subs, 'Borstal Breakout' by Sham 69 and, most surprisingly of all, 'I Lost My Love to a UK Sub' by The Gonads!

Oi had come to India and nobody noticed.

Wild cheering greets the intro tape of Carl Orff's *Carmina Burana*, which sounds as if it should be on the menu next to the Chicken Bhuna but it works as well in Bombay as it did for Ozzy Osbourne in the US

Bible Belt. The mood, like the hotel carpets, is electric.

Simple but effective Spirograph lighting illuminates the stage, revealing Razzle whose solitary drum beat is soon joined by Monroe's mouth organ for an impromptu version of that main street exile 'Do the Hip Shake Babe'. Unusual but necessary, because these punters won't accept anything less than a two-hour set.

When the full band storm into their infectious opening anthem 'Oriental Beat' the crowd start to surge forward and I realise what a red-hot live band these boys can be, and why their London audiences span everyone from skins and punks to bikers, boot boys, metal maniacs and New Romantic mannequins.

Groping for an adequate description, the rock writer Dave Roberts labelled them "part Stones, part Gary Glitter, part Clash, part early Japan and part Kiss", which hits the nail as close to the head as anything I could throw at it. Except to say, if you want it neater, this is rock 'n' roll, as subtle as a prize fight and as tasteful as a Lime Street ponce. It's the Stones via New York Doll, or, in the case of Andy's duck-walk, Berry by way of Johnny Thunders (through his stage persona he is pure Keef meets Mick Jones). And when you add castrato harmonies, hooks handsome enough to solve the Danish fishing crisis overnight and the pure trash delivery, you've got something distinctive from all the influences – the whole is greater than the parts. And then I realise that's why Andy bangs on about punk. Hanoi Rocks are punk just like the New York Dolls were punk's biggest influence. They just throw in the garbage, the untuned guitars, the false harmonies … They're flash-trash, brash, loud and they don't give a fuck. They'll be megastars by the end of next year, or else they'll be dead.

Monroe is the first focal point, preening and careening around the stage in his mosquito net vest and later a red feather boa. His voice is nowhere near as pretty as his face; live especially, he comes over all Jagger-yob, which makes Andy's Keef poses all the more suitable. He even flicks back his right wrist and cuddles Mike to share a harmony before cavorting off on another amp-climbing spree. This man's got the energy of a hundred chorus lines.

But Razzle is man of the match, supplying the drum solo he swore he'd never do when the power cut out six numbers into the first set. (Similarly, Andy McCoy is forced to unleash a killer metal solo during the second set despite his professed "total hatred" of guitar solos.)

By the time the opening set has thundered to a titanic close with a magnificently punky rendition of 'My Generation', the crowd are going seriously barmy. The boldest are already jammed down the front and their enjoyment grows to Millennium Eve party proportions during the second set. The trouble is the stagehands have got no idea how to handle it. Kids start jumping on stage for a dance or grope and the bouncers start overreacting. Fists fly into fans' faces and the odd bottle whistles back. Before long the stage is lined with cops armed with lathis (long sticks), which dampen the old enjoyment considerably - despite a belting rendition of The Stooges' 'I Feel Alright'.

During the final two encores there are constant invasions, severe lashings, and the odd plod is incapacitated by flying missiles. A great night had been needlessly marred by ridiculous heavy-handed crowd control due to bouncer inexperience. But it gets worse. On the way out the police lay into the punters with SPG-style abandon. Or, as the Bombay Daily reports the next day in an article headlined "Music Fans Caned, Cops Run Amok":

"The police ruthlessly lathi-charged large sections of the audience at Rang Bhavan towards the end of a wholesome performance by the Scandinavian-English band punk metal rock 'n' roll quintet Hanoi Rocks."

It goes on to report small groups being badly mauled by mobs of cops and people "displaying terrible weals".

Despite band disgust at the police's actions, the fantastic reception they earned tonight cheers everyone up no end. Even Mick Staplehurst got a rousing chorus of "For he's a jolly good fellow". Razzle is beside himself; "What other band do you know who appeal to bikers, Mohicans, Indian peasants and hysterical Finnish loonies?" he asks rhetorically, and I'm forced to answer absolutely sod all. Firstly because no other band appears to; secondly because I'm now too rat-arsed to make conversation.

Such is the local morality, not even Hanoi Rocks can pull here – they're out for a Bombay duck, folks. So instead they turn to recreational narcotics, which in turn are my undoing. I'm not a lover of hard drugs. When I was a kid I tried puff and acid and liked neither. I took cocaine, again by mistake the first time, with Eddie & The Hot Rods. Speed was the only stimulant that floated my boat. I loathe heroin and that whole *NME* junkie worship culture.

But here in an Indian hotel Andy McCoy offers me "brown sugar" and I naively ask, "What's that?"

I'd only heard it as slang for attractive black women and there are none of them here, unfortunately. I thought heroin was white; this stuff was brown.

"Oh," he replies, "it's like a cross between cocaine and speed."

"That's handy," I say. "That'll perk me up …"

And that's how I ended up snorting smack.

The feeling of well-being was almost instant.

"Here," said Andy, "have some cake."

And I merrily chomped on some opium cake, too.

I can't tell you which of the drugs made me paranoid, but I suspect the opium made me hallucinate, because as we walked around the market that afternoon I became convinced that I wasn't me in India at all, but rather a GI in Vietnam, with an Mk.16 over my shoulder, and that the bemused locals were actually hostile villagers. Somehow I got back to the hotel room, threw up and crashed out for 20 hours straight.

Everyone thought it was hilarious. Hanoi Rocks? Chinese Rocks are what these bastards are into.

* * *

After the hurly-burly of Bombay, Delhi is a revelation. It's cooler, there's no smell, a better class of beggars, good roads, beautiful architecture and a much cleaner hotel. This is Ghandi's showcase city, though paradoxically its relative richness only serves to emphasise the absolute misery of the masses elsewhere.

Tonight's gig is a Delhi first. There's never been a rock band here before, mostly because promoters have to pay taxes on local stage shows. Consequently, the equipment at the indoor venue, a mini-Albert Hall called the Shankerial Auditorium, makes Bombay's look relatively complex. Mike the mixer reckons, "It's not so much a PA as a home stereo." A main power point held together by strategically placed matchsticks doesn't do much to inspire confidence. Neither does the stage barrier - one limply stretched rope. After the riot at the previous show, this looks positively ominous, especially as it almost kicks off big time as soon as the doors open. But, unlike Bombay, the Delhi crowd have no idea about rock gig behaviour, having been brought up on jazz and classics, and they sit cross-legged on the floor, their numbers swelled by Yank- and Euro-hippies, until Mike succeeds in haranguing them to their feet six numbers in.

By 'My Generation' there's even a couple of kids pogoing – turns out one of them had been in London in '77 and he asks me to complain to John Peel about playing too little punk and Oi on the world service.

The best numbers are the sheer raunchy rock 'n' rollers like 'Motivating' and 'MC Baby', the Alice Cooper reminiscent 'Wild and Free' and the newer song 'Sailing Down My Tears', a Stonesy saunter that goes down a monsoon.

One old codger complains it's "just noise", but the majority are well into the experience (Hanoi for India!) and I even get handshakes and the odd "Thanks for a good programme". Anytime, pal. You got a sister?

Back at the hotel our initial horror's virtually completely forgotten. "I love it," Andy enthuses, "I'm definitely coming again. We'll be doing the new album before we go to the States and 'Dead in Delhi' is definitely on it, plus 'Raped in Bombay By Billy Boys'. Put in *Sounds* that we came here for the opium."

Yeah, yeah. They're an odd bunch. McCoy, born 20 years ago in Finland, is the son of a "fat banker" (according to Nasty) who grew up in Sweden, swapping a football for a cheap acoustic guitar at 11 years of age. Before finding chart success with puny band Miljoona Oy, Andy scratched a sordid living as a gay prostitute in Stockholm. "I needed the money," he shrugs. "The first time I went down on a bloke I felt like throwing up – after that it didn't bother me."

Back in Finland Andy recruited Monroe on the basis of his looks, adding ex-school mate Nasty (real name Jan Stenfors, now 20) and original drummer Gyp Casino to form the Rocks less than three years ago. They canned Gyp last year after his nerves were shot and he'd taken to walking offstage halfway through the sets. He was replaced by rib-tickling Razzle, a 22-year-old refugee from the Isle of Wight living in North London, who long ago ditched the name Nick Dingley and who, despite a brief respite in the Dark, is most infamous for a two-year stint with a legendary if peculiar semi-punk pathetique outfit called The Fuck Pigs. He eats pint glasses as a hobby and is blessed/cursed with total Python recall, spending most of his Bombay time wandering around markets shouting, "Okay big-nose, let's haggle."

To date the Rocks' legacy to the world has been three flawed but spirited albums (the last, *Self-Destruction Blues*, being a collection of b-sides, singles and demos) released by Finnish label Johanna.

They all moved to London last year. In Japan the first album, *Bangkok*

Shocks, Saigon Shakes, Hanoi Rocks, had sold a healthy 15,000, while the newly released second album's sales will be boosted this month by their first Japanese live gigs, which follow India and Hong Kong and precede a hole-a-day holiday in Bangkok, where they're incongruously signed to WEA. Their greatest successes were in their native Finland where all the albums have been number ones, clocking up between ten and fifteen thousand sales apiece, with the single 'Loves An Injection' making number one for a month in September 1982.

In India the promoters cheekily have brought out a cassette entitled *Hanoi Rocks' Greatest Hits* but discreetly leaving off 'Love's An Injection', which is felt to be too 'risqué' for the authorities to tolerate.

Despite the promoter's fears, the 'Hanoi' in their name was picked purely for the exotic sound of it rather than for its Vietcong implications.

The nearest the band comes to politics is a cover of the old Hoyt Axton classic 'Lightning Bar Blues': "I don't need no diamond ring/I don't need no Cadillac car/Just want to drink my Ripple wine/Down in the Lightnin' Bar ...'.

"It's a big lie that song," laughs Nasty. "I do want a diamond and I do want a Cadillac car."

"It's an old country song," Andy informs. "I do love country for its harmonies, Dolly Parton, Crystal Gayle ..."

How about Johnny Cash?

"I thought that was the change from a Durex machine," Razzle cracks.

"We wanna meet him down Covent Garden for a fist fight," guffaws Andy.

"Seriously," says Razzle, "we're the only band like this getting back to '73, that whole Alice/Mott period was the best rock era ever."

"Not '73," Andy counters, "we're pure 1954!"

Indian morality is closer to 1854, however, and despite the hotel being used by a shedload of Miss India beauties there will be no debauching of locals on this part of the tour either, although special mention must go to the delightful Phooni from Mauritius for services beyond the call of expectations for one lucky band member.

Yeah, India is certainly the place to come if what you're after from foreign travel is hashish, dysentery and the opportunity to lust after unavailable Asian women.

As I leave them they're already talking about coming back in October and travelling by train for more shows, including Madras, Goa and Calcutta, no doubt in pursuit of the black hole.

"There's no hurry for anything," their laid-back manager Seppo Vesterinen assures me. "We're just taking things as they come, everything's cool. You don't even have to write this feature up if you don't want to."

Oh I want to. But could you imagine Peter Grant coming out with something like that?

PS: When I wrote the words, "They'll be megastars by the end of next year, or else they'll be dead," I had no idea how prophetic they would be.

On 8 December 1984, Razzle was killed in a car accident – the car was being driven by Vince Neil of Mötley Crüe. They'd been partying all day and had popped down to the local liquor store for more supplies. Drunk, he lost control of his car and smashed into an oncoming vehicle. The two occupants of the other car were seriously injured. Neil was charged with vehicular manslaughter and driving under the influence – his blood alcohol level was more than double California's legal limit. He spent fifteen days of a one-month sentence in a minimum security prison and was ordered to pay Razzle's family $2.6 million in damages. Nick was replaced in the band by Terry Chimes from The Clash.

Hanoi Rocks never achieved the fame they felt destined for, but they were a major influence on bands as important and diverse as Guns N' Roses and the Manic Street Preachers.

McCoy and Monroe re-formed the group in 2002. They've had a Number One hit in Finland but nowhere else, and broke up again in

2009. Sami Yaffa is currently playing in the New York Dolls. Nasty Suicide now works as a pharmacist.

Over the Rainbow

November 1982: Finland, of all the international rock stars I've known, Ritchie Blackmore of Rainbow was indisputably the most disturbed. And disturbing. Blackmore liked to portray himself as a miserable bastard: mean, mysterious and macabre, with a heart as black as his stage clothes. In *Rock Dream* terms, Ritchie would have to be painted as the murderous and gloomy funeral director of Rainbow's *Death Alley Drive* video. Only one thing would make him smile: an open grave. If one day he jacked in this rock 'n' roll lark to start twiddling thumbscrews in a South American dictator's torture chamber, you wouldn't be at all surprised. That was his image - and one that he had worked hard to create and perpetuate. But it's actually as close to the real man as *Coronation Street* is to real life in Salford.

I knew from insider gossip that there was more to Ritchie than that. Rock hacks assigned against their will to cover Rainbow would blanch at the thought. Blackmore had a reputation for getting writers merry and then setting them up with dodgy hookers. And that was if they were lucky. The unlucky ones enjoyed a less salubrious fate. Ritchie once fixed up a virginal, plate-faced *Kerrang*! journalist with a real babe. He left the happy couple locking tongues in a dark subterranean bar a few blocks off New York's Times Square. The poor sap had no idea that his date was actually a beautiful transvestite. He didn't discover the additional organ until his own had been in 'her' mouth. What happened next was an area rife with lurid speculation.

Then there was the *Sounds* hackette who was still spooked by the time Ritchie had handcuffed her to a hotel bar and cut off a lock of her own hair for some never explained reason, which she sincerely believed involved the black arts. Every time she had a period pain after that, she imagined the rock god cackling as he stuck pins into a model of her.

Guests at a party at Blackmore's New York home had been well plied with liquor and then spooked out by a series of bizarre apparitions projected by electrical devices he'd planted in his back garden.

Even being a pal was no safeguard against his pranks. The first time Ross Halfin went on the road with Rainbow he returned to his hotel room characteristically as legless as a boa constrictor, only to find it sys- tematically stripped of all furniture and personal belongings. Months later a box he was perched on in a photo pit exploded as the band came on stage, sending the fat fool flying, singed and stunned, into the shocked audience.

Ritchie liked people to think he was some rock 'n' roll Baron Frankenstein, but in reality he was the ultimate prankster, addicted to wind-ups and mind games. He was closer to Beadle than the Baron. But make that an Evil Beadle, the kind who might be hired for an adult channel version of the US hidden camera show *Punk'd*.

Now I prefer to think of him as a hit man for the Goons, but when I got off the plane at Helsinki to meet him for the first time I was far less certain. In fact, I was desperately doing deals with God, trying to get an estimate on a guardian angel. It must have worked, because as we shall see it was Halfin who got stitched up spectacularly on this trip …

We were met at the airport by a Finnish record company man, who asked politely whether we were "the men from *Melody Maker*". The wind- ups had begun. Calmed only by the cool chill of the early evening air, we were driven straight to the gig, itself a giant ice hockey stadium, and plunged into the lunacy of the Rainbow dressing room. Almost immediately, drummer Bobby Rondinelli, a thick-set, fast-talking filth hound, whipped out his penis and poked it into Halfin's hand. Ross is unimpressed.

"Ha ha ha," Rondinelli cackled. "Ross is the only bloke I know you can't gross out! C'mon, let's see the warts on yer dick. Jee-zus, they must work like a French Tickler."

It's possible that this sort of thing went on backstage with the Gang of Four, but somehow I doubt it.

As the burly Brooklynite and the wimp from Wimbledon immersed themselves in perverse peaks of mutual appreciation, handsome Rainbow singer Joe Lynn Turner grabbed my hand and promised me "two dumb days and two numb nights". I was still reeling at the possible implications when I got summoned to meet Ritchie. Gulp.

Blackmore insisted on a separate dressing room from the band and the two female singers, which emphasises both the 'lone wolf' side to his character and the fact that Rainbow are very much his baby, the band he formed back in 1975, after walking out on Deep Purple, and has steered through an apparently endless stream of line-up changes in pursuit of his own highly individual vision of what he wants to achieve with his music.

Meeting Blackmore was a big event for me, and not only because of the challenge of emerging unscathed. In common with millions of other kids, Ritchie was largely instrumental in shaping my taste and my teenage years back in those grease and greatcoat days. It was watching Purple live on telly that gave me the first clue that there might possibly be more to music than Bob & Marcia and Desmond Dekker. Seeing Purple perform 'Black Night' and Black Sabbath belt out 'Paranoid' on one incredible October 1970 edition of *Top of the Pops* soon after completed the process of satori. Shortly after, *Deep Purple in Rock* took pride of place in my album collection – a position previously occupied by *Tighten Up: Volume Two*.

I paid homage by snapping up every piece of Purple vinyl I could find/afford and filling in Ritchie's name under 'Best Guitarist' on every pop opinion poll I came across. He was as big a hero to me in my musically formative years as Hendrix, Hunter, Holder, Marriott, Bowie, Ozzy, Jagger, John Lennon and Rod The Mod had been. And it's hard to put that into words without sounding like a brown-nosing phoney, so I let Halfin do most of the talking (or, more exactly, drag up a cesspit of slanderous gossip) while Ritchie went through his near-religious pre-gig rituals – clipping his nails with a pair of pliers, drinking a limited amount of Scotch (about four doubles) and loosening up with finger exercises on a cream Fender Strat, unleashing several stunning runs even in warm-up.

If I had any fears that his prowess had diminished with the years, these put paid to them, and my suspicions that Ritchie had watered down his sound into some AOR bland-out were blown clean away by the gig. 'Land of Hope and Glory' thundered out of the darkness – yeah, Elgar, Helga - before Judy Garland's disembodied voice announced, "We must be … over the rainbow," and Blackmore's guitar oozed like syrup into the heavy riff of 'Spotlight Kid'. Smoke bombs and sparklers joined the fast-forward rhythm as giant mechanical eyeballs descended from the heavens, beaming surrealistically into the bowels of the quilt-coated crowd. We ain't in Kansas anymore, and we ain't in the Roxy either. This is rock as escapism. Spectacle. A high decibel Disneyland.

The band makes an impressive unit. And okay, the obligatory ballad left me colder than Don Arden's heart, but Rainbow's massive jukebox hits were magnificently heavy live. The only pain was Dave Rosenthal's over-long organ solo – he was definitely at his best on the *Close Encounters*-style call and response passage with Blackmore, at the opening of 'Power'. Ritchie sparkled most brightly on the blues intro to 'Can't Happen Here' or the 'Lazy F' passage before 'All Night Long', with his guitar teasing and flirting like an LA streetwalker or swooping to attack like a hungry hawk. But, for my money, the finest moment came with their droog-approved reappraisal of Ludwig Van's 'Ode to Joy', which preceded the set-closing 'Long Live Rock 'n' Roll'.

The crowd wanted more. Of course. And minutes later Blackmore's Fender was ringing out a beautiful melody line from the darkness, joined one by one by the other instruments until the guitar built into the spine-tingling opening chords of 'Since You've Been Gone'. This was cut short after the first chorus for a more nostalgic retread of 'Smoke on the Water', the rock riff equivalent of Beethoven's Fifth, and suddenly I was a teenage boy playing air-guitar in my boxroom bedroom again. A fine nostalgic end to a mammoth show.

Backstage, Joe Lynn helpfully suggested lines for my review. "Put 'the singer sucked again'," he smiled, "and make sure you mention the 'Ian Gillan screams'." I saunter over to Blackmore's room, where the guitarist had been joined by about sixteen attractive female autograph hunters.

"Any of these lumps you fancy, just tap 'em on the shoulder," Ritchie remarked generously, with a casual wave of his hand.

Lumps? Oh, I see. No I'm fine, thanks.

Lumps! Outrageous. I found myself wishing Germaine Greer or Sounds' resident feminist Robbi Millar had been with me just for the small joy of seeing the shock on their faces. They'd be lumps with the hump; grumps, in fact, and Blackmore would be getting clumped ...

Mind you, it would have been funnier if he'd asked me, "One lump or two?" Or offered me some lumpy-pumpy.

Several of the lumps, blessed with attractive bumps, joined us back in the hotel bar, where a somewhat more intoxicated Blackmore was revealing his early teen promise as a javelin thrower at White City.

"You ever thrown a javelin, Garry?" he asked.

"I threw one 100 yards once," I lied. "Well, that's not strictly true. I threw it 70 feet and the bloke it hit crawled the rest of the way."

Blackmore smiled. Blimey. I'd made the mad monk crack his face.

"What about you?" he asked an attractive would-be groupie. "You ever had a javelin up the arse?"

Not speaking English, she just smiled sweetly. Reliable reports suggest that, later on, what went up her arse was not a javelin.

Like it, lump it, rump it ...

Scandinavian tour promoter Eric Thomsen was Ritchie's wind-up target this night. A tall, bespectacled dipstick of a man, so thin he could have been made out of pipe cleaners, Eric had been strung up naked by the band before but didn't appear to bear any grudges. Tonight he'd announced his intention of performing his party piece – drinking a glass of Coca Cola while standing on his head. Naturally, Ritchie had the coke laced heavily with Dead Sea levels of salt. The effect was horrible. Eric screwed up his face in disgust, spitting out the drink while mucus streamed from his nose and mouth followed swiftly by vomit.

Even this didn't spell the end of the poor bloke's torment. Blackmore had got hold of his passport and superglued a picture of a skull over his face. Eric was due to clear Swedish Customs shortly after I'd returned home. For all I know, he could be languishing in a Swedish jail to this day.

The next evening we arrived in Copenhagen for a night off. We were booked into an old and prestigious hotel called the Kong Frederick (named after a royal gorilla perhaps) rather than its more customary modern rival, after Ritchie had fallen out spectacularly with the hotel manager. Rainbow had been recording in Denmark and Ritchie kept getting woken up at godforsaken hours of the morning. When polite protests made no difference, Blackmore had simply moved some of the amps back from the studio and demonstrated how to really make a racket. At 4 a.m. Non-stop. For an hour.

So in place of the usual saunas and jacuzzis we got: Atmosphere! History! Dark wood! Rafters! Suits of armour! Portraits of chinless royalty! And brasses! (Horse brasses, not hookers.) The hotel combined the classic East Sussex Olde Worlde pub feel with nouveau riche prices. Naturally, Blackmore loved it. Even though the rooms reeked of ancient institutions, too – mostly Dartmoor Prison.

Rondinelli was horrified. "No TV," he moaned. "And the rooms are so goddam small. All I wanna do is jerk off and go to sleep. In here I'd hit the freakin' ceiling and it'd drip on my head all night."

A lovely image, redolent of Halfin at his most poetic.

Later that evening Ritchie took me, Ross, his sidekick Barry Ambrose and Dave Rosenthal out for a beer and a chat in what was an, in retrospect, amazingly straight disco. Blackmore was sporting a suitably arrogant badge announcing 'Everyone has the right to my opinion' and I duly took him to one side for the interview, taking great care only to order beers in bottles that were opened in front of me. Ritchie would not be slipping me a Mickey Finn tonight.

Blackmore spoke honestly about his confusion over the band's direction, admitting that he was losing interest in heavy rock just for the sake of it. "I refuse to play heavy just for the sake of it like, say, AC/DC do. There has to be some sort of subtlety as well. There's no one I look towards for inspiration now. I'm bored with looking towards Hendrix. I find myself listening to Tull, though obviously that's not a direction Rainbow will go in, and Abba. I love Abba's heavy classical progressions, they're brilliant writers."

He had time for Jeff Beck - "Probably the best rock 'n' roll guitarist in the Yardbirds days"; Randy Rhoads – "Slightly clichéd but very good"; and Eddie Van Halen – "Very impressive though sometimes he lacks sophistication." Pete Townshend, he said, was "over-rated".

He was surprisingly soft-spoken, but he radiated a rare intensity, a charisma if you like, and took the interview process as seriously as he did his music, granting only one interview a year for quality control and playing it really straight.

Like Hendrix, Blackmore was more than a virtuoso, he created a style, although his direction has concentrated on the assimilation of Western classical ideas into the rock format. He uses classical scales and progressions. His guitar parts are often similar to classical violin parts. Rainbow's sound was "very European", he said. The Bach and Beethoven influences are obvious - *Difficult to Cure* was largely half-inched from

Beethoven's Ninth. But Wagner was "too heavy", he said. "I'm more into the Baroque people and Handel. I like some of the Renaissance music, and medieval music. I think a lot of 16th century music could be used in rock; it's very similar in many ways. Mostly I listen to organ recitals, especially in churches. They have a majestic quality that can root me to the spot, whereas with rock 'n' roll I often feel 'what's the point?' Church music makes me feel proud to be part of music. I find I've got nothing in common with rock 'n' roll people."

When he left Purple he insisted on his new contract specifying that he'd record a maximum of one album per year. "In Purple they wanted us to do three a year," he said. "That's why every other one was sub-standard."

Looking back at my interview notes, the non-musical quotes are the most entertaining. Certainly the most provocative. He backed Thatcher, saying she did "a very good job". If you'd told me Blackmore had dreamt up the Poll Tax as one of his spectacular wind-ups it wouldn't have been at all surprising.

Ritchie reserved special venom for UK Customs officials. "They are the worst in the world," he fumed. "It's like they resent you for having got out the country! It's one thing to clamp down on drugs, but I hate the way they come down on people who've been to Spain and are bringing in an extra bottle of wine or something. It's disgusting. I feel really strongly about that. And I hate the way people are always eager to run England down."

Away from the formal interview set-up, Ritchie spoke passionately about old castles, folklore and the paranormal. At Copenhagen airport he produced about twenty different vitamin bottles and gave me a lecture on their properties – just as Bob Monkhouse would do two decades later.

Few of the Bobby Rondinelli quotes were printable then, or now. And frankly, if you want to read about that sort of thing, it's what the internet is for. Bobby did take me and Ross on a shopping expedition (which was turned, against my will, into a 'lump hunt', with stolen concert passes used for nets) and explained his theory on women at some length. "If they're nice to you, they love you; if they're not nice to you, they love you even more. Never ever accept no for an answer."

Several cavemen have since offered the opinion that Bobby was a tad old-fashioned.

Later he gave me a graphic book on anal sex, which he claimed would spice up my marriage. I suppose you'd call that trying to score brown-eye points with the press.

There was certainly something rotten in the state of Denmark that day, but it was definitely imported.

You may be thinking I got out of this all remarkably lightly, but in reality only years of hard drinking saved me from a fate worse than 'Death Disco'. After the Copenhagen gig, Blackmore took us all out on the town as a parting gift. His chosen destination was a club called Madame Arthur's – and if you think the name sounds like a clue, you're dead right. It was another gay/transvestite club, full of bearded men snogging away like nobody's business. Thankfully, by refusing once again to drink anything other than bottled beer opened in front of me, I survived with my dignity intact.

Ross Halfin was not so lucky. After we got back from the club, Blackmore sent a lady-boy up to his hotel room, a burly creature wearing a peroxide wig and more slap than Barbara Cartland. A bit like Bela Emberg but more feminine. Ross didn't want to know, but his date became quite irate because Ritchie had paid for his services in advance.

The next morning the wretched Halfin confessed over breakfast that he'd let the pre-op transsexual give him oral sex. When I called him sick, Ross couldn't understand it. He just shrugged and said, "Well, a mouth's a mouth …"

I told that story years later to Al Murray and it ended up as a line in his Sky 1 sitcom, *Time Gentlemen Please* ...

POST SCRIPT

A fortnight later, over in New England with Rose Tattoo, I met a girl who claimed to have been Ritchie's babysitter. Once, she said, she'd been sitting alone with him in a room when he pointed at an empty chair and said, "Who's sitting there?" "He could really see someone," the girl explained. "He's really psychic." Yeah? Maybe he is, maybe he isn't. I don't pretend to know. But I'd bet good money that Blackmore had a bloody good laugh after she'd gone.

Down the line I heard about more of his wind-ups. For example, on tour in Japan a while later Ritchie had agreed to meet up with the corporate head of his record company after a concert. The big boss duly arrived backstage, flanked by minions. But Blackmore didn't answer his dressing room door, despite repeated knocks. Eventually, the local promoter, Mr Udo, opened the door himself. Nobody was in the room. All they saw was an open window and a rope descending from it, tied to the leg of a table. Rather than meet the man, Ritchie had lowered himself out of the first-floor window by rope and made his getaway. The snub, and the loss of face this caused, is apparently still spoken about today.

It got worse, however. Roadies on Rainbow's next European tour told me that they'd discovered Ritchie had miked up their room purely to hear what the crew were saying. The other side of his deliberately awkward and aloof nature appeared to be a growing paranoia. He rejoined Purple, briefly, but according to the other band members was impossible to work with. The last I heard of Ritchie Blackmore, he was making Renaissance-influenced folk music and playing a hurdy-gurdy. Maybe that was his problem all along: pre-minstrel tension.

UFO: Close Encounters of the Blurred Kind

April 1982, I was with UFO when the Falklands War started. We were snowed in at a Ramada Inn, in Portland, Maine, and watched the British fleet sail with the kind of watery-eyed pride that only normally overwhelms long-term ex-pats, who are also very drunk. And UFO were always drunk. X-rays of their livers would come served with bar snacks. Bass player Pete Way is the only man in rock to be banned by Sharon Osbourne from working with Ozzy, on the grounds that he was "a bad influence". Which is a bit like being told you can't spend time with the Devil because you might lead him astray.

Even sober, the news footage of the Taskforce had the same effect on me. British citizens had been overrun by a fascist junta and our lads were going to sort them out. That some sections of the far Left felt that we were in the wrong merely demonstrates how far these self-professed socialists were out of step with working-class opinion.

Back in the bar, UFO singer Phil Mogg is of the opinion that a visit to Port Stanley of an advance party consisting of me, Ross Halfin and the Cockney Rejects would settle the matter in hours … and, being smashed, we waste a good few minutes visualising Halfin trying to negotiate a backstage pass for behind enemy lines, and promising admirals front covers in return for paying for his trip.

"You're not worried about getting called up yourself, Phil, are you?" I ask innocently.

"No, no," he says, falling into the trap. "I'm too old."

Slowly he twigs what he's said. "Don't print that," he hollers. "Don't you DARE print that …"

Severe weather has temporarily frozen their current US tour, supporting Ozzy in huge stadiums, to a standstill. Outside, the snow is two stoned St Bernards deep and the hail pellets sting like rubber bullets. At one stage me and guitar ace Paul 'Tonka' Chapman nipped out to the tour bus to watch *Apocalypse Now* and were lucky to get back.

Two feet of snow had risen to crotch level in just three hours. Ronnie James Dio would have been buried alive. I hadn't seen so much white stuff since I last saw Tonka chopping out lines. (He's called 'Tonka' because he's indestructible; the only person I ever saw drink him under a table was Phil Lynott's mum ...)

So, naturally against our will, we're forced to sit and drink ourselves silly - sorry, that should read 'warm' - for two whole and very hazy days. And all we had to do was watch the news on the hotel bar's ten-foot telly and tot up the number of times the impish Mogg did a runner on a bar bill (seven, I reckon; good, but no Jock McDonald).

Our latest adventure began a couple of days earlier in New York, the Big Apple, though in this brass monkeys weather it's more like a withered Cox. Insert your own Ross Halfin joke here.

The adventure began in New York a couple of days earlier, where I bumped into Phil as he tried to embarrass a nice make-up girl at MTV.

"Do you want it with the trousers on or off?" he asked her, before his TV interviews. 'Trousers off' had landed him in hot water down in Texas earlier this tour. Mogg got slung in the slammer for "exposing himself to minors" on stage.

"The whole thing was farcical," he tells me later over his usual double Jack Daniels. "All I did was moon – Angus Young does it every night."

The incident had happened the day after Ozzy had pissed on the Alamo. "The cops wanted blood," says Phil. Frankly, I don't blame them. If some drunken Yank had piddled over the Cenotaph, would we not feel like clumping him?

Mogg was banged up for five hours, probably the longest he'd gone without a drink in years. "I was in this cell with twenty-four hookers cos they'd cleaned the streets up that night," he tells me. "And there was this real lunatic who kept shouting, 'Hey girls, d'you wanna see my burrito,' and flashing his cock at them."

"Was it Halfin?"

Four generations of Bushells,
with my dad George at the front

And a generation on, with me at the front

Me and Mum

On a family holiday,
dig the crazy deluxe caravan

Nin and Uncle Bern in festive mood

The Wager boys, with great-Gran May

My eldest kids: Danny, Julie,
and baby Robert

Above: Danny with the wolves from
ITV's *What's Up Doc?*

Below: On the road with rock legends Thin Lizzy

The great Joe Strummer
studies my tattoos

Def Leppard's Phil and Steve
salute the revolution

I had Lloyd Honeyghan worried –
he thought he'd killed me

Sweet dreams are made of this: the
Eurythmics toast my boxing victory

His name was Benny – one of
the nicest guys in the business

During my stint on GMTV

On the razz with comic
genius Peter Cook

Mike Reid meets some kind
of double-yoker

Bob Monkhouse – the master
humours an unworthy apprentice

Oi Grant, no! In training for
pantomime in Southend with
Ross Kemp

Fairy Bowbells meets Hairy Bow-Locks - backstage
at panto with Falcon from the Gladiators

Lesley Joseph admires my bulges
on Muscle Beach, LA

Above: Maybe I
shouldn't have told
George Wendt it
was opening time

Left: With
Peter Stringfellow
and pal

Derek 'Charlie Slater' Martin and I take a
tea-break while filming Bushell On The Box

With Shane Richie filming Win Lose or Draw

Vic and Bob join me for a pub crawl

Dee Ivens thought she didn't
stand a chance with me – on
the set of Bushell's Blue Xmas

Right: She ain't heavy
... she's Jet! I'd love
to see her taking off...

The difference between Frank
Carson and the M1? Eventually
you can turn off the M1

My Big Big Variety bill with (from left) –
Tania, Lisa Valente, Stephen Mulhern
and Francine Lewis

Country legend Reba McIntyre checks
out my Wimbledon panto

With Al Barr from the Dropkick Murphys
when the Gonads toured the USA

The first place Dale came out of
the closet was in my bedroom!

A nice day for a white wedding, me and Tania,
Graceland Chapel, Vegas 2000

And here we are with the maids
of dishonour: Fleur, Francine, Angelique
and Christine Peake

The Vegas stag night with my best man
Mickey Pugh (left) and funny-guy Rikki Jay

The Gonads live! Me with
flag-girl Vikki Thomas

The Face book launch, 2001: Tony Lambrianou,
Gilly, me and Billy Murray

My Jenna and her proud godfather,
Dale Winton

Of course it wouldn't be a christening without
the girls – Dee, Angelique, Francine and Fleur

Jenny Powell and Melinda Messenger
give me a TV grilling

Lovely Linda Robson at the book launch
for my crime novel Two Faced

I rarely venture out these days without my
fearsome minders Winton and Windsor

The stars come out for Ciara's christening –
Billy Murray, Bradley Walsh, Robert, Ciara,
me and Terry Alderton

My family: Robert, Julie, Tania, me,
Ciara, Danny and Jenna

New York shock jock Howerd Stern
appointed me his English ambassador

Back in Vegas for my fiftieth, with brother
Terence (left) and our pal Whippo

The Unidentified Cockney Gonads:
Pete Way (left) and Mickey Geggus

Jo Guest loved my up-right; she wasn't
so impressed with the organ

Movie star Dave Legeno politely
request a good review

"Sadly, no. The cops came in and thumped him. It was horrible. I didn't think I'd get out alive. But eventually they brought this UFO fan in for an unpaid parking ticket, so I had someone to talk to. I might have to make a court appearance later in the year ..."

I found Pete Way having breakfast in the hotel bar, a large double breakfast served in a glass with a slice of lemon for vitamin C. Tonight's gig is at Madison Square Gardens, where Pete comes into his own, on stage and off. On the way out he asks if I fancy a drink, and before I know it he's nicking full bottles of wine from Ozzy's dressing room and making me an accessory. We both come round in the hotel bar a few hours later when Pete's wife Jo catches up with us and shoves the sozzled rock god into a lift while belting the living daylights out of him with her handbag, *Carry On* style.

"We call Pete Mr Medinite," confides Ozzy, who had somehow joined us along the way. "Cos he gets so out of it the only way he can get to sleep is to drink five bottles of Medinite straight down. They call me a madman, but compared to Pete Way I'm outta my league; he's fucking mental! But at least he's a good bloke – unlike that fucking singer. I can't say a bad thing about him, cos he hasn't said a word to us for two months. What's wrong with him?"

Well, let's think. 1) He once told me that Sid Vicious was "a wimp who couldn't take his drugs". 2) He has a nose that could get him dates with pachyderms. 3) I once found myself at the Lyceum bizarrely surrounded by German autograph hunters because the sniggering Mogg had told them I was Judas Priest singer Rob Halford. 4) He gets his gay mates to ring you up first thing in the morning with outrageous propositions. 5) In Texas he tried to hurl me into a swimming pool. I swerved and he went flying in fully clothed. 6) Once Halfin tricked him into blowing a whistle that moments earlier had been stuck up his arse. 7) In Greenville, North Carolina, in 1981 he totally trashed a dressing room because other band members ate two pieces of his pizza. 8) At McAllen he became convinced he could fly, jumped off a first-floor landing and knocked himself out. Phil was woken up by the promoters, whom he promptly decided to 'do'. They called the cops and Mogg had to run off and hide, coming to the next morning with a broken arm.

But other than that, what's wrong with Phil Mogg?

Pretty much everything.

* * *

UFO were always a byword for rock 'n' roll excess. Some bands employ PR weasels to drum up outrageous tour stories. UFO never had to.

When they first hit the States in 1976 they went down a storm.

"Everything was there for the taking; drink, drugs and women, in glorious excess," recalls Phil. "You'd get girls knocking at your door every night, saying, 'Hello, my name's Lisa,' or whatever, and you'd end up saying, 'Go away.' She'd say, 'But you haven't seen me yet,' and she'd be beautiful, but they were all stunners. And you'd be saying, 'I don't wanna see ya, I just wanna sleep.' It was non-stop and we were like kids in a candy store. We'd gone from the Marquee to that and it was full-on."

Drummer Andy Parker added, "I remember walking into Phil's hotel room in California and there was a girl bouncing around on top of him, singing 'Doctor Doctor' at the top of her voice … She had quite a nice rhythm going. You notice these things as a drummer."

Shouldn't it have been 'Shoot Shoot'?

Phil: "There's a better Schenker story. We caught Michael lying naked on his bed with a cute girl from the gig on top of him, pumping iron so to speak, and he's got a cigarette and a pint of beer going, and he's listening to that night's show on a battered old cassette player."

Andy: "She's screwing him and he's calling up the tour manager saying, 'John, tonight we used too much echo …'"

Phil: "We asked him about it afterwards, and he said, 'For me the woman must do everything.'"

Heroin was Pete's downfall. He still has scars on his ankles from the injections. It got to the stage where he couldn't get any more in because all of his veins collapsed. He came for a beer in Chislehurst with me and my father-in-law Vic in 2004, and his hands were swollen up like inflated Marigolds. A terrible waste of his considerable talent.

His fourth wife, Jo, an American doctor who shared his habit, died in 2000. It had a cathartic effect on Pete. When he first met his current missus, Rashida (wife number five), she was his dealer. Back in the early eighties cocaine was the band's drug of choice. On one US tour a dealer arrived not with a bag but with a suitcase half full of it. None of them thought of saving any. When they got to the gig Phil Mogg was rigid.

The Spinal Tap scene, where the band got lost backstage, was based on UFO at a stadium gig at St Louis.

They blew their takings for a whole US tour by missing their tour bus due to excess partying and having to hire planes to get to the next venue. Phil's drinking had become such a problem on their 1981 US tour that the record company insisted he saw a doctor. Mogg sent Halfin in his place. The quack found cocaine up his nose and told him, "Philip, that's a no-no". Naturally, this became a tour catchphrase.

Probably his cruellest wind-up was on keyboard player Neil Carter, who caught a dose early on tour and then had his pills stolen. He got an anonymous message telling him that the only way to get them back was to pack his bags and hurl them out of a sixth-floor window. Desperate to clean up before his girlfriend arrived, Neil complied. He got the pills back, but two days later he was told that they had been substituted for garlic tablets. It wasn't true, but it was too much for Neil; the poor sod broke down in tears.

I caught up with UFO again nearly a quarter of a century later, in November 2006. It was the same band and the same banter, but different problems. Problem one was Peter Way's bladder. Pete couldn't get through a set now without having a slash, and consequently he had to leave the stage three or four times a night to relieve himself in paper cups in the wings. Andre, the bass tech, had to hold the cup. He was naturally christened the 'Guardian of the Golden Goblets'.

Problem two? Pete's trousers. He only took one pair of ancient stage strides on their latest UK tour, and they were an optimistic 31in waist. At Newcastle he was lying on the floor during 'Rock Bottom' and they split. He was wearing nothing under them, so the audience saw rather more of Pete than they expected – cock bottom you might say.

Rashida refused to fix them. So the next night he was still wearing them on stage. Of course they kept sliding down. Phil and Andre were taking turns to pull 'em up on stage. He was showing so much butt crack that Paul Raymond was keeping a guitar pick in there …

Rock 'n' roll! Glamorous, no? No. Not really.

Chapter Four
Borstal Breakout - The Hooligan Years

Prison Break-in

April 1979, Gerry the roadie hangs up the band's banner on the stage. It's a Union Jack embellished with the words 'Upstarts Army' and an angry clenched fist. The banner also boasts the motto 'Smash Law And Order' and a drawing of a pig in a helmet cruelly entitled 'PC Fuck Pig'. The audience starts to laugh and cheer. As well they might. They're convicts, we're in prison and the punk rock band about to play is the *Angelic Upstarts*. That's right. THE BAND THE POLICE LOVE TO HATE IS PLAYING A PRISON GIG.

Singer Mensi isn't the only one not sure that we'll get out alive. Or at all. It seems that the prison chaplain - nice fella, reminds me of Mr Barrowclough from Porridge - has booked the notorious South Shields punk band on the strength of their name alone. They're angelic, see; he has yet to discover that this lot are not wholly holy. But then, as Voltaire knew, you have to have the devil in you to succeed in any of the arts.

Mensi has invited me up here "for the crack, like". He's a big lad with a face straight out of the *Beano*, but right now he looks as worried as I feel.

"What's the matter with you, man?" asks Keith Bell, the Upstarts' stocky, barrel-chested manager as the gates of HMP Acklington close behind us.

Mensi shakes his head and mutters, "They always said I'd end up inside, but I - *aa* - never thought it'd be like this."

Bell laughs and Mensi grins, but that's just to hide the fact that he's shitting himself. We all are.

"Hey, what if they don't let us out, man?"

Keith takes no notice. A self-confessed former gangster, he's been here before – when he stayed a lot longer than we intend to. After visiting his house last night I'm not too convinced about the 'former' part of that previous sentence.

Bell, a one-time North Eastern Counties light-middleweight boxing champ, maintains order at their gigs on the basis of his reputation alone. The windows of his terraced home are attractively lined with metal grilles on account of the fact that someone threw a petrol bomb through a downstairs one not so long ago. Well, it could happen to anyone.

The band and their entourage are eleven strong and the inmates are genuinely pleased to see us. Only Keith seems totally at ease.

Acklington Prison in Northumbria is less than an hour's drive north from the Upstarts' hometown in Tyne and Wear. It's a fast-growing 'semi-open' jail, a limbo where men come, like Keith Bell had once come, to finish their sentences, though recently lifers have started to number among the clientele.

We stroll across the grounds to meet the poor, unsuspecting chaplain, who outlines some rules and regulations and smiles when Keith asks if he knows they're a punk rock group. He still thinks he's getting Christian rock. So why is it happening? Certainly not for the dosh – the fee doesn't even cover the Upstarts' expenses, and I know them well enough to know that this isn't just a lame publicity stunt. For starters, I'm the only one here from the rock press and the pen anjd pad were optional.

This gig was entirely the band's idea, partly because there was virtually nowhere else left in the North East of England that they could play, and partly as a favour to the men inside, some of whom they knew from the Shields. The cons testify that this is the first entertainment on offer in Acklington for many a long month. They're grateful and excited. Scores of blokes pack into the tiny hall as soon as the gear's set up, cheering the band through a soundcheck version of Sham 69's 'Borstal Breakout'. Gigantic geezers of 30-plus, who make Meat Loaf look like Lionel Blair, wander in with their hair spiked up with Brylcreem, the laces all removed from their plimsolls, and grins as wide as their biceps.

Soon there are about 150 in, with a few screws watching from outside. A fella with 'cut here' tattooed across his throat eggs on an ex-busker inmate to jump up and jam with the band in a 12-bar soundcheck muck about. Roadie Gerry unfurling the stage banner makes the men laugh out loud and the colour drain from the poor old chaplain's boat race. He couldn't look more shocked if Mensi had produced a small nun from his holdall and started banging her over the guitar amps.

Still nervous, Mensi takes the stage and the band wham-bam into the opening number, 'Police Oppression'. This has got to be the ultimate irony – the Angelic Upstarts, a band who the Northumbria cops view as being about as welcome as Crippen serving mystery cocktails, are guests of Her Majesty's government for an exercise in subversion.

Rows of lumps with tatts that make mine look like heat spots watch the stage antics intensely, the younger ones swaying with the beat, the older ones a bit bemused, but all of them clapping a thunderous approval at the end of each song.

And the more they enjoy it, the more Mensi starts to loosen up, dropping in the odd "My name is Sue, how do you do?" throwbacks to Johnny Cash's pioneering 1969 San Quentin gig, swearing at the mixing desk, stripping his shirt off, spitting at the ceiling (they loved that) and bellowing along like a wounded bison to the raw rock 'n' roll that makes the Upstarts one of the handful of real punk bands left in this country.

"There's crooks everywhere, but it's always the wrong ones get nicked," announces Mensi to much applause, introducing 'We Are the People', the band's savage put-down of police corruption and social double standards.

"This is one you've got to sing along to," he smiles as the band power-drives into a specially amended 'There's Gonna Be an Acklington Breakout'.

"This one's for all the screws, 'Fuck Off and Leave Me Alone'."

The chaplain looks as if he's praying to be struck down by a heavenly thunderbolt, and even the cons who aren't into the band's primal din are loving the spirit, looking over their shoulders – they always look over their shoulders – and grinning at each other. Never more so than on the emotive set-closing 'Murder of Liddle Towers'.

This was the Upstarts' first single, about electrician Liddle Towers, an amateur boxer from Birtley, Gateshead, arrested for being drunk and disorderly, who died after a spell in police custody three years previously. Mensi's lyrics leave the listener in no doubt as to whom he blamed for the 39-year-old's untimely death: "He was beaten black, he was beaten blue/But don't be alarmed, it was the right thing to do/Police have the power, police have the right/To kill a man, and take away his life/Who killed Liddle?/Did you kill Liddle?/Who killed Liddle?/Police killed Liddle Towers …"

And Mensi reinforces his opinion, as he usually does, by subtly unveiling the fresh head of a pig, which he leaves gurning from atop the amps. The prison hall explodes with cheers and whistles as cons leap up and punch the air. An encore is inevitable and the Upstarts slam through 'Acklington Breakout' one more time, before the screws let them know it's time to stop. Some of the inmates wander out on cloud nine, still shouting the chorus, while others hang back to chat and thank the band.

"That WERE G-R-E-A-T," one young con enthuses to me.

Why do you like them? I ask.

"Cos they're just like us. We can identify with 'em."

It's a sentiment that Mensi echoes in reverse when we finally, and thankfully, shamble through the prison gates into cars for home:

"That's what frightens me. It could so easily have been me in there.

When I think of some of the things I've - *aa've* - done ... if I wasn't a singer in a band, I'd probably be an inmate."

And if certain sections of the Northumbria Police get their way, he still could be. A few of the prison officers today would have been happier if they'd escorted us from the stage to the cells, and you can't really blame them for that. But instead they just clear us off the premises as quickly as a stray Celtic fan might vacate a Loyalist rally.

The Upstarts claim that unofficial police activity has left them banned from every club in the area; this is a long history of personal and group harassments and the Northumbria force were charging the band with incitement to violence at the time of the prison gig.

"They always get me when I'm by myself, right," spits Mensi. "Two weeks ago I was walking home from my girlfriend's at 4 a.m. and this police car pulls up and they start shouting abuse, 'Wanker, fucking poof.' I just ignored them, and they followed us about half a mile down the road at walking distance. Then one of them shouts, 'Hey cunt,' and I just lost me temper and shouted, 'Fuck off.' They jumped out and chased us, but I hid in a coal bunker. I went to the police - *poliss* - inspector and complained the next day and he said, 'To tell you the truth, son, you haven't got a leg to stand on. You've got no witnesses and a criminal record.' Since I've seen him I've had no hassles, mind, but it's only been a week ...

"I'm not anti-poliss. Nobody's got more respect for an honest policeman than I - *aa* - have. You have got to have law and order, but when the poliss become the law, when they start making the law, that's when it's wrong. They're so corrupt up here they can get away with fucking murder."

Mensi gets heated as often as a spinster's kettle, though he doesn't strike me as violent - just strong in his convictions and outraged by what he sees as injustice. But it's easy to see why some feel the need to prove themselves by taking him on, and others are outraged by what they feel he stands for.

Appropriately, we get back to Keith Bell's drum to find that the rest of the band have been stopped and interrogated by the police on the way back ...

An everyday story of South Shields folk.

PS: Mensi, who'd been an apprentice miner for three-and-a-half years, was resolutely anti-racist ("We're all black men down the pit," he says) and anti-Tory. Not that this prevented the *Daily Mirror* from turning the band's prison gig into a front-page shock-horror story (headline: 'Punks Rock a Jailhouse') a few days later and quoting me as "band spokesman". (Even funnier, the local Tory MP condemned it as "an incredibly stupid thing to allow". His name? Neville Trotter.)

An accurate record of the event appeared in the *Socialist Worker* – I wrote it – quoting the things that Mensi actually told the inmates, like they'd be better off in the nick if Mrs Thatcher got elected later this year, and urging punks to vote Labour on the accurate grounds that the "Thatcher's Government will destroy the trade union movement". Although you might argue that Scargill was the man who hit the self-destruct button, bringing the unions down with him.

Music was Mensi's escape from a lifetime down the pits. At the time he was on £15 a week from the band's new WEA advance – Warners snapped them up after Polydor dropped them over a fight that Mensi had with a security guard. Bassist Steve and drummer Sticks were on the dole, having packed up bricklaying and bakery work respectively at Christmas; and guitarist Mond was still working as a shipyard spark, saying, "I'm packing it in if the single charts."

The single 'I'm An Upstart' peaked at 31, and the follow-up 'Teenage Warning' managed 29; and that was as high as they ever got. So Mensi was never really in his dream place of "being in a position where I can say things and be listened to" by millions. But he carried on speaking out against racism and capitalism in the music press, while quietly making a fortune from the used car trade. He was the biggest socialist in Oi, and the only one who ended up minted.

The Upstarts' relationship with Keith Bell did not last long. Sacked by the band when he started to knock them about, Bell and his henchmen set about trying to intimidate Upstart fans, even assaulting people buying their records, before threatening Mensi's mother, smashing her house windows and making threatening and abusive phone calls to her. Reprisal incidents included Mensi and one-time Upstarts drummer Decca Wade smashing one of the Bell firm's car windows and a midnight visit to Bell's own home by Decca's dad, club comedian Derek Wade, and Mensi's brother-in-law Billy Wardropper, who blasted one of Bell's henchmen in the leg with a sawn-off shotgun. Hitting back, Bell threatened to kill Wade Senior. Three of his cronies set fire to a stable belonging to Mensi's sister, causing almost £5,000 worth of damage. In ensuing court cases both Bell and Billy Wardropper were jailed, while Decca's dad copped a year's suspended sentence. Presiding Judge Hall told the Upstarts' team: "I accept that all of you suffered a severe amount of provocation, which was none of your seeking. But at the same time I have a duty to condemn the use of firearms, particularly a sawn-off shotgun."

The Upstarts recorded their opinion in a song called 'Shotgun Solution': "Shotgun blasts ring in my ears/Shoot some scum who live by fear/A lot of good men will do some time/For a fucking cunt without a spine."

A Fairy Tale of New York

June 1982, I went to New York with the Angelic Upstarts in 1982. The Yanks all mistook me and Mensi for Australians – me because of my accent, him because he looked like a convict. In a hurry to get to Tim Sommer's punk/Oi radio show, we got ourselves more lost than Atlantis. And what do you do when you're lost? You ask a policeman.

The three uniformed cops leant against the street corner, chewing matchsticks. Three times I asked them how to get to Rhode Island. Three times the cockiest one replied, "Whaaa?"

Then his chubby mate added, "Are you sure you don't mean Queens?"

The penny dropped. With our cropped hair, combat jackets and 'fag' English accents, the cops had mistaken us for pillow-biters. I explained this to Mensi as I dragged him away.

"Fucking cuunts!" he exploded. "Let's do 'em, Gal."

"Tommy, mate," I said, "they've got *guns*."

He still fancied his chances. "They're WIMPS! Do I look like a fucking poof? We could smash them to fuck."

But I managed to calm him down with the promise of beer. If I'd had me wits about me, I'd have blown them a kiss.

We had breakfast with Joe Strummer the next morning, who thought it was hilarious. We asked him why he'd recently done a runner from The Clash. Strummer shrugged and said, "I just thought, what the fuck …"

Joe and Iggy Pop both came down to the Upstarts' show at the Peppermint Lounge. But the most incisive review came from the punter who told Decca Wade, "Your singer's ugly and he can't sing. He just shouts and he doesn't do that too well." He could have been talking about The Gonads.

Cops were a frequent factor on Angelic Upstarts tours, but it wasn't always their fault. I was on the road with Jimmy Lydon's band the 4 Be 2s in Scotland once. Jimmy is John Lydon's younger brother. They were managed by 'rock entrepreneur' Jock McDonald (real name O'Donnell), a legendary music biz chancer. The band were *supporting* the Upstarts, but they were staying in the best hotels and tucking into steak and champagne every night. Jock even treated me to a fine Cuban cigar. How was this happening? Mensi was mystified. It turned out that Jock had simply half-inched a load of WEA headed paper, forged the MD's signature and produced a letter guaranteeing that all of their expenses would be met by the record company – who they weren't even signed to. They got away with it for a week before Jock was led away in cuffs. If he'd been really clever, the prison governor would have then received a letter from the MD of EMI demanding his release.

The 4 Be 2s were pretty much a Lydon family in-joke. John's other brother, Martin, appeared with them occasionally, as did John Stevens, better known on the Arsenal terraces as Rambo. McDonald was great company but a terrible influence. He took John to Dublin in 1980, where the ex-Pistol was banged up in Mountjoy Prison – known as 'The Joy' - for four days after getting roughed up by two off-duty garda in the Horse and Tram pub. They falsely accused John of assaulting them (he wrote Public Image Ltd's *Flowers of Romance* album as a result and didn't go back to Eire until the Pistols played the Electric Picnic in Stradbally, 28 years later.) It was an outrage; the only thing Lydon ever did that merited choky was the *Country Life* ad campaign.

Talking of banging up, Jock led me astray in 1980 too, although I wasn't aware of it for years. He invited me out for a dinnertime drink with Jimmy Lydon, Mensi and a couple of young girls. We started in the White Lion and, nope, I don't remember anything else about it other than at the time it had seemed a very agreeable lost day. Twenty-eight years later I had a surprise reminder of what had actually occurred. A young man turned up and said I was his dad. We've yet to call in Jeremy Kyle for DNA tests to confirm the story, but when he showed me a picture of his mother in her punk heyday I recognised her immediately as one of the girls ...

I've not seen Jock for more than 25 years, but when my band played Berlin in January 2010 Jock's own band, The Bollock Brothers, were due in town the following week. Gonads, Bollock Brothers ... it's all a load of balls; grown men who should know better, veteran punks growing old disgracefully.

OTT in the OC

Orange County, October 1980, The Cuckoo's Nest club in Costa Mesa, about fifty miles south of Hollywood, was the largest punk venue in Orange County. It claimed to have the world's first mosh pit, and every West Coast band worth their salt would play here, including Black Flag, The Vandals and TSOL. Everything seemed fine when we pulled up outside. I was travelling with the all-girl punk pop band the Mo-dettes. Virginia Turbett was taking the snaps, not Halfin, and so the chances of the trip degenerating into a Ross-style gross-out seemed minimal.

We pulled up early for the soundcheck and breezed into the next-door bar, a kind of cowboy joint called Zubies, to shoot some pool while Louis, the slaphead US road manager, went to recce the venue. The locals were down to earth and friendly. Well, why not? The band members Kate, Jane, June and Ramona were pretty, as was Virge; while me and their roadie Chris, a young skinhead from East Ham, were clearly no threat. We had a beer and a laugh with the resident bar-flies.

Then Louis stormed in spitting feathers. The club was trying to charge the band extra for the PA and the sound guy, and he wasn't having any of it. He had pulled the gig. The mood changed in a moment. The faces of the friendly locals clouded over. We weren't just two geezers with a gang of stunners in tow, we were a band. A freakin' asshole punk band.

The guys playing pool stopped and started to tap their cues across their palms menacingly. The odds weren't good. They were twelve or thirteen fully grown geezers. We were five girls, me, Chris, and a "fucking prick with ears". We headed for the door; the whole bar followed. Pool cues were being tapped harder, as hard as our hearts were beating. As we stepped out, two cop cars pulled up in the parking lot. Hurrah, we thought, the cavalry. Uh-uh. Glaring at us, the cops left their cars, pulled out their night sticks, crouched down and started to drum the ground. They began to chant: "Punk rockers go home!" The crowd joined in. "Punk rockers go home!" Huh? The girls looked moddish, me and Chris had crops, and Louis was still a bald prick.

What we didn't know was that, despite the two buildings being owned by the same guy and sharing a car park, there was an ongoing war between the Zubies regulars and the Cuckoo's Nest punters.

We headed for the tour bus and were relieved when it started first time. The nightmare didn't stop. We drove off; a cop car drove after us. They trailed us for an hour, all the way back to la-la land. We convinced ourselves that we'd be pulled over and left for dead in a ditch. Those with us with any bottle promptly lost it, along with various pills and small wraps of whizz and Charlie. Legs were vigorously crossed; there was no way we'd be stopping for a roadside slash. All this for trying to play a gig. Imagine the fuss if we'd knocked them for the beer as well ...

The Cuckoo's Nest was later targeted by a twelve-man police team. The following January one of the punks tried to run down two cops in the parking lot. The city council revoked its live entertainment licence soon after. The Vandals immortalised the hostilities between the two clubs in a song called 'Urban Struggle'.

What Have We Got? Sham 69

I was a fan of Sham 69 long before I started working for *Sounds*. Their angry anthems were righteous outpourings from the gutter aimed at the soft underbelly of what punk was becoming. 'Rip Off' laid into the McLaren myth, attacking Talcy Malcy's overpriced boutique: "It's just a fake, make no mistake/A rip-off for us and a Rolls for them." All of their choruses punched like Rocky.

But Christ, their audiences were scary. Nick Kent described them as "a sight to curdle the soul – skinhead behemoths with prison tattoos and someone else's blood on their Doctor Martens". When Jimmy sang "There's gonna be a Borstal Breakout" you could well believe it'd happened already and all the young hoods were there in the audience.

"Hey Little Rich Boy," Jim hollered. "Take a good look at me." One

Sham anthem summed up their message succinctly: "What? Have we got?" Pursey would shout, and the roar would come back from the hardcore faithful: "FARHK ALL!" Pursey was aiming his words directly at kids at the bottom of the scrap heap. He got the mood wrong occasionally (Jimmy would sing about not needing a flash car, cos he could get the bus, but the smarter kids were already thinking how they could get one of their own – either by working or thieving or other semi-legal enterprises) but he meant it, mannn.

Sham seemed fresh, dangerous and new. Tony Parsons gave them a rave review in the NME. Danny Baker declared them to be his favourite band. And they let the hooligan genie out of the bottle. There had been other punk bands with hard followings, but Sham 69 attracted the hardcore terrace element; the ruckers; the lunatics; and, in parts of London town, the Nazis.

Pursey, from when I knew him well, 1977-80, spent a lot of his time arguing with the racist element among the London skins. The worst were the hardcore Hitler-worshipping British Movement – we called them the German Movement – who in the end destroyed the band.

Sham's ferocious following fuelled several rumours about the singer, who cheerfully sent himself up. When 'Hurry Up Harry' charted in October 1978 I went along with the band to *Top of the Pops*, and watched Jimmy introduce Sham to passing BBC types along the lines of, "Hello, we're the gay roughs, we're a black NF band and I'm 47 ..." And then he was off chatting up waitresses, hurling sugar cubes at roadies and crawling under canteen tables. He was well meaning, generous and likeable, if you could suffer the verbal diarrhoea.

When he wasn't banging on about "the kids", Jimmy's real obsession was betting. He lived above a bookie's in his hometown of Hersham, Surrey, where I spent many an hour watching him pore over racing form while his minah bird squawked away in the corner. He'd previously worked at Wimbledon Dog Track, and in the early days of Sham's success he'd bought himself a greyhound called School Graduate. That was the difference between Sham and the bands that the NME crowd usually liked; he blew his money on horses, not Horse. But the pressure was immense and more than once he told me that he was thinking about jacking it all in.

Fast forward to July 1979, and I am up in Glasgow at the Apollo for 'Sham's Last Stand', along with 3,500 others. The strain of being seen as a 'yoof leader' to Britain's warring teenage tribes had worn Jim down. Tonight was supposed to be the band's last ever show. His exit on his own creation; his grand finale; his goodbye ...

The stage at the Apollo is about twelve feet high, and ten feet in front of it a thin line of bouncers restrain the front ranks of the crowd, kids who know they'll never see Sham again and who intend to wring every drop of enjoyment from what turns out to be a 100-minute show, comprising three different sets. And a definite false turn in punk rock history. Set one was the past; all the old hits: 'I Don't Wanna', 'Rip Off' (dedicated to McLaren, as ever), 'Angels With Dirty Faces' (for the Upstarts and the UK Subs), 'Everybody's Innocent', 'Ulster Boy', 'Borstal Breakout' (with a kid risking broken limbs leaping on the stage from a side box), 'Hurry Up Harry' ... finishing with 'If the Kids Are United'. Set two - the present – begins minutes later with Ricky Goldstein, late of The Automatics, replacing Doidie Cacker on drums for a taster of the new album and Jimmy explaining that tonight's gig is being recorded for a live album. The crowd go nuts, but the bouncers are bastards and when the band strike up 'Borstal Breakout' one more time it's like Grunwicks all over again down the front. Jeez.

Only one song could possibly round off this part of the set – the mighty new single, 'Hersham Boys', with its rousing "Robin Hood, Robin Hood, 'ere we go again" intro for a full-scale football-punk outing of outrageous Top Ten proportions. Hey ho, let's gooooo, and off the stage they troop to a touch of the old tumultuous applause till ... SET THREE. Jimmy's idea of the future. Enter the Sham Pistols. There's now five men on stage: Pursey, Dave Parsons, Kermit, Steve Jones and Paul Cook. Pursey steps forward to the mike and grins. "I once met these two geezers and I said ain't you the geezers with that cunt McLaren who's killin' punk off ... but they got rid of 'im and now, together. WE ARE GONNA MAKE SURE PUNK COMES BACK ALIVE!" The crowd roar out their approval, and Jonesy steps forward, ringing out the unmistakeable opening notes of 'Pretty Vacant'. It's a bit of an anticlimax cos the guitar lead goes, but Pursey smiles "just testing" and they belt through 'Vacant', a dynamite 'White Riot' and an orgasmic 'If The Kids ...' They sounded so tight, so strong, so goddam impressive that I was just foolishly filled with optimism for what they could become.

Backstage there were a load of Sham veterans, the Sheffield Boys, the Benfleet Boys, Dean representing QPR and Ladbroke Grove, and some lads from Tooting. All of them agreed with me that tonight was one of the best, if not THE best Sham gig they'd ever seen; but then we were all pissed and something new was obviously going down. Also backstage were Sham's manager Tony Gordon and Virgin supremo Richard Branson, who were clearly both sold on the lucrative possibilities of a permanent Sham/Pistols link-up. I spoke to Branson. He was amicably non-committal, optimistic but as vague as a medium's insights. Polydor still had an option on two Sham albums after the next one, one of which would be a live album, and Virgin were trying to talk them out of the second so that Cook, Jones and Pursey could start recording as the Pistols immediately. The lads themselves were heartily pissed off with the whole affair, Paul moaning how bad it gets when the lawyers take over ("they're the only ones what make any money") and Jimmy saying they were being treated like bits of paper.

On the long train journey home, I pumped Steve Jones for tales of his days as a teenage tealeaf (all in my book *Hoolies*), then got them to open up about what the new punk supergroup of Cook, Jones, Pursey and

Kermit would amount to. They would be called the Sex Pistols, they'd already written six or seven songs, and they were planning to be on the road by October. Cooky, who confessed that last night was the first time he'd played live since the Greedy Bastards gigs with Phil Lynott, told me (rashly), "Jim is the only person who's come along who we can get on with. He's the same as us, see. We'd have started gigging again long ago if we'd found the right person, but now we're ready. Apart from the fact that he's a country bumpkin, Jim's all right. The great thing about Sham was that they appealed to the kids, and that's what we wanna do. The kids come along for a great time, they don't care what some wankers and trendies in the music press say."

Everyone was so pumped up with enthusiasm that nobody listened to Dave Parsons, who correctly observed, "I don't think it's gonna last long because Jim always likes to be 100 per cent in control." Cook and Jones walked out of a recording session with control freak Jimmy the following month. Steve Jones said working with him was "worse than working with Rotten". Next summer, they launched the Professionals.

Pursey's biggest mistake, though, was to announce a farewell gig in London as well, at the Rainbow in Finsbury Park. I knew it would go tits-up as soon as I left the tube station. The first thing I saw was BM bully-boy Matty Morgan smash a pint glass into a kid's face for his ticket.

There were only about forty of the knuckleheads, but they turned the show into a disaster. By the time Sham came on stage, they'd built up a small army of some 200 skins around them and were running amok through the unseated venue. Jim had hired in a bunch of Road Rats to do his security and they didn't want to know. The set lasted for four numbers before the embittered ex-fans invaded the stage. The safety curtain dropped and Sham retreated.

The band did come back, eventually, but after seven numbers the Neanderthal Nazi tide surged onto the stage again. Pursey finally cracked. He demolished the drum kit, grabbed a microphone and shouted, "I fuckin' loved you! I fuckin' did everything for you! And all you wanna do is fight!" A tear rolled down his cheek. It was all over. Robbi Millar wrote in Sounds: "Jimmy said goodbye to London, and London kicked him in the teeth."

My own open hostility to the BM made me a target too. I was at the Bridge House in Canning Town for a *Cockney Rejects* gig when I found myself surrounded by Matty Morgan, his brother Steve, Dick Barton, Glen Bennett and a couple of others who constituted the hardest of the twisted hardcore. Matty started on about me being a commie. I was in trouble, and I knew it. At that moment, Kevin Wells, the Rejects' beefy roadie, walked right through them and put his hand firmly on my shoulder. "Are you okay, Gal?" he said, glaring at the Morgan brothers. "Yeah," I said. "Thanks, Kev." The neo-Nazis scowled and backed off. By doing that, Wellsy had let them know that if they'd started on me they'd have to face him and the entire Rejects entourage. That simple gesture was all it took for BM to turn from British Movement to bowel movement.

The Morgans were seriously nuts. Steve once stuck a bayonet through Matty's shoulder over a row they had while watching *World of Sport*. These were not people you could reason with.

Later the Rejects firm would take on the BM and batter them twice – see my book Cockney Reject for details - ending their psychotic menace for many a year. The 'Movement' were formed and were originally led by Colin Jordan, a crank whose public life came to a pathetic end when he was collared for stealing three pairs of women's knickers from Tesco's in Leamington Spa. I'm not sure what was the biggest humiliation from a Nazi point of view – that the knickers were a bright Communist red, or that the store was Jewish-owned. For God's sake, man, if you must nick panties at least make them gym-class black and British-made.

I Am Der Management

My association with the Cockney Rejects began in 1979 when I took a phone call at Sounds from a young kid called Mickey Geggus. He told me he was from Canning Town and had a band. I liked the sound of him so I told him to come up the office; but he and his brother Jeff came up at dinnertime, and between the hours of midday and 3 p.m. my office generally relocated to the White Lion pub in Covent Garden.

It was only a small pub, but everyone from Chrissie Hynde to Phil Lynott via Shane MacGowan, John Peel, Alan Moore and Malcolm McLaren had drunk in that bar – McLaren never bought a drink though. I was knocking back a few with another Sounds writer, Robbi Millar (aka Margaret Ann Forester), when the Geggus brothers waltzed in, two fast-talking teenagers sporting West Ham paraphernalia and brimming with confidence, with a barrow boy's gift of the gab. They were both boxers, Jeff was in training for the ABAs. He was just 15 – he'd bunked off school to meet me. I liked them immediately and knew that Jimmy Pursey would, so I said I'd get onto him about them doing a pukka demo up at the Polydor studios for his new JP Productions venture. What I didn't know was that they'd never played a gig, didn't have a drummer, and the bassist could only play three notes. It was all front. Chutzpah.

Jimmy liked the sound of them as much as I did. We booked them in for a session, unaware that they were busy writing their first four songs as we spoke. The cheeky sods told the engineer, Pete Wilson, that their drummer had been in a car crash, so Pete played drums on what was to be a seminal recording session. The songs were 'Police Car', 'Flares and Slippers', 'Fight Song' and 'I Wanna Be a Star'. Incredibly, they were excellent - raw but exciting, totally punk. 'Police Car' was about Jeff getting wrongly arrested at Upton Park. It started with a holler of: "Freedom? There ain't no fuckin' freedom," and the lyrics began, "I like punk, and I like Sham/I got nicked over West 'am …" 'I Wanna Be a

Star' ended with Jeff adlibbing about wanting "twenty new Gibsons, playing Hammersmith at £10 a ticket with Iggy Pop supporting".

They were instant classics and it caught on in the Sounds office. Me, Dave McCullough, Robbi Millar and Eric Fuller all put 'Police Car' on our weekly published playlists. The boys took the demo to Small Wonder, an indie label in Walthamstow, run by Pete Stennett. He also loved it and instantly stuck them in a studio to re-record it as their debut EP. They managed to knock over Les McKeown of the Bay City Rollers with a broom in the process. The lads asked me and Pursey to pose for pictures, which they put on the sleeve - four rejects together – and I got them what turned out to be their first ever gig supporting the Little Roosters at the Bridge House, Canning Town. About thirty of Jeff's schoolmates, styling themselves the Rubber Glove Firm, turned up. Vince Riordan, a former Sham roadie who was the nephew of Jack 'The Hat' McVitie, joined as bassist in time for their second gig, supporting my mates the Tickets, also at the Bridge. I brought Robbi along and got her to review it – she was the talk of Canning Town after turning up in see-through plastic trousers. They didn't go in for that kind of thing back then.

Vince's presence attracted a different, older crowd of hardcore hooligans, including the ICF, former Glory Boys, ex-skins and other terrace regulars. Among the faces were such infamous characters as Carlton 'Rise of the Foot-soldier' Leach, Gary Hodges and Hoxton Tom McCourt. Robbi's review accurately dubbed them "the new Sham". The EP sold out its first pressing of 5,000 in a fortnight and went on to do 30,000 copies.

I introduced Jeff to Mensi, who gave them a support slot at the Electric Ballroom in Camden. It ended in a barroom brawl, with the Rejects and their entourage – about a dozen in all – taking on and battering about ninety BM boneheads who were picking on punks. It was a taste of things to come. Yet when Mick and Jeff asked me to manage the band, I agreed.

Even their road crew were fearsome – Wellsy, H, Binnsy, Skully. They would chill the blood of a hired assassin. Skully, aka Andrew Russell, whom I'd first met in Glasgow at the Sham Pistols gig in '79, ended up doing 15 years for hijacking a helicopter and springing gangland boss John Kendall from Gartree Prison in Leicestershire in 1987. Their entourage included the likes of Andy Swallow, Gary Dickle, Johnny Butler, the Meakin brothers and Danny Harrison, all of them notorious in their own way. By November 1979 their support on the Upton Park terraces was so strong that chants of "Cockney Rejects – oh, oh" to the tune of Gary Glitter's 'Hello, Hello, I'm Back Again' were clearly audible on *Match of the Day*.

I tell the whole story of the band in *Cockney Reject*, the book I wrote with Jeff. Managing them was never going to be easy. One showcase gig for record companies at the Moonlight Club in West Hampstead was interrupted by H and Wellsy throwing Mad Dicky Galvin – a fan, but also by then a drugged-up nuisance - down a flight of stairs. Journalists sent to interview them were routinely persecuted. One poor sod was even stripped, and to add to his indignity he had toothpaste squirted up his arse. But live they were one of the most exciting punk bands I'd ever seen. Just listen to early songs like 'Fighting in the Streets' and 'Bad Man' and you'll know why Joe Strummer called them the real deal, and why it was so easy for me and Jimmy Pursey to get them signed up to EMI for £135,000 and a four album deal.

Now it was getting serious, and I knew I had to choose between full-time management and rock writing. Maybe I made the wrong decision, but I chose to stay at Sounds. Definitely the wrong decision was to let Jimmy Pursey talk the band into signing up with his manager, Tony Gordon. The Rejects needed a Peter Grant or a Frank Warren to keep them under control. Tony Gordon, a marshmallow blob of a man, just wasn't up to the job. He was much happier with his next client, Boy

George. So little was money my motivation that my price for signing the band over was a £100 meal at the Park Lane Hilton – not a patch on Manze's (I went with Hoxton Tom and our wives; Tony begged us to get him a receipt).

The band's later violent demise has been well documented. Less well known are the sexual shenanigans, including Mick's affair with a rock star's gorgeous model girlfriend. Or the time Vince got bored with a girl he'd pulled on the road. He told her he wanted to shag her from behind while she looked out the hotel window, and then got his roommate Wellsy to take his place. The poor woman only realised what was going on when she looked down mid-coitus to see Vinnie waving up at her from the car park below.

While the band were staying at a posh Retford hotel, roadie Binnsy was so irritated to find some of the entourage bedding an obliging punkette in his room that he threw her out of the first-floor window straight into a rose bush. Johnny Butler shot straight down there to help her out and ended up receiving a blow job for his gallantry. Unfortunately, this Mills and Boon moment was in full view of *Terry and June* TV stars Terry Scott and June Whitfield, who were downstairs having dinner at the time … and all of this was before the gig. I don't know what Terry thought of the scene, but odds-on June found it "absolutely fabulous".

People sometimes ask me why the Cockney Rejects weren't a bigger band. The truth is that *they* are the one and only reason. I love the crazy bastards like brothers, but they were set on auto-destruct. Two examples:

1) Ozzy Osbourne was about to break big again after the demise of Black Sabbath, and The Rejects were lined up to be the support act on his 1982 UK tour. Accounts vary slightly, but the general consensus was that while horsing around in his hotel room Ozzy kicked Ross Halfin off his bed. Mickey Geggus immediately chinned Ozzy. That's right. The about-to-be support band's guitarist punched the star turn on the chin. In fairness, Ozzy had been leading Ross around the room on a lead and

making him bark like a dog, and Oz did say a week later that Mick had been in the right. But once Sharon knew about the incident there was no coming back. The Rejects were off the tour.

2) Sounds, my rock paper, were hugely supportive of the band. They rewarded that support, firstly, by slapping staff writer Pete Silverton in our Long Acre office and, secondly, by decking a harmless Chelsea-supporting punk called Pat Marc, also in our office – from which they were immediately, if temporarily, banned.

There are many other examples: times they snapped at Iron Maiden and Def Leppard or ran amok at EMI – that helps explain why the band never got as far as they could have done. It's frustrating for all of us who believed in them, and a lesson for other bands to learn: if someone is on your side, do not piss them off. But, then again, if they'd been diplomats they wouldn't have become legends. At one stage I did get them to play a couple of Prisoners' Rights benefit gigs that I'd set up with Hoxton Tom at the Bridge House. When Jeff asked why, I said simply, "Insurance".

Shane MacGowan reckoned that the Cockney Rejects were one of the Top Three most important bands to come out of punk. They were certainly the start of something new, something different. Punk had sold itself as the voice of the tower blocks. It wasn't. Most of the forerunners turned out to be middle-class pretenders. In contrast, the Angelic Upstarts and docker's sons Mick and Jeff were for real. They didn't need invented backgrounds and faked accents because they really were the cul-de-sac, council estate kids that the first punk bands had largely only pretended to be. I called them New Punk or Real Punk to begin with and then settled on the simpler term 'Oi!'

Where the first punks had been top-heavy with pseuds, pretenders, posers and charlatans, this new wave was more about boxers, building workers, headcases and thieves. Oi was raw, brutal and utterly down to earth. But it wasn't all violent. There were poets, artists, fanzine writers, cartoonists, touts and radicals in the ranks too. The kids at the gigs weren't the 'fick fascist fugs' imagined by media snobs either. A significant number ended up running their own businesses; although some are dead, some became armed robbers and quite a few did serious jail time. One or two ended up on the streets. Legend has it that, when it kicked off badly between West Ham and Chelsea at Upton Park a couple of years ago, a pile of what looked like dirty washing rose from a corner and steamed into the Chelsea mob. It was Mad Dicky, now sadly a tramp.

The first standalone Oi scene developed around the Cockney Rejects and their regular gig venue, the Bridge House in Canning Town. It became the focus for an entire subculture. None of these faces were 'Nazis'. Most of them weren't political at all. A tiny percentage was interested in the extremes of either right or left. As a breed, even the Labour voters were natural conservatives. They believed in standing on their own two feet. They were patriotic, and proud of their class and their immediate culture. They looked good and dressed sharp. It was important not to look like a scruff or a student. Unlicensed boxing was a big draw, as were the dogs, legal boxing and stag comedians like Jimmy Jones and Jimmy Fagg. And, of course, they liked to fight around football matches – the West Ham ICF (Inter City Firm) were fully represented at most local Rejects gigs.

More bands followed; more tearaways and hooligans, who were inspired by and attracted to the new movement, including The Business, Blitz, The 4-Skins, The Blood, The Exploited, Splodge, The Violators, The Last Resort, Criminal Class, Peter and The Test Tube Babies, Red Alert, The Toy Dolls and The Oppressed. The hungry and the hunted exploded in rock 'n' roll bands. The Business, from Lewisham, wrote terrific pop-punk anthems, but what was more amazing was that their following encompassed reprobates from pretty much every London team – and consisted of terrace geezers, not skins or punks.

The idea that Oi was just for skinheads is a myth. The truth is we were a magnet for nutters and bad boys of all persuasions. On paper, many of them were terrible people. They drank and fought too much, talked too fast, wolf-whistled pretty girls and probably voted the wrong way – not many of them were Michael Foot fans. But, for hard work and good times, they beat the hell out of a squat load of *Guardian*-reading, lentil-eating layabouts and hand-wringing liberals.

Working with people like Lol Pryor and Dave Long, I set out to make Jimmy Pursey's 'kids united' dream into a reality. We had Oi conferences for the bands, one being held at the Conway Hall in Red Lion Square, where we talked about doing benefits for strikers and the unemployed. We wanted to marry backstreet bands to working-class protest. Instead, the Southall Riot happened and the *Daily Mail* went into lie overdrive. Three Oi bands, an immigrant area, a burnt-down pub ... who were they going to blame? In a retrospective piece by Alexis Petridis published in 2010, the *Guardian* claimed that the Oi fans were guilty of arson, as if they'd been in the pub throwing petrol bombs at themselves ...

The funniest story of the night involved Steve 'Rockabilly' Pear, the staunchly socialist guitarist of The 4-Skins, who was trying to call his dad to come and pick him up. He knocked on a door to ask to use a phone; an Asian gent opened it, took one look at Steve and smashed him over the head with a frying pan.

Pretty much everything written about Oi in the mainstream media is built on lies and invention. The true story is told in minute detail in my book, *Hoolies*. I compiled the first four Oi albums, and when Southall happened in July 1981 I took most of the flack. I even found myself on *Newsnight*, speeding out of my head, being interviewed by Joan Bakewell, the thinking man's crumpet, whose son turned out to have been a fan of some of the bands.

Stunned by the backlash, Lol and I took a weekend break in Amsterdam with our wives, Maureen and Carol. Not long after we arrived, we turned a corner into a square and walked slap bang into a skinhead riot. Dutch skins were fighting with the cops. Here we go ...

We decided to walk round them, but a young skin called Hugo recognised me from *Sounds*. "Ah," he said. "Look, it's Garry Bushell from England," and he ran over to shake my hand. I turned to Lol and told him that I didn't want to get blamed for another riot.

The girls went off shopping while we took shelter in a nearby bar. The locals seemed friendly - two big geezers even bought us drinks, but as neither of us spoke Dutch we had no idea what they were saying to us. Not until Lol remarked how odd it was that there were no women in there at all, and I spotted an unambiguous poster on the wall. It was a gay bar. Bottoms up? No thanks. We downed our beer and took our chances back on the street.

The Blood were the second band I managed. They were a bunch of yobs from Charlton who were touched with genius, but who ultimately squandered their talent. Colin Smith and Jamie Cantwell – who called themselves Cardinal Jesushate and JJ Bedsore – were bright boys and gifted songwriters with plenty to say. Their first single, 'Megalomaniac', was an attack on the Pope. The second, 'Stark Raving Normal', savaged apathy and the blind worship of pampered elites. But they preferred drinking themselves senseless to touring. They didn't fall off the wagon, they were never ever on it. I mean, I drank, but when I watched them knocking back cleaning fluid mixed with Coke at 3 a.m. in the recording studio I knew they had gone beyond problem drinking and had entered the realm of mental disorder. Jamie finally drank himself to death. And yet they had something magical, especially on stage when the Cardinal became this deranged carnival barker and JJ unleashed blistering lead runs.

Their early songs were very Damned influenced, but they progressed quickly, expanding beyond the narrow confines of punk and experimenting with moods and keyboards. If they'd toured, they could have built up a massive following. But they were lazy bastards and were more interested in making it through McLaren-style hype and bad behaviour.

Colin had gone to the same school as me – Charlton Manor in Indus Road – but he was a few years younger and I didn't get to know him until 1982 when I put them on the fourth Oi album under their earlier name of Coming Blood. I interviewed them for *Sounds* that year too, which should have been enough to warn me off. One of their roadies Eric, was so blitzed that he started to kick his way through the glass office door because it wouldn't open outwards (it opened inwards). Their other roadie was darts legend Andy 'The Viking' Fordham, who back then was as thin as a whippet. Later JJ and Colin got on a boat at Westminster Pier to get home to Woolwich. Col came round the next morning under Tower Bridge. Jamie was gone. He thought he'd drowned. He'd actually resumed drinking with porters in a pub in Borough Market …

They asked me to manage them in 1984, and I got them a headlining gig at the Marquee. I then asked my friend Spanner to lend us a blow-up doll from his Soho sex shop. We filled it with butcher's offal and Colin took an electric chainsaw to it on stage, giving the front row punters a psycho shower with a side order of botulism. It was horrible, but no one who was there ever forgot it.

The next big London gig was at the Walthamstow Royal Standard. I placed a small ad in the agit-prop pages of *City Limits*, calling on feminist sisters to come and picket this vile sexist band, and a handful of scruffy wimmin turned up with placards. The gig itself went well, until the end. I asked where the designated driver was, and Colin pointed at a comatose figure under one of the tables. I was the least drunk of all of us, so it was down to me to drive the lorry with all the gear, the band and the entourage back to Charlton. I'd never driven a lorry and was used to an automatic car. So I drove with Jamie changing gears. We went right over the top of one smallish roundabout but somehow managed to get home in one piece.

I was shifting at the Daily Mirror office at the time and sent them on the road with Brian Collinson, who managed Darlington punk band Major Accident (and ended up co-managing Jürgen Klinsmann). They hated every moment and, in a gesture of defiance, sprayed 'Fuck off you cunts' all over the van. Despite driving hundreds of miles with this charming message on display, they never once got pulled over. They weren't even pulled up for urinating and puking out of the back. But they wouldn't tour again, and fell apart a year or two later still dreaming of hyping themselves into the headlines.

After Band Aid, The Blood wrote a Bob Geldof-bashing song called 'Still Looking After Number One', which I don't think was ever released. Jamie and Colin fell out badly. Col and drummer Wild Thing ended up on Sky's Star Search as the Wise Guys – they won their heat. And Jamie toyed briefly with the idea of becoming a stand-up comic. He certainly had the acid wit. He re-formed the band without Colin in 1995, and I had them on my *Bushell on the Box* ITV show a year later, playing live in my back garden.

It looked as though The Blood could finally come into their own, but sadly Jamie inherited half of his parents' house and proceeded to drink the profits. He died in 2004 of multiple organ failure caused by years of chronic alcoholism. Colin re-formed the band two years later, releasing a protest song about human trafficking called 'Kill The Pimps' and recording a self-penned punk opera. He's still plugging away to this day.

* * *

I have to be honest - I wish I could tell you more about the *Sounds* days, but too much beer and too many uppers have dulled my memory. I look at back copies and see that I've reviewed gigs I don't even remember being at. A whole weekend with Max Splodge in Amsterdam has slipped entirely into some mental void. Henry Rollins asked to meet me once and I know I must have disappointed him because he was asking me questions about things I just couldn't recall.

I'm saving some of the great stories – time on the road with bands like Iron Maiden, The Exploited, Madness, Motorhead and The Selecter - for the second book. Other memories exist semi-formed in a kind of timeless haze. I recall Cock Sparrer re-forming for my 25th birthday bash at the Bridge House, but Hoxton Tom thinks I might've had another party the following year when Judge Dread topped the bill. Tom was with me when a Mod band called Seventeen, who became The Alarm, tried to abduct me as a publicity stunt outside the *Sounds* office. They came up to me and said, "Oh, hello Garry Bushell, we're going to kidnap you." Tom growled, "Fuck off, we're going for a beer," and they did. But then we took pity on them and called them back for a pint.

Other attentions were considerably more welcome. I was in LA when I met up with rock scribe Sylvie Simmons and her tall, stunning, blonde friend. I ended up making a date with the friend to see her that evening, but, half thinking it was a wind-up, I continued to drink in Barney's Beanery. I managed to demolish a bottle of Green Chartreuse with one of the Bay City Rollers, and someone gave me a Quaalude (a sedative-hypnotic drug). I made my excuses and left. Sylvie's mate came back an hour or two later for our date. She was done up to the nines but nobody could wake me. I was out for the count.

It wasn't always glamorous. I went from being in Texas with UFO one week to pushing The 4-Skins' tour van after it broke down on the rain-lashed M1 a week later. It's no fun pushing foreskins uphill in the rain, believe me, although Boy George might beg to differ.

I was in Pennsylvania with Rose Tattoo when Steve Tyler snorted so much cocaine between songs that he collapsed and had to be carried off stage by his security men. And in San Francisco I once had to fight off the unwelcome attentions of a drunken female musician. I was there with the Mo-Dettes on the hottest day in a hundred years, so I ended up in the bar, where one of Delta 5 started an argument with me about the Cockney Rejects. She was a typically arsey middle-class feminist, and she absurdly likened the band, whom she had never met, to "student rugby types". I can't remember if she was Julz the singer or Ros the bassist, but she was skinny, quite pretty and had short black hair. I'd soon had enough of her and went to crash out in the hotel room I was sharing with Mo-Dettes roadie Chris. A while later he came back with this nuisance in tow. She stripped off and tried to get in bed with me. I politely resisted her charms, but ended up having to turf her out of the room, followed by her clothes. It wasn't that she was unattractive, just that I found her hypocrisy unappealing. Imagine the outcry if I'd leapt into her bed uninvited. The story ended up in the *Sounds* gossip diary, Jaws. Delta 5's record company rang up complaining and were invited to check its veracity with the band. That was the last we heard about it.

Sounds liked to wind up feminists anyway. The *NME* was outraged when Eric Fuller dug up old topless pictures of Gaye Advert posing as an 18-year-old called 'Mella'. Eric went on to publish *Nuts* magazine. The *Sounds* staff went on strike for about a month in October 1981, and somewhere I have pictures of me and Eric on the picket line – just before he drifted away for his usual mid-morning spliff.

A year earlier *Sounds* had held its tenth anniversary party and ironically laid on strippers. Debbie Hodges, then wife of 4-Skins singer Gary, couldn't get her head round it. "Why are those women taking off their clothes?" she asked. "Are they all drunk?"

I must have upset a lot of people with my views and reviews. I've lost count of the songs that were written about me. Adam Ant started the trend with 'Press Darlings' (see 'Feuds' in Chapter Seven). Crass had a pop with 'Hurry Up Garry', The Exploited recorded 'SingalongaBushell' and The Notsensibles wrote 'Garry Bushell's Band of the Week'. Then there was 'The Man Who Came In From The Beano' (Angelic Upstarts) and 'Garry Bushell' by The Warriors. I even got name-checked in the Cockney Rejects' Top 30 hit, 'The Greatest Cockney Rip-off'.

None of this hurt half as much as getting jumped by a mob of BM Nazis at the 100 Club. I was with Tony Barker and another one of the Tilbury skins, but there were two dozen of them and I ended up with a blood facial. I was lucky – they stabbed Si Spanner.

It may sound corny, but what I cherish most from those days are the friends I made - people like Tom, Lol, Garry Johnson, Bev Elliott, Joanna Burns, Steve Whale, the Geggus brothers, Jenny Torring, Spanner, mad Frankie Flame, Eddie Piller, Paul Hallam, Pete Way and Terry Hayes, who have remained good pals for decades.

John Peel was a regular drinking buddy back then. He'd turn up at the White Lion most weeks, usually with his hilarious radio producer, the former jazz trumpeter, John Walters, who was always full of anecdotes. He reckoned working Peel was "like taking a dog for a walk - you just have to make sure he doesn't cock his leg at any musical lamp post for too long". He also said their relationship was "a bit like a master and his dog", except each of them believed the other was the pooch. John himself was great company. He was an absolutely genuine enthusiast for new music and delightfully indiscreet. His appeal to teenage girls bemused him, but he rarely turned down their advances.

Garry Johnson deserves a special mention. A brilliant speed-freak poet, Hackney-born Garry was another street socialist at the heart of the Oi movement. A Borstal Boy, he'd dropped out of school at 14 and struggled with spelling and grammar, yet his verses managed to conjure up vivid pictures of life at the bottom. Gal began his career as a punk poet and naturally graduated into rock journalism. He was the first person to write about and champion The Stone Roses, and he ended up rubbing shoulders with A-listers like Bowie, Ozzy, Sade, George Michael, Freddie Mercury, Neil Kinnock, Bob Geldof, Jacko and Georgie Best.

After a period working as a taxi driver (without a licence) he turned to the easier job option of making things up for profit. Garry made a small fortune selling stories to Fleet Street (see next chapter). His career as a press manipulator began by accident on the rock press when he reviewed a gig he hadn't attended after missing his bus. No one noticed and so before long Garry was reviewing bands that didn't exist in venues that didn't exist. Or sometimes he'd write about made-up bands in bars run by his mates to give them a bit of publicity. I was the only one who was in on it.

Together we created an act called Bert and Col – based on my sister-in-law's boyfriend, a swimming ace, who drummed with his dad in pubs around The Oval. In reality, they did old cockney songs, but in our version they were eccentrics who took to the stage in swimming gear and snorkels, singing electro-synth numbers all based on things that Col actually said, like 'Tunnel Vision' ("Why should I pay to get through the Dartford when I can get through the Blackwall for free?"). Items about them appeared in *Jaws*, in the live review pages and on the news pages. They started to build up a following of people who'd never seen them! Business bassist Mark Brennan rang up once in utter frustration because they were due to play the Cock Inn in Chislehurst and he couldn't find it - for the very good reason that it didn't exist. Eventually, the local London 6 p.m. ITV show got in touch and wanted to film them. With great sorrow, Bert and Col hung up their trunks a week later. The dream was over.

Garry had no O levels, or CSEs, or any journalistic training. Yet at one stage he lectured students about journalism and was employed by the editor of a national newspaper to read the morning papers for her, as she was too busy to do so.

Gal became part of the family, even babysitting for us – he'd be speeding out of his head all night, writing reams of indecipherable poetry and talking to the budgie. He came down the CCC, drank with Uncle Bern and the rest, and naturally came on our annual coach trips to the Derby along with my brother Terry, Frankie Flame and later cockney comedians Mick Pugh and Willie Thompson. Traditionally, we'd eat a fried breakfast at Gambadella's at the Royal Standard, troop into the Newbridge for the first pint of the day, and get to Epsom in time to set up the beer barrels by 10 a.m. One year we even cooked a mega-curry in an empty barrel. Frankie Flame got so sloshed the first time he came that he wandered into Gypsy Rose Lee's caravan to have his palm read. He came back ten minutes later with his eyes streaming, claiming that the gypsy had touched his soul. Touched his wallet more like. He'd come back £20 lighter and we hadn't even had the first race yet.

In 1985 Garry very nearly got Frankie a spread in the *News of the World* when he convinced showbiz reporter Annette Witheridge that Frank was going to be signed up as the regular Queen Vic pianist in *EastEnders* - he told Frankie she just wanted to write a piece on him as a Londoner. She wined him, dined him, had pictures taken of him and interviewed him at length about his views on the soap and cockney culture in general. The scam only fell through at the last minute when, on deadline, Annette rang back to check when exactly he'd be seen on screen. Frankie said, "Eh?"

Frankie was a true eccentric with a heart of gold. But we did play some cruel pranks on him. Once Lol and I called him up from the Watt Tyler pub on the Ferrier and told him to get down there as Phonogram exec Tracy Bennett was there and was keen to sign him up. Frank turned up in minutes, wearing his leather jacket over his pyjamas. We pointed to a near empty pint glass and said, "Sorry, Frank, you've just missed him."

I was loving life back then, until my wife's infidelity shook my world to its foundations and left the good times as shattered as a greenhouse on a beginners' golf range. Shortly after we'd moved to Ockendon in 1984, I came home one day to a 'Dear John' letter. Carol had gone and she'd taken the kids, then aged five and three. I was devastated and dumbly swallowed a bottle of sleeping pills. If I hadn't phoned my parents earlier to tell them she'd gone, and if George hadn't driven straight over, that might have been it. As it was, I just took my anger and frustration out on my knuckles and Dad's wooden fence.

Believing my long absences from home to be the root of our marital problems, I quit *Sounds*. Yeah, I walked away from the best job in the world and a life I loved. We'd just got our first mortgage, but I wasn't thinking straight. All I had was a commission to write Iron Maiden's official book, *Running Free*. I took Carol with me to Florida and stayed with the band for a week, trying to repair the damage.

It was gutting to leave *Sounds*, and I've occasionally played the what if game, wondering about the bands I never met – Nirvana, Guns N' Roses, Green Day, Oasis. But a small part of me believed it was the right time to go anyway. I didn't want to turn into another bitter old staffer kicking his heels and waiting for his pension.

My leaving do, at the Nags Head in Covent Garden, was riotous, with members of Tank, Terraplane, Conflict, The Business and The Blood adding to the chaos, and peroxide bombshell Bev Elliott at one stage invading the gents for a drunken encounter in a cubicle. "Bev," I said, as she grabbed me intimately, "it's traditional to shake *hands*," adding quickly that it was cold, I'd been swimming, that speed has that side effect and hadn't she heard of shrinkage?

Carol did come back, and in 1986 we returned to South London – to 132 Greenvale Road in Eltham. My son Robert was born two years later, at Queen Mary's in Sidcup. But nothing was ever the same. The trust had gone. You forgive, but it's hard to forget, and it certainly affected my attitude to life. I had two full-blown affairs that decade, one with a breezy blonde Essex girl called Lesley, and one with Antonia Moore, a model I met at Stringfellow's on Garry Johnson's stag night, who called herself 'the black Marilyn' and did things to me I'd only ever read about in books they don't stock in reputable libraries. But the things she was into – strangulation and the like - were too weird for me. I'm not choking.

How do you know when to stop? And what if you strangle her too hard? At least you wouldn't have had to worry about knocking her up.

If Garry hadn't intervened and talked me out of it, I would have left home for Les. As it was, my marriage hung together for another decade, but we grew increasingly apart until it got to the stage that we were strangers sharing a house. I turned to work, Carol turned to the bottle.

That wasn't the only relationship in trouble either. I'd joined the Labour Party in '83, but didn't like what it had become. The Greenwich branch in particular was overrun with middle-class professionals. The party had been lost to the well-heeled liberals: lawyers, accountants, lecturers. Tony Blair was elected MP for Sedgefield this year - the shape of things to come. I didn't like the members much either. The ones I met were the kind Attlee had identified years before as being feminists, cranks, anti-sport, anti-jollity, and general wet blankets.

The People's Party? They weren't my sort of people. But who were?

Chapter Five
The Beast of Fleet Street

It's 16 December 1986 and I'm in a boxing ring at the Eurythmics end-of-tour party at a Covent Garden health club. I'm supposed to be fighting John Blake, the editor of the *Daily Mirror*'s White Hot Club pop page, for Annie Lennox's amusement and the added sweetener of five grand for the charity of the winner's choice. As a boxer, I'm more Tommy Cooper than Henry, but I've got a good feeling about this bout. I've spent the last few weeks training for the fight with my old friends Glen and Terry Murphy from the Bridge House, both great pugilists in their day, and I've had a few solid tips from Stinky Turner, too. Blake is going down, I'm sure of it.

The first clue that things aren't going to go to plan comes when I'm standing in the ring, waiting to go, and I spot Blake still dressed in a tuxedo. What the f ...?

All of a sudden, the theme music from *Rocky* rings out and a hooded figure flanked by two huge trainers enters the room. Even now, I'm not worried because I've seen Bruno there earlier in the evening and I know Frank, he's a good bloke, and if he gets in the ring we'll have a laugh. But the figure who climbs through the ropes isn't as tall or as wide as Frank. He takes off his hood and grimaces in my direction. It's Lloyd Honeyghan, the welterweight boxing champion of the world ... whom I happen to know is eight weeks away from a title fight against Johnny Bumphus. He looks as happy as a shark with toothache. My legs start to wobble, but Glen and Terry Murphy are in my corner and Glen says, "Go on, Gal, it'll be all right ..."

Well I throw a left and a right, an uppercut - I'm dazzling … until the bell rings for the start of round one and he joins in. I move forward, jabbing with my left. A red mist comes down over Honeyghan's eyes and he goes for me. Blam, blam, blam. He throws a right to my face, followed by two vicious left hooks that connect with my chest and collarbone. I hit the canvas.

I have him worried, though. For a moment he thinks he's killed me. I see a face in the third row that I recognise. It's me.

The bell goes for the end of round one and I stagger back to my corner. "Right," says Glen, "this time, when you get in there, move more, duck and dive and …"

"Fuck off," I say. "I'm not getting back in there with him."

"Gal," he says, "do it. You'll be fine. Trust me."

I get back in and Lloyd's a changed Ragamuffin man, a real honey in fact, pretending my punches are hurting. Glen had known that his worried corner would have reminded Lloyd between rounds that he's fighting an amateur and will lose his licence if he doesn't ease up.

As the bell rings to end the bout, Annie Lennox and Dave Stewart enter the ring and declare me the winner. Dave apologises profusely. I get a £100 prize and Help The Aged get the £5K. But that isn't the end of the story. The papers go nuts and *The Sun* runs the story over the whole of Page 5 under the headline 'Chump Champ' with two pictures – one of me on the canvas ('Down but not out … Bushell hits the deck') and one more flattering shot from the second round ('Take that … Honeyghan ducks as Bushell prepares to lay one on him'). The funniest thing is that the editor has made the art desk blank out all my tattoos.

All of the papers take the line spread by Lloyd and his manager, Mickey Duff, that he'd lost his temper because I'd tried to knock him out. Lloyd told reporters that I'd hit him on the chin "and no one gets away with that". It was cobblers, flattering cobblers, but cobblers all the same. I'd gone in, jabbing and moving, fully believing that it was going to be a fun charity bout. But they had to protect Lloyd's licence and it didn't do me any harm to be known as the nutter who tried to KO the world champ. My quote in the papers was "Bring on Tyson!"

It wasn't the hardest fight I ever had. That was the divorce in 1999. At least Lloyd didn't take my house, my money and my youngest son. But I had several pints bought for me on the strength of it.

I met up with Lloyd at a TV show in 2008. He's about three times his fighting weight these days and has taken to wearing a Fat Pat style fur coat. I reminded him about our bout and he said he'd gone for me because he'd thought I was a big bloke like Lennox Lewis and might punch like Lennox too. I was quite flattered, until I remembered that Lennox Lewis wasn't even heard of back then.

I would fight Lennox now, though. Annie Lennox. Anything to stop her squawking.

My next big fight was with Rod Hull in a pantomime in 1994 - actually on the stage in front of screaming kids who thought it was part of the show … but more of that later. Panto was one of the many strange experiences that came as a direct result of working for *The Sun* – the good old, bad old Currant Bun.

My Fleet Street career was entirely accidental. I was never a journalist. I was a rock writer who got lucky. I'd never even learnt shorthand. I just scrawl my own version. (I stopped using a tape recorder after interviewing The Skids back in 1978. They were young - I think Richard Jobson was 16 - with really heavy accents. I understood them face-to-face, but the resulting tape proved as hard to decipher as alien hieroglyphics. If a haggis could talk, it would have sounded like Jobbers did back then.)

My arrival in the Street of Shame happened completely by chance. Bruce Foxton's wife, the lovely Pat Stead, RIP, had rung up out of the blue with the news that *The Sun*'s Bizarre column was looking for people with rock and pop contacts to work shifts. I didn't even read *The Sun* at the time, as my family had taken the *Mirror*, but I liked George & Lynne and Welsh wonder Sian Adey-Jones so I thought, why not?

On my first day in February 2005, Bizarre's co-editor, Nick Ferrari, took me down to the newsroom, where a loud, angry bloke was blowing his top at the men manning the news desk. They weren't just cunts, they were fucking fuckwitted cunts. The guy was swearing like a mad tramp who'd spilt his last glass of Meths while being buggered against his will by an angry Rottweiler.

"Who's the nutter?" I asked Ferrari.

"That's the editor," he replied, deadpan.

That was my introduction to Kelvin Calder MacKenzie, one of the last remaining living legends of Fleet Street. The liberal press at the time tended to paint MacKenzie as the devil incarnate and The Sun's Bouverie Street HQ as the seventh circle of Hell. The jury is still out on that. He was a monster, but an engaging one. I quite liked him. And the feeling was clearly mutual, as I was one of the few people that Kelvin never bollocked. He seemed to adopt me as a kind of pet, inviting me down to the canteen every now and then and treating my jokes and daft ideas as though they were great insights.

For example, coming up to the 1987 general election, I wondered in passing how famous dead Britons might vote if they could. This led to the classic, deranged Sun headline: 'Why I'm Voting Labour, by Joe Stalin', which I had to write with the help of a fairly obscure Kent psychic called Nella Jones. Boadicea, to no one's surprise, was backing Maggie.

Back in 1985 I wasn't sure what to make of the paper. This was new territory – for me and for them. Up to that point the tabloids hadn't employed writers from the rock press. So initially I played Bizarre for laughs while I carried on contributing Lord Waistrel's Diary and the occasional review to *Sounds*. Speeding out of my nut for my first shifts, I knocked out between forty and fifty stories and gossip items over my two-day trial, and then went back to my normal freelance life at home in South Ockendon. That was probably that, I thought. But then the phone rang and the *London Evening Standard* asked me to work some shifts on their Ad-Lib column. Bizarre had me back soon after, and then John Blake asked me to work the summer at the *Mirror*. Once you were on the shift circuit and had demonstrated that you weren't a complete moron, word got around and the gigs kept coming. I quickly realised that there was nowhere like *The Sun*.

On Bizarre the team got in early and MacKenzie would be at us all day long. What did we have? What were we working on? Did we have anything for the main paper? And, "If that's a story, my prick's a bloater." Bizarre was an overnight page – Wednesday's column, for example, was written on a Monday and Kelvin threw most of it out on Tuesday morning at the 'pages' conference.

I expected the *Mirror* to be the same. So, on my first day at the White Hot Club, I got there at about 8.30 a.m. No one else showed up for two hours. John would read the papers, we'd write the stories, then at 12 noon he'd look at what we'd done, choose the lead, ask us to rewrite bits and bobs and then disappear for three hours, either to a restaurant, a hotel bar, or occasionally our local, The Stag – known as The Stab in the Back. Granted, we drank at *The Sun* too – four or five pints of Stella were the lunchtime norm – but the atmosphere at the *Mirror*'s Ludgate Circus HQ was entirely different. In my six weeks there I don't recall a single column lead being chucked back at us. There was no editor screaming abuse at us or offering to "show my arse in Woolworth's front window" if what we'd written was newsworthy.

You may think that this could explain why *The Sun* now outsells the *Mirror* by more than two to one.

I still thought of myself as a visiting rock writer and kept a foot in both camps. As well as Ferrari, the turnout for my 30th birthday party that May at the Blackheath & Newbridge Working Men's Club included Beki Bondage (plus whip), Buster Bloodvessel, Upstarts bassist Ronnie Rocker, Colin from The Blood and Hoxton Tom.

Some elements of the old lifestyle remained constant. I'd be lying if I didn't say that sex and drugs were available on Fleet Street in abundance. One *Mirror* exec would casually ring his dealer from the office and have it picked up by the company couriers. Three future editors loved a crafty snort and one *Sun* high-flyer would disappear for a cocaine break every mid-afternoon – 'Charlie up the bugle' - and then come back and jump backwards onto the desks. Kelvin just thought he was clowning about. He had no idea about the narcotics, but he did have a very clear one about the levels of shagging, which would have been front page news if those in any other industry – BBC presenters, Premier League footballers – were getting up to it.

One now famous former News International employee, a notorious womaniser, pulled a barmaid from the Dome wine bar the night before his wedding. Sun female journalists were subjected to sustained sexual harassment, often from senior executives, right up until the Noughties, while women reporters from the regions who were known to be 'up for it' were transferred to the London office so that senior staff could have a go. This applied to certain Page 3 girls, too. The air was thick with talk of rumpo, rumpty, dingly-dongly, sausage and the serving of the salami. Any woman deemed INOS – In Need of Sausage – was brazenly invited to partake. At the Virginia Street plant there was sex in the lifts, in the car park, in toilets, and even in the editor's cupboard. That probably surprises nobody. It's life. And it would be a dirty trick to name names. The non-sexual cock-ups are funnier.

I was at the *Mirror* when I heard wind of Martin Dunn's Boy George disaster. Jock MacDonald (yes, of Bollock Brothers fame) had tipped off *The Sun* that the pop star had bought a deluxe mansion in Hampstead. Some Irish builders were his source. Martin Dunn duly rang the builders, who assured him that, yes, the house had been bought by "the Boy George". Dunn dispatched Dave Hogan to photograph the house and the story duly appeared as a Bizarre exclusive. Only it wasn't.

The house belonged not to Boy George but to a young, unknown, rich fella whom the builders had called 'the boy George' because of his age. John Blake got wind of it and decided to piss all over Dunn the next day.

In my one act of disloyalty I let him know. Well, I liked Martin, he'd given me my first shifts, and I knew how badly he would be bollocked black and blue if the first Kelvin knew of it all was a page lead in the *Mirror*.

I met Mart in the Printer's Pie in Fleet Street and told him what was going to happen. The colour drained from his chubby hamster face and he decided to confess immediately. He went straight back to MacKenzie's office. Roy Greenslade, the ex-Maoist features editor, was the only one with him, but Kelvin was in such a fury that Martin couldn't bring himself to say a word. Instead, in a moment of madness, he pretended to faint, throwing himself on the floor and starting to dribble from out of the corner of his mouth. It cut no ice with Kelvin, who just walked over and started kicking him.

"Dunn," he screamed. "You fucking moron, you'd better be dead because if you're not you soon will be."

I got Martin in more shit that summer by filing a joke story to Bizarre, claiming that George Michael had been slung out of the Video Cafe in the West End for hurling chicken burgers at other diners. Mart had just read the story when Kelvin came up and demanded, "Oi, Dunn, you lazy fucker, have you got any fucking stories, eh, eh, eh?" Of course he told him his George Michael tip, hoping for a temporary reprieve. Kelvin loved it.

Unfortunately for Martin, he loved it a little too much. Fuck all was happening, so the chicken burger exclusive was earmarked for the next day's splash – front page story. MacKenzie was getting increasingly excited about it, and Dunn more and more worried. His only source was the filed story from me at the *Mirror*, which came with a fake phone number. The Video Cafe were pleading ignorance, and George

Michael's people were denying it. But, convinced of the story's veracity, Martin finally tracked down the rich and reputedly villainous restaurant owner on the sixteenth hole of an exclusive golf course. He was extremely disgruntled to have been called away from his game, and his displeasure escalated to Kelvin-style levels of wrath when Mart put the story to him. "Dunn, you cunt," he hollered "We don't even serve chicken burgers."

Martin can't have found out that I was behind the prank, because a few weeks later he offered me a six-month contract.

It was the start of an association with the Currant Bun that, aside from a three-month defection to the *Daily Star* in 1990, was to last sixteen years and see me transformed from a writer to a minor celebrity, a regular TV broadcaster with my own shows on ITV and Granada *Men & Motors,* and a hate figure for gay militants, telly executives and piss-poor alternative comedians. Muslim extremists, too. At one stage I was given 48-hour police protection after the paper received graphic death threats from Islamic nut-jobs. CID officers followed me to and from work and watched the house overnight. Nothing occurred, but the threats had been so precise that they had to be taken seriously.

I had a brief, misguided period where I parodied my own views in my writing, becoming a caricature of myself either for devilment or comic effect. But not everything I wrote for *The Sun* was trivial. Whenever I could, I slipped in articles on things I felt strongly about, such as the Billingsgate porters fighting to save their market, and the case of the UDR 4 – Ulster soldiers who had been wrongly charged with murder. I also stuck the boot into the EU and its slippery apologists as often as possible.

My biggest achievement was the 'Let It Be' charity single, which I put together with the help of Dave Nicholson and Sue Humphries after the terrible Zeebrugge ferry disaster.

The *Herald of Free Enterprise* had capsized on the night of 6 March

1987, moments after leaving Belgium, killing 193 passengers and crew. I came up with the idea of doing a fund-raising record and chose the song. Then we set about making it happen, recruiting Pete Waterman and a huge squadron of pop stars ranging from Gary Moore and Mark Knopfler to Boy George, via Kate Bush, Mark King and Mel & Kim. (I fancied Hackney stunner Mel Appleby like crazy, but although I made her laugh the passion remained sadly unrequited.)

I had to get permission from Michael Jackson to release the record because he owned the Beatles back catalogue. The message came back from Michael in LA: "Go ahead, make a fortune."

Paul McCartney even took the time to record a video inset for the song. I also sneaked Mickey Fitz from The Business in for the promo video. The support from the pop world was overwhelming. The only one who didn't seem best pleased was the editor. Kelvin was on holiday when I'd come up with the idea and his deputy, Dave Shapland, was running the paper. He came back in a major Stygian sulk because he hadn't been the one to green light what he saw as a major tabloid event.

The single, released by CBS, went straight to Number One and stayed there for three weeks, raising £1 million for the survivors and the families of the victims. And I was given a staff job as a reward.

On the back of the smash hit, we put together a Ferry Aid Comedy Gala at the Palladium, featuring Jim Davidson, Jim Bowen, Bernard Manning, Hale & Pace and a host of other largely working-class comedians. It sold out on the night and was released on video, raising more dosh for the pot.

The Socialist Worker had long claimed to be the voice of the working class. *The Sun* actually was. It was *the* British working-class newspaper, speaking to millions daily. The formula was to achieve a clever balance between bawdy, down-to-earth humour and a brand of radical right-wing politics that were populist and thoroughly anti the elites who ran every sector of British society. Of course, the only interests the paper genuinely represented were those of its tax-dodging Australian-born proprietor, Rupert Murdoch, and his business empire. Murdoch's politics are generally misunderstood. He is a serious right-wing radical, a Calvinist who believes in the work ethic and the market. At election times, he either wrote the editorials himself or rewrote them – I have one of them at home, which Rupe had faxed to the leader-writer, covered in his handwritten amendments. Naturally, he was for Maggie and for Reagan.

And, although there's no justification for a foreign national having such a huge influence on UK politics (especially when he used it to help push us into unjustified wars), there was much about *The Sun* that appealed to me. Liberals, the middle classes and the media class – the culturati, as I called them – all hated it. It was as far removed from the new disease of Political Correctness as it was possible to get while remaining in business. It thoroughly distrusted the European Union. And it had intelligence. Professor John Vincent and the philosopher Roger Scruton wrote articles for it, having their university lectures invaded by Bolshevik storm troopers as a consequence. It was a grade A irritant.

I never made the leap from Marxism to Maggie in the way that Julie Burchill did, but by the time my TV column Bushell on the Box was launched in July 1987 my disillusionment with the far Left was absolute. Why did I hate them? Let me count the ways. Their intolerance, their mania, their economic naivety, their ignorance of human nature, their double think, their hatred for the white working class coupled with the rose-tinted glasses they insisted on wearing whenever it came to minorities, their endorsement of the barking-mad, self-defeating creed of multiculturalism, their hatred of Britain coupled with their unwavering support for foreign nationalists ...

On every social issue, from patriotism to paedophilia via the State and terrorism, the hard Left were wrong time after time. And the Old Left were no better. Socialism had been a disaster wherever and whenever it had been put into practice. I still looked at the left-wing press occasionally, but the only ones I had any sympathy for were the RCP (Revolutionary Communist Party) – the group who went on to publish *Living Marxism* and are now behind Internet magazine *Spiked*. They continued to make sense throughout the nineties, challenging the New Labour orthodoxy, Western military intervention in the Balkans and the growth of Big Brother-style snooping.

For me, the Tories weren't the answer because, among other things, they'd destroyed Britain's manufacturing base, our farming and fishing industries, and sold us out to the EU. But I liked the principle of a property-owning democracy, of people running their own businesses and taking control of their lives. My own politics had crystallised into something new and different. I thought of myself as a patriotic libertarian, an anarchist. Not in a hippy Crass way, but in the sense of believing in the widest possible spread of power and ownership, the hacking back of the nanny state and bureaucracy, increasing democracy and liberty, and the importance of national identity to guard against the antisocial chicanery of the globalised ruling elite.

It's pure punk politics, and it's still what I believe today: be true to yourself, question everything, small is beautiful, look after your own. Roots, nature and people matter; live and think as freely and as creatively as you can without encroaching on other people's rights ...

Establishment politicians say that too much freedom makes people irresponsible. The opposite is true. Having the State make our choices for us encourages us to feel and act irresponsibly. What we needed, and still need, is a New England, radical, independent and free.

Of course, when Kelvin found out about my humble IS beginnings he asked me to write an article about it, which he headlined: 'I Used To Be A Looney But I'm All Right Now'. My last paragraph, which said quite clearly that things were getting worse, was changed at his instruction to say the exact opposite, which I soon found out was par for the course.

* * *

Until you work on a newspaper like *The Sun*, you have no concept of the editor as tyrant. But the liberal media's attempts to satirise MacKenzie always miss the target. In BBC2's *The Crying Game* Anthony Sher portrayed a Kelvin-style editor as a sleazy, unshaven slob. Wrong, wrong, wrong. The real Kelvin was smart, clean-shaven, and as bright as a button. His shirts were crisp and he wore decent suits and a discreet watch. Only his black loafers and gold tooth betrayed the South London soul-boy within. He didn't often partake of 'the falling down potion' – I never saw him drink much. Diet Coke was his tipple of choice. His interests were golf, Millwall and making money – at which he was notoriously bad. Kelvin would later encourage staff to join *The Sun* Share Club, but he took charge of the investment choices and cost club members a packet. He might have spoken like a yob, but Kelvin – 'Kelly pops' to some of the girls – was a driven man, taking pride and a keen interest in every aspect of the paper. Woe betide anyone whom he considered was trying to patronise readers or pass off press release drivel as a story. We were constantly urged to "lift your game" and anyone who didn't copped "a fucking bucket load". Libel lawyers were laughed at. Back then Kelvin's reaction to a writ arriving was to tear it up and chuck it in the bin.

At heart he was almost as puritanical as Murdoch. Wapping was a dry plant. And long boozy lunches were actively discouraged. In fact, we rarely left the building, and half the time when you did make it to the canteen to eat you'd be summoned back up mid-meal. It was far safer to get a takeaway and eat at your desk.

Kelvin wasn't working class. He was the son of two journalists educated at Alleyn's, a minor public school in South London. His mother sounded very posh. Later, when I co-edited Bizarre with his brother Craig (aka

'The Bouncing Bogbrush'), she would ring up and ask for him in a cut-glass accent. It was like taking a call from Clarence House. Yet somehow Kelvin had a connection with the man in the street. He made his decisions on gut instinct. Sometimes he got it spectacularly wrong – *The Sun*'s coverage of the Hillsborough disaster was a shocking disgrace. But often, with headlines like 'Gotcha' (about the Belgrano), 'Up Yours, Delors' (about the EU) and 'It's Paddy Pantsdown' (about Lib Dem leader Paddy Ashdown's affair), he caught the popular mood bang on.

Kelvin's most expensive cock-up was the Elton John rent boy splash, which cost Murdoch £1 million in damages – all because Neil Wallis, later my editor at *The People*, made up a date ...

We all make mistakes, of course. It was while I was running *The Sun*'s Bizarre column that I did the most unforgivable thing in my career, something that I deeply regret to this day. I employed Piers Morgan.

Despite his monstrous reputation, Kelvin was often very funny, instigating things like National Fish Week, or National Syrup Week, devoted to men who wore wigs (syrup of figs - wigs). He dismissed the Scots as "Tartan tosspots" and peppered his conversation with strange phrases. "'Ere," he said once, "I'm on Radio 4 tonight. I'll either sound like I've been at the sherbert or that I'm being rogered by a rhino."

One of his funniest pranks involved a promotions exec called Brian Clouter, who, in a bid to get *The Sun* tied into a campaign involving the Odeon cinema chain, had claimed that there are "Odeons in every town in the country," going on to mention specifically the one in Carlisle. Kelvin immediately stopped the meeting and ordered a hack to go and check the number of Odeons in the country. It turned out that there wasn't even one in Carlisle. When Clouter left the company, Kelvin got hold of a blue Odeon usherette's outfit to wear at his leaving do. He came in holding a tray of popcorn and reminded him: "Clouter, your career took a left turn at *The Sun* when you said the words, 'I think ...' and I said, 'No one gives a fuck what you think!'"

MacKenzie's phone manner was the stuff of legend. He'd roll his eyes and pull faces for the benefit of whoever was in the office while putting on a sincere voice. At one stage, during a conversation with a puffed-up MP, Kelvin held the earpiece over his arse. In playful moods, he'd phone hacks at 7 a.m. and ask what they thought of the Page 11 lead story in the Mirror just to hear the panic in their voice. He once rang Piers Morgan on Boxing Day to ask why he wasn't in the office. Panicking, Piers drove in from East Sussex only to be told, "I was only joking."

Kelvin once took a phone call from a reader complaining about something in that day's paper. MacKenzie immediately told him he was banned from buying The Sun. A few minutes later the man's poor wife called back and asked if she was banned too.

* * *

Kelvin loved the humour of my reviews in Bizarre, and the fact that I was "a free thinker". So when veteran telly critic Charlie Catchpole quit the paper he asked me to have a pop at writing a TV review column. Bushell on the Box was born in July 1987, back when variety was televised, Coronation Street was cosy and Judith Chalmers was white.

It's been running ever since, puncturing the pompous, kicking up a stink and generally pissing on the electric fence of destiny.

The column generated controversies in the way that trees pump out oxygen, and MacKenzie contributed to my bad reputation as much as I fuelled his madness. One week I wrote a couple of throwaway topical gags about gays on TV, tying in gay programming to a news scandal that had just broken involving a corrupt homosexual ring in the Scottish judiciary. The jokes appeared on the overnight pages. I was out of the office on a job the next morning and got the call from the chief sub. "Kelvin loves the column," he said, "but he wants to lead on the poof stuff. Can you rewrite it as a lead and sling in some more gags?" What

Kelvin wants, Kelvin gets. When it was published all hell broke loose. A gay campaigner made an official complaint about the throwaway use of the word 'poofter' in the piece. The Press Council ruled the word taboo, and I was widely denounced as a homophobe.

I was bemused, but, loving the outrage, I responded like a bull to a red rag. I appeared on Radio 4's *Today* programme, where I said that if I couldn't use the word 'poofter' I'd be happy to substitute 'shirt-lifter'. Then the Oxford Union got involved and at their invitation I found myself marching into battle, alongside a crusty old judge who would have been horrified to know I was high on speed, and cheered on by the university rugby club who might not have been.

I was up against the journalist Duncan Campbell, who shut me up with just a few magnificent words. It wasn't the strength of his argument that silenced me but the fact that he quoted the lyrics from an old Gonads song. "Mr Bushell," he said sternly, "is it not true that you wrote the words, 'Hitler was an 'omo, a snivelling little queer, he never got his round in, he never bought a beer, he never had any fags, he was always on the ponce, he was rotten to his mother too, the dirty little nonce...'"

I was helpless with laughter. Guilty as charged.

A while later, gay activists burnt an effigy of me at Covent Garden, unaware that the real thing was sitting with Kelvin in Luigi's restaurant just fifty yards away. Far more frightening was getting introduced to Rupert Murdoch at the height of the uproar as "the one who got you in trouble over poofs ..." Rupe smiled wryly. Murdoch, according to Kelvin, was against employing homosexuals at the time, on the grounds that "once you get one in they become a fucking colony". And Kelvin himself was always banging on about them. David Hancock, Bizarre's gay team member, would roll his eyes theatrically. (He was a funny guy whose favourite trick was to get straight men back to his house, get them tipsy and encourage them to strip off. He had the hots for Garry Johnson, but Gal was having none of it.)

The 'poofter' controversy didn't discourage the closeted comedian Frankie Howerd, whose TV return I was campaigning for, from making unwanted advances to me in a restaurant. I politely declined. Patrick Newley, the writer and walking showbiz wikipedia, was the first gay man to come out in my support. He contacted me and wrote a piece in my defence. Newley knew that there was nothing malicious about my jokes, and he despaired of the humourless gay activists who saw 'homophobia' everywhere.

For the record, I have no problem with people's sexuality. I couldn't have spent years in the rock business if I had done. I've liked and worked with gay comics and journalists. Live and let live, I say. But I kicked against TV's liberal desire to shove it down our throats (insert own joke here) and was deeply suspicious of the paedophile-driven campaign to lower the age of consent to fourteen, or even eleven.

The most offensive thing I wrote was at the height of the government's ludicrous and misguided "We're all at risk" AIDS propaganda, apparently, when I suggested that gay men should have a luminous message tattooed at the base of their spine: 'Abandon hope all ye who enter here'. On stage I used to say, "If you're a fella and you prefer Christopher Biggins's hairy arse to Linda Lusardi's tits, don't tell me I've got a problem."

One of the strangest things to adapt to at *The Sun* was the way that small things could have major significance. One Monday, for example, Ferrari asked what I'd done at the weekend. As it happened, I'd taken a Mensa exam at Avery Hill College just for the hell of it, and had passed with a recorded IQ of 153. Nick mentioned this to Kelvin, and suddenly it was a page lead in the paper. When the Greens did well in the opinion polls I quipped, "In power they'll go from green to red faster than a frog in a blender," and the quote ended up in a book 'exposing' the newspaper.

This worked to my family's advantage, too. When my sister-in-law

Sandra's new husband Colin (of Bert and Col fame), who swam at national level, dumped her on their honeymoon, the story made a full page – 'What A Drip! Swim star ditches bride and runs home to mummy'. Sandy, a very attractive blonde, politely rejected an offer to appear on Page 3.

Anything you said to Nick or Martin would find its way back to MacKenzie. And, in turn, intimate details of Dunn's 'cocktail sausage' were known to all of us the morning after he made the mistake of sleeping with glamorous news reporter Antonella Lazzeri. The place had more leaks than a sinking ship. Letters sent to me from my friend Andy Russell, in prison, found their way from my desk drawer into *Private Eye*. There was a culture of grassing. Stories were stolen; colleagues were shafted. There were weasels with more integrity. The lesson was: trust no one.

It certainly added to the mood of paranoia that Kelvin deliberately cultivated and Murdoch encouraged. Even his jokes had an underlying tone of menace. One exec had a memo from Kelvin pinned to his wall that read: "I have seen your memo regarding a holiday request in October. What makes you think you will still be working here in October?" (Funnier was the letter he sent to sack the paper's astrologist for recycling his horoscopes; it started: "As you will already know ...").

Stuart Higgins, an exceptionally good reporter who succeeded MacKenzie as editor, seemed immune to his rages. This pushed Kelvin to new heights of lunacy. "Higgie, you take it all, don't you?" he fumed mid-rant. "You just sit there soaking it all up ... You're like a fucking sponge." Next morning 'Higgie the Human Sponge' made his debut. Readers were invited to call his direct line and slag him off: 'He can't live without a tongue-lashing.' Poor old Stu had to do his news desk job while fielding a stream of calls from readers, some of whom were colleagues putting on accents. One extremely posh lady, claiming to be from Essex, told him, "My God, you're so ugly. I've never seen anyone so ugly in my life." Many of us believed the caller to be Camilla Parker-Bowles, whom Higgie had befriended as a newsman in Wiltshire. She was almost certainly the source of Stuart's big exclusive exposing the Princess of Wales's fling with James Hewitt.

Not too surprisingly, I didn't socialise much with journalists. I made a few close friends whom I still see today, but I'm not a networker and I kept my private life largely to myself. The exception was my son Robert's christening in 1988. Nick Ferrari was godfather (a spectacularly bad one as it turned out), and Craig MacKenzie came too. Unfortunately, my brother Terry turned up after four hours in the Newbridge – his back teeth were floating. His wife Lynne, who was just as pie-eyed, started accusing people of stealing her handbag, which was found where she'd left it, by the side of the settee. In the end I physically had to subdue Terry, who wanted to deck everybody, and it all got reported back to the office as a "Cockerney christening cum catchweight wrestling card", much to Kelvin's delight.

My favourite haunts after work weren't journo pubs or West End clubs but the Phoenix Apollo in Stratford, a favourite hang-out for Page 3 girls, football players, boxers and ex-ICF hooligans that I knew from my days managing the Cockney Rejects. Set to the right of a bijou knocking shop, it was run by an ambitious pair of Greek-Cypriot brothers, Panny and Gilly. Carlton Leach did the security. Panny famously dated Samantha Fox and was widely (jokingly) credited for having turned her off men. It was here that I met and befriended the likes of Suzanne Mizzi, Terry Marsh and Nigel Benn. Of all the boxers I met, Frank Bruno was always the most fun. We went to see a *Rocky film* once and the big chuckling fool covered my eyes during the love scenes so I wouldn't get corrupted. Frank, mate, I said, you're about ten years too late.

* * *

MacKenzie was feared for his bollockings, but Murdoch's were far worse. In the spirit of Monty Python's Piranha Brothers sketch, even Kelvin was scared of Rupert. The man he called "boss" roasted him over the phone almost every day. Despite the success he made of the paper and the fortune he was making Rupe, he was still a "fucking idiot".

In 1993 Kelvin had enough. In the middle of a face-to-face tirade of abuse from Murdoch, he stood up, put on his jacket and walked out. A few hours later Kelvin faxed through his resignation from his home in Kent (appropriately enough, not far from Fawkham). He then refused to take Rupert's calls or answer his faxes. Murdoch knew he'd gone too far and had to get Gus Fischer, his top man in London, to intervene. It took days to change MacKenzie's mind. In the end, Murdoch promised him, "I'll change," and Kelvin returned. But not for long. A year later, Rupe moved him to Sky TV.

Some said that this was because the balance of power between them had changed and Rupe couldn't cope with it. Others claimed that Murdoch had done a deal with John Major to get shot of both MacKenzie and Andrew Neil at the *Sunday Times*, who had both been persecuting the Tories mercilessly.

The ERM debacle was the cause. Major called MacKenzie in his office to say that he hoped he wouldn't be too hard on him. Kelvin replied, "Well, John, let me put it this way. I have a large bucket of shit on my desk and tomorrow morning I'm going to pour it all over your head."

Major thought he was joking. He wasn't.

Moving Kelvin to Sky, where he inevitably fell out with tough Aussie boss Sam Chisholm, was Murdoch's way of firing him without firing him. Kelvin came good, however, bringing mayhem to the *Mirror*'s cable station Live TV before buying Talk Radio in 1998 as CEO of The Wireless Group and turning it into the hugely successful TalkSPORT. He had a plaque put on his office door, which read: 'Anger management course (failed)'. But Kelvin could take it too. Back in '93, after twelve glorious years exposing shagging politicians and pop stars, Kelvin got caught on a Caribbean beach by the *Mail On Sunday* with an attractive blonde who was not his wife but a secretary from News International. Kelvin held up his hands, posed for pictures and congratulated them for "absolutely great journalism".

Dealing with Rupert was always tough. Bill Wyman's extremely dodgy relationship with precocious wild child Mandy Smith was the unlikely catalyst for a deeply uncomfortable night. Murdoch was in a great mood while entertaining *Sun* executives at Covent Garden. The only thing bothering him was "bloody Bill Wyman". Every time he opened a paper there were pictures of Mandy and "bloody Bill Wyman" and he was "bloody sick of it". The execs all nodded in agreement and tried to move the conversation on, but Murdoch kept coming back to his irritation over the wrinkly old rocker's prominence in the press. What the execs knew, and Rupe didn't, was that the next day's paper featured a centre spread devoted to the newly married couple. The meal ended pleasantly and the party trooped out into the streets. Kelvin breathed an audible sigh of relief. He'd got away with it. At that moment, Ray his driver came up and offered Murdoch a first edition of tomorrow's paper fresh off the press. Murdoch laid it on the top of Kelvin's jag and opened it up, nodding approvingly at the headlines and the editorial. Execs drifted off into the night, knowing what was coming next, but MacKenzie was trapped. Rupert reached the centre pages and unleashed a cry that could be heard in Maiden Lane: "BLOODY BILL WYMAN!"

* * *

January 1994 saw the end of the MacKenzie era at *The Sun*. Higgie the Human Sponge became the new editor and made a very good one. He certainly believed in the paper's core values and fought tooth and nail against the management when, in a bid to cosy up to New Labour, they demanded that *The Sun* changed its mind on everything from Mandelson to the Millennium Dome. Part of the paper's insolent charm was that it was anti-Establishment, but now it was becoming *Pravda* for the equally corrupt new leftish Establishment. Higgie's instincts were on the button every time; management made *The Sun* a laughing stock.

Stuart made his biggest ever mistake in 1996 when he ran the 'Di Spy Video Scandal' under the byline 'By The Editor'. It turned out to be a hoax. The faked footage was of Princess Di and James Hewitt, supposedly filmed secretly at Highgrove. It cost the paper £100K and was actually shot in the back garden of a Wandsworth terrace. *The Mirror* had a field day. The lookalike playing Diana said she felt "embarrassed" kissing the less convincing James Hewitt double, "and wished I hadn't had a chicken tikka sandwich." The quote from Kensington Palace was a doozy. "The Princess of Wales does not recognise herself or James Hewitt from these photographs," it said.

* * *

My mum had always wanted me to end up on Fleet Street, it was her ambition for me, but in my bull-headed way I'd always pooh-poohed the idea. One of my great joys was being able to show her the page that said 'Bizarre by Garry Bushell and Craig MacKenzie' with my byline picture, in the weeks before she died of fibrosing alveolitis on 28 April 1987. The nursing staff of the Brook Hospital were wonderful, but that image of my mum in that bed, looking skeletal and in constant pain, still haunts me. The night she died, me, Dad and Terry opened a bottle of malt whisky and drowned our grief to a country soundtrack. Nin was naturally heartbroken, and she too was gone within a year. One by one the great-uncles and -aunts followed suit; my dad went in '96, following a stroke, and Uncle Bern a few years later. The strokes left them unable to communicate, and visiting them in hospital was heartbreaking.

Nin had been the cornerstone of the family, and after we lost her it all unravelled. Of all those wonderful Wagers only Aunt Mag is still alive, and her memory is totally shot. Soon that whole exuberant community of kin and close friends will live on only in family photos, and this book.

* * *

I ran Bizarre, first with Rick Sky, and then with Craig MacKenzie, employing such keen young whippersnappers as Andy Coulson, Peter Willis, the Big Bird lookalike who is now a high-flyer at the *Mirror* and, of course, Piers. What was he like back then? The same as he is now. Full of himself. A former prep school boy, Piers Stefan Pughe-Morgan was bursting with ambition and utterly slappable, but was also somehow likeable. His taste in music was appalling, he took his briefcase to gigs and his motives were often suspect. When he ran Bizarre himself, for example, Piers kept plugging the extremely naff novelty pop act Jive Bunny. We couldn't work out why until it emerged that Jive Bunny had agreed to play at his wedding. For nothing.

He is shameless. Anyone else drummed out of a high-profile job after publishing faked pictures of Queen's Lancaster Regiment soldiers torturing Iraqi prisoners, and breaching the financial code of conduct in a shares scandal, might reasonably have retired permanently from public life. Piers reinvented himself as both a celebrity and an expert on variety entertainment – about which everything he knows could be engraved on Ronnie Corbett's foreskin. As former *Sun* promotions exec Ellis Watson once said, he is the ultimate proof that self-confidence and self-belief can become a self-fulfilling prophecy. If I had a hat, I'd take it off to him.

Back in the eighties, the reaction of rock stars and music press mates to my new high-profile job varied dramatically. Elton John went out of his way to ask me how Sham 69 were doing during an impromptu press conference at a Paris airport, while Elvis Costello rang up the Bizarre desk and berated me over a story I had not written. "You used to be a good writer," Costello ranted, recalling my review of him at the second ANL Carnival. "What happened?" But Ozzy was delighted and warmly congratulated me when I met up with him in LA in '87. Others, including The Blood and Hoxton Tom, would regularly come for drinks in my new work local, the Sydney Smith in Leman Street. And, when my old pal Glen Murphy from the Bridge House joined the cast of *London's Burning*, I made sure that *The Sun* helped catapult him to celebrity status. I even dreamt up a UK version of the Brat Pack, whom I called the Brit Pack, and whose ranks featured Glen, Ray Winstone, Gary Webster, Jamie Foreman (actor son of gangster Freddie) and Perry 'Billy Mitchell' Fenwick. One thing that hadn't changed was my ability to spot talent.

My good friend Garry Johnson was particularly delighted by my move to the tabloids and eked out a subversive and lucrative career flogging entirely made-up stories to a variety of papers for two decades. Johnson was a one-man Press Association, flogging tips on everyone from Princess Diana to Baroness Thatcher. His CV includes published World Exclusives on Tony Blair, Michael Jackson, Prince, Kylie, Madonna, Rod Stewart, George Michael, Dirty Den, Catherine Zeta Jones and The Kray Twins. Highlights included 'Maggie The Movie', 'Mick Jagger to spend £60K on new lips' (a Sun splash), David Bowie's breath being sold in bottles and Kylie Minogue combusting in front of a TV. Incredibly, he was never sued over a made-up story. Equally incredibly, some of his inventions became true.

We estimate that he made more than £1 million from his imaginative enterprises. And Garry got to rub shoulders with everyone from George Michael to Michael Jackson, whom he persuaded to try pie and mash.

Gal finally got rumbled just a few years ago when *Private Eye* caught him out over his claim, published by *The People* as fact, that Robbie Williams was learning cockney rhyming slang to star in the film of a book

Garry had written. There was no film. But *The People* still paid him ... Garry should write a book about it all.

My own rise through the ranks was mercurial and, to me, baffling. I went from Bizarre editor to Showbiz editor to TV editor in less than a year. Often I felt like Chauncey Gardiner in the film *Being There*. Simple things I said were interpreted as profound insights by senior management. It was really very odd.

Eccentrics and mavericks flourished under MacKenzie. During the Falklands War Tom Petrie, the news editor, took to wearing an army helmet. He once sacked my entire team of Bizarre reporters – including Jonathan Ross's future wife Jane Goldman, and future *Shooting Stars* producer Lisa Clark (then known to us as Lisa Fuckwit) – on a whim. He finally quit in 1992 after being stitched up by Neil Wallis, who was then known as 'Wolf Man' because of his whiskers and dark aura of evil. The beard has gone; the darkness remains.

Much of the paper's content in the 1980s was trivial, full of Kelvin's odd obsessions such as the 'cursed' Crying Boy pictures or the case of Blackie the Donkey, who became the victim of a tug-of-war between *The Sun* and *The Star* as to who could save him from a Spanish village. *The Star* won. I once had to buy up a grotty single bed that George Michael had slept in from his uncle so we could give it away to readers. *The Mirror* hit back with a hotel bed he'd slept in. Not so personal, but it looked a lot more impressive.

Probably the daftest thing I ever had to write was 'Ten Ways To Spot If Your Next Door Neighbour's A Werewolf'. (The purple urine was the big clue, obviously).

One of my dinnertime fish and chips canteen chats with Kelvin had more serious consequences, however. I told him about my GB75 escapade. It excited him. Murdoch was obsessed with fascism, as well as royalty and bizarrely the abolition of UK mortgage relief. The rise in votes for Jean-Marie Le Pen's Front National in France had convinced

Rupe that the far-Right could gain a foothold here. Kelvin asked me to infiltrate the National Front and write a piece on them. I contacted *Searchlight,* the anti-fascist magazine, and told them what I was doing, and they supplied me with NF publications like The Flag. I attended a branch meeting and, within weeks, I had met their eccentric and misanthropic Oxford graduate leader, Ian Anderson.

On one occasion I found myself watching TV with a fanatical anti-Semite, who ranted that all the kids in the adverts were Jews. Then the TV news came on. There was an item on Gorbachev, whom this guy insisted was Jewish, saying, "All Jews are Communists, all Communists are Jews."

Then Bush Senior came on. "He's not Jewish, is he?" I remarked innocently.

"No." came the response. "But he's controlled by Jews."

I gave him a funny look. "If the Soviets are all Jews and the Yanks are run by Jews, how come they hate each other?" I asked.

"Where did you read it?" he shouted. "In the papers! And who runs the papers? The Jews!"

It was a perfect conspiracy theory, as self-contained and irrefutable as it was bonkers.

Several problems rapidly developed, however. Firstly, I was no longer an unknown face in the crowd. My byline picture had run in Bizarre daily and now graced Bushell on the Box every week, so I was frequently recognised by NF members. Secondly, far more worrying was that one of the Beckenham organisers, Matthew Collins, lived next door to Ogden Hodge, a chirpy black librarian who was a close friend of mine – her brother had been one of the Lewisham crew who followed The Business. Collins had seen me arrive and leave her house more than once. This put me in an awkward spot, so I made up some garbage about slave owners in the Confederate South being able to do things with black 'bed-warmers' that you couldn't do with a self-respecting white woman, and he swallowed it. Thirdly, and this is where it all went tit-shaped, Collins turned out to be a turncoat and pretty soon *Searchlight* splashed with a picture of me and the headline: 'The Front's Chum On *The Sun*' – even though Gerry Gable knew exactly what I was doing for Kelvin because I'd told him before I started! So I sued and we ended up settling out of court – they paid my legal fees. And then they leaked a picture of me at a dinner for Lady Diana Mosley sitting next to an NF member, which the *Mirror* printed to embarrass The Sun. Yeah, because who did they expect you to be sitting next to at a fascist dinner? Tariq Ali and the Lady Boys of Bangkok? It didn't help that the piece I'd written on the Front hadn't run, largely because my conclusion was that the enfeebled British NF was clearly not in a position to ape the success of Le Pen's mob in France. Murdoch had wanted 'Nazis on the rise' sensationalism. To make things worse, Kelvin was spitting feathers over the picture in the *Mirror*, even though he'd asked me to do the piece in the first place.

I was pretty angry about being the fall guy, so when I was invited to meet Brian Hitchen, the avuncular editor of the *Daily Star*, I agreed. Brian came and picked me up in a chauffeur-driven Jag, handed me a Romeo y Julieta Cuban cigar and poured drinks down my willing throat at the Prospect of Whitby pub. I started to moan about the *Mirror*'s stunt, vehemently denying the implications, and he just winked and said, "it's good to have a bit of fascism in the paper. Now what I want to do is make you assistant editor …"

When I handed in my resignation to Kelvin a few days later, it was the first and only time he ever lost his rag with me, ordering me to "fuck, fuck, fuck right off" immediately. So I did. Bushell on the Box began running in *The Star* straight away, followed swiftly by a current affairs column called Walk Tall With Bushell and a series of big interviews with the likes of Benny Hill, who became a good pal, and a splash given to me by Reggie Kray. Sales of *The Star* shot up by 30,000 copies.

Almost immediately, Kelvin started to send over my female friends from *The Sun*, like Antonella and Mad Sue Evison, to talk me into coming back. They wanted me back, he wanted me back, Murdoch wanted me back. I was flattered. But I'd done a deal with Brian. I liked the bloke and his Lou Grant braces. He'd treated me well, so I resisted the sirens' lure.

The Star was a different place altogether back then, though. The executives used to start their lengthy morning conference with a triple brandy. I shared an office with the executive picture editor, who always brought a briefcase in to work with him but never opened it. One day I had a look inside. All that was in there was two bottles of Scotch. Take two bottles into the shower? Yes he did ... Peter Hill (now editor of the *Express*), who wrote the editorials, once came back from an extended lunch as drunk as a sack and fired a pencil from a crossbow at my colleague's chair and then collapsed like a poleaxed mule. I had to step over him and write his leader column.

The paper was afloat on a sea of alcohol.

Brian Hitchen was a lovely fella, but he loved a tipple too. One night we were in the bar when the first editions dropped. Brian, who was as drunk as a thousand sailors, took a copy and started going on about how good it was. Page 3 was great. The stories were terrific. He loved it. Very gently we had to tell him that he was looking not at *The Star* as he thought but at the next day's *Sun*.

It was fun, and it worked on the music press, but it was no way to run a national newspaper.

Eventually, Kelvin himself called and arranged to meet me at the Charlton Conservative Club. We did the deal about me going back very quickly and I told him I wanted to work my notice in fairness to Brian. He nodded quietly. Then, to make conversation, I told him all the drinking stories from *The Star*. What was that I said earlier about not trusting anyone in journalism?

Two days later it was all over *The Sun*: "Garry says there are more drunks at *The Star* than you'd find under the arches at Charing Cross."

I left the paper that day. Execs were coming past hammering on my door all morning. I thought, Christ, what are they going to be like when they've had a few?

I came back the following night with my brother Terry and our mate Big Jim Cheatham. I cleared out all my personal belongings and took off to Lowestoft for a few days with my mate Paul Devine (known to music lovers as the maniac behind my band The Gonads' 'Stop That Drumming'). And that was that.

The Star sued me for breach of contract, but they'd made the mistake of suing *The Sun* for libel first, which apparently took legal precedence. I had to give a lengthy statement to *The Sun*'s lawyer, detailing all the drunken stories and - lo and behold - they all turned up word for word in *Private Eye*. Only three people had copies of the statement: me, the lawyer and Kelvin. I doubt the lawyer leaked it and I know for sure that I didn't.

My dad was pretty angry about it; he thought I'd let Brian Hitchen down. And he was right. I had. But there was little I could do once Kelvin had set the ball in motion. Bushell on the Box was back at Wapping within days, along with the Big Bushell Interview, a regular two-page spread with me profiling major TV celebrities – it launched with Bobby Davro in Blackpool. That week, at Murdoch's direct behest, I also wrote up my manifesto of how I'd run Britain. A new era had begun.

Within weeks of returning to the paper, I was set up live on TV by *Noel's House Party*. I'd done TVs before, shows like *Riverside* and even *Newsnight* in the early eighties, and *Through the Keyhole* more recently. But, from 1991, the bookings came through in floods (see Chapter Seven, Celebrity Squared).

Working at *The Sun* turned out to be a radically life-changing decision. The mid-eighties were a turning point in the newspaper industry, and the print unions were the losers. It was hard to have much sympathy with them. The print unions were arrogant tossers. They didn't give a damn about other trade unionists. They had crossed *Sun* journalists' official picket lines in 1984 (just as they had when *Sounds* writers went on strike a few years earlier), and when the Wapping dispute kicked off they had the cheek to call us "brothers". They dug their own graves and invited us to jump in with them.

Up until the mid-1980s British newspapers were printed with hot lead – the print unions had put an absolute block on technological advances; they were dinosaurs, and they abused their power totally. 'Spanish Practices' abounded. Print workers were paid full time for working half-shifts. One of them owned a vineyard! 'Ghost workers' was the name given to the pay packets that had to be given to men who didn't exist – Mickey Mouse, R. Poon, etc. – and these were then shared among the other workers. The *Sunday Times* was disrupted by "the 6 o'clock smell", which print workers claimed made their work intolerable. It only ever happened at 6 p.m. on a Saturday night, only they could detect it, and it only disappeared when wads of £5 notes were waved under their noses.

This wasn't union power; it was a protection racket.

Ultimately, the unions' own arrogance was their downfall. If the NGA (National Graphical Association) and SOGAT (Society of Graphical and Allied Trades) had agreed to work in Wapping, if they'd got a foot in the door, Murdoch would have been up shit creek. They refused.

I'd supported the miners throughout their long, bitter strike, and had slung shrapnel in every collecting bucket I passed, even though I thought Scargill was nuts. It was impossible to sympathise with the pig-headed printers, however.

Sun journalists held a chapel meeting in January 1986, addressed by Kelvin at his most populist, stressing the joys of computer technology and improved working conditions. "If I bend over any further for you," he joked, "I'll end up in *Gay News*." The chapel voted overwhelmingly to move to the new plant. The Electricians' Union did a deal to man the new machinery and the rest is history. Wapping opened the door for a technological revolution, making newspapers cheaper and easier to produce. The hated new technology liberated and revolutionised the industry. The hot metal days were over, and no one misses them. Like old-style socialism, they were outmoded and out of time. In fact, all of the old certainties – *my* old certainties – were now out of the window. My teenage idols had feet of clay. I was facing life without a safety net. Everything was going to be different.

Chapter Six
Profession of Violence

The doors of Broadmoor closed behind me with a clang that could have come straight from the soundtrack of a Hammer horror film. My immediate irrational reaction was to think - what if I never get out again? - followed swiftly by - why the hell did I agree to this?

I was here, as it happened, at the personal invitation of Ronnie Kray, and my companion was the notorious former Black Sabbath manager Wilfred Pine, a man I had met years before when he worked for Don Arden. There were many dangerous men involved in the lucrative business of rock 'n' roll. Led Zeppelin once hired John 'Biffo' Bindon as a security man, but there is little doubt that Isle of Wight born Wilf was the heaviest. In the sixties, when the feud between the Krays and the Richards was at its peak, Wilf and his gang would carry out audacious robberies in both of their territories, letting the warring firms believe that their rivals were responsible.

Wilf contacted me in 1989 on behalf of Ronnie Kray, who wanted me to visit him. Not the sort of invitation you decline. Ronnie wasn't what I'd expected. He was softly spoken – he sounded exactly like my Uncle Harry - and very dapper. He was wearing a £500 handmade Italian suit, silk tie, solid gold Gucci watch, gold and diamond pinkie ring and solid gold cufflinks with the initial 'R' engraved on one and 'K' on the other. His face, much thinner than it was in the sixties, lit up when he spoke about his brother.

I visited Ronnie five times – four times with Wilf - and the routine was always the same. He would drink alcohol-free beer and chain-smoke, and introduce me to inmate friends. Once, as we waited for him, Wilf leant over and said softly, "In a minute, turn around discreetly and have a look who's sitting behind you." It was the Yorkshire Ripper. He'd piled on loads of weight and sweated profusely as his little old mum held his hand.

Another time, as I was leaving, Ronnie asked, "Garry, can you bring little Kylie Minogue along with you next time." I said I'd give it a go. Ron loved Kylie. She never came, but I am one of the few people alive that have heard 'I Should Be So Lucky' sung by Ronnie Kray. He had a terrible singing voice himself. But I wasn't going to tell him.

On my first visit, though, the tone was entirely serious; Ronnie was furious that the paedophile gang who had abused and murdered 14-year-old Jason Swift had received recommended sentences of just 15 years when Reggie was serving 30 years for one gangland killing. He wanted to use *The Sun* to attack the paedos and also to campaign for Reg's release. I agreed with him.

By that time Reg had served 21 years for the murder of Jack 'The Hat' McVitie (the uncle of Vince Riordan, the bassist in the Cockney Rejects, who I had managed ten years earlier).

I was happy to do so, and Kelvin MacKenzie published the piece uncut, with a You The Jury phone line. Thousands called and the over-whelming result was that Reggie should be released.

I understood why the Krays were jailed, of course. They were undeniably villains and I believe in the death penalty for murderers, but as we don't have that in this country the Krays should have received the same treatment as other killers. I believe they were singled out for extra-harsh treatment because their links with Lord Boothby terrified the Establishment. To a degree, they were political prisoners.

Oddly, I found Ronnie a lot easier to get on with than his sane brother. I visited Reggie three or four times, in Lewes Prison and Gartree. Reg just had a list of things he wanted to say and pretty much stuck to it. In contrast, Ronnie was chatty and listened to what you had to say; he definitely had the business brains – Wilf says he made more money with Ronnie in Broadmoor than with any other business venture he was ever involved with. Apparently, Ron took a liking to me, and he even introduced me to his boyfriend, Charlie Smith, who seemed like an easy-going musician. I asked Wilf what he was in for. "Oh, he's a double murderer," he replied cheerfully. "He killed a drug dealer, but got transferred to Broadmoor after he strangled his cell-mate while the other fella was asleep." Nice. I also met and liked Ron's bubbly wife, Kate, although quite what that union was about escaped me.

Kate was a Kent girl who had first contacted Reggie after flicking through John Pearson's book, *The Profession of Violence*, in WH Smith at Charing Cross Station. A few evenings after sending a letter with her phone number, Reggie called her up from Gartree. Prison visits followed, and Reg asked her to visit Ron in Broadmoor. Kate resisted because she was intimidated by the reputation of the place; even the words 'hospital for the criminally insane' gave her the jitters. But when she eventually plucked up the courage to go she found, as I had done, that Ron was incredibly easy to talk to. A week later Wilf called her and said, "Ron wants to see you again." Kate went and, within minutes, Ron had proposed. Kate laughed it off, but over the next year, she says, Ron "courted me in a lovely, gentle, old-fashioned way, sending me flowers and presents, and soon I was visiting him twice a week." Finally, she gave in and agreed to marry him. Ron bought her a Cartier engagement ring, with 33 white diamonds. Some say she did it for the money, but that wasn't entirely the case. Kelvin did pay £30K in total for Ron's two weddings, but Robin McGibbon, the journalist turned author who brokered the deal, agrees that the fondness between the odd couple was genuine. What was in it for Ron? Good question. I don't think he loved Kate, but he did like her a lot, because he told me so. I'm sure he would have thought that the ongoing publicity would help keep the Kray name alive, and the bunce came in handy. He also had a sense of humour …

But Ronnie proved his depth of feeling - utter hatred - when she betrayed him by having an affair with an old flame. It sent him into a deep depression, lasting many weeks. He wrote to Rob McGibbon twenty-four times in less than two weeks, asking him to "put it in the papers" that he was hurt by what Kate had done and was getting a divorce. I got the same message via Wilf, and the job was done.

Ronnie was, in his own words, "a nice person with nice people, but a bastard with bastards". Reggie was much tougher to fathom. Off-the-cuff conversations with him were hard work. He didn't do small talk, although Reg did tell me once that he read my column and that he liked it. I asked him about Skully and his audacious Gartree break-in. Naturally, he had heard of his exploits and thoroughly approved of his cheek. But, as ever, Reggie was more interested in getting over a message – and often it was a good one. He was particularly adamant that crime didn't pay and always asked me to emphasise that kids shouldn't follow in his footsteps.

In many ways, Wilf Pine was a more interesting, and deadlier, character. Wilf was the only Englishman ever to be admitted to the heart of the Mob. He became a 'made man' of the New York Gambino family. Joe Pagano adopted him as a son. (His book, *One of the Family: the Englishman and the Mafia*, by John Pearson, is still selling steadily, even though he tells me, "I left three-quarters of it out.") Wilf went from managing Black Sabbath to fighting gun battles alongside John Gotti. I'm not going to pretend that he's a Samaritan, but he's loyal. When I fell out with *The Sun* in 2001, Wilf was one of the first people on the phone to make sure that I was okay and to ask if there was anything he could do for me.

Incidentally, as well as working with Edgar Broughton, The Groundhogs and Amen Corner, Wilf had also launched the career of my great mate Clyde Ward, who became a mainstay of my band, The

Gonads, when he was in a combo called Cagey Bee.

In the mid-1980s Wilf got involved in rock music again and invited me down to see a band called Shogun at the Limelight and the Marquee. They didn't pull the normal rock audience. For starters, the faces in the audience included the Twins' elder brother Charlie Kray, Johnny Nash, Roy 'Pretty Boy' Shaw and Joey Pyle, who was acknowledged as the Mr Big of the London underworld at the time and a serious drug baron. It later transpired that, although Wilf and Don Arden claimed to be managing the band, the hidden boss and the owner of the tape-lease agreement was Joey. It was all a scam. They'd got the band signed up, pocketed a big advance, then broke up the group and never repaid a penny. Cheers! Who was going to argue? Justice finally caught up with Joey in 1992, when he copped a 14 stretch for masterminding a drug smuggling ring.

Wilf's biggest earner was a prog rock band called Judas Jump, a supergroup made up of members of The Herd and Amen Corner – he and Don negotiated a £100,000 advance from EMI and the band split after releasing three singles. The advance was spent, and the money was not recouped.

I went on to meet more serious villains, and several others who were merely wannabes. I met characters like Mad Frankie Fraser, Lenny McLean, George Dixon (Craig Fairbrass's uncle) and Tony Lambriano, as well as several other bigger criminals who would not appreciate being named. Kenny Tyler became a friend – but more of him in Chapter Eight, The Great Escape. Some of the faces I met were conmen, naturally, but mercifully I was shrewd enough to see through them.

I had a lot of time for Charlie Kray – Champagne Charlie, they called him. He was a proper East End gent, who was more likely to throw a party than a punch. He was nothing like his brothers at all.

In 1996 Lenny McLean was appearing as an actor in ITV's *The Knock*, so it made perfect sense to invite him onto my late-night *Bushell on the*

Box show. Lenny had a reputation of being a bully, but he was great when he came to my house in Greenvale Road, lecturing the local kids not to do drugs. "Shit up here," he'd say, tapping his nose, "nut don't like it." A problem arose, however. Lenny's old prize-fighting rival Roy Shaw was watching and he wasn't happy. I got a call from Billy Murray. Roy said if Lenny had been on the show then he should be too. The argument that Lenny was on TV whereas he wasn't didn't cut much ice with him. So Roy came on, with Billy, who was then in *The Bill*, and proceeded to challenge Lenny to a rematch. It was a minefield. And it was the same higher up the food chain too.

I befriended John Nash one night at the Circus Tavern – the North London gangster was known as the gentleman of sixties crime, because he would put iodine on his bullets. John had been to the same borstal as Garry Johnson. He was a funny guy with a dry wit, and was great company. I spent many nights with him, Kenny Tyler and our wives at the Tavern, the New World Inn and my own local Chinese restaurant, Good Friends. They supported my variety campaign, and took a table when I ran it for a week at the Green Room in Regent Street in the West End. John also came to my 2001 book launch for *The Face* at the Phoenix Apollo, Stratford, mingling with a host of rockers, comedians, Page 3 girls and TV stars. But the happy atmosphere was shattered when he caught sight of Tony Lambriano, whom he disliked – he thought he was "the tea boy" of the Krays firm, someone who was making a living on their name.

Dave Courtney was another controversial character. I'd known Dave since the nineties and understood that he was scamming book publishers, TV producers and magazine trendies with his underworld stories. But a lot of heavy villains didn't like him. John warned me to drop him, but I'd already agreed to be in Dave's film *Hell to Pay* and didn't like to let him down. My friendship with John cooled as a result, but Kenny kept in touch. He was a big supporter of my campaign for talent shows and even put on his own showcases at the Tavern. Unfortunately, Kenny wasn't the most diplomatic of blokes and didn't suffer moaning Billies (Billy Bunters – punters) well. One night he was at the bar when he was surrounded by an irate mob of relatives, angry that their singer hadn't won. Mickey Pugh noticed a strange acrid smell in the air. Kenny had taken the top off the bottle of ammonia he kept in his pocket and was preparing to use it. Mercifully, Mick intervened and calmed down the situation before anyone got hurt.

* * *

It's 31 March 2000 and I'm in Plumstead, South East London, for my stag night. Fatty Lol, one of my oldest pals, is outside the pub making a call when the Bentley pulls up. A sinister bald-headed bruiser steps out. He opens the boot, takes out a shotgun and walks purposefully towards the saloon bar. Lol recognises him as Dave Courtney and thinks the worst; Courtney has been hired as a hit man to bump me off. He ends the call, grabs a tool and chases after him.

Mercifully, the action inside the pub is nowhere near that dramatic. Dave is a guest, the gun is a wedding present, and the blonde WPC who turns up moments later is merely a stripper, who (irritatingly) refuses to give me a personal lap dance when she clocks the boat race because she thinks I'll 'expose' her in the tabloids. Daft mare. That wasn't the kind of exposure I had in mind, but no matter …

Courtney is soon holding court, swapping gags with my comedian mates and anecdotes with the assorted punks, slippery so-and-sos and football herberts who make up my inner circle. We end up in a black club, where the DJ indulges us with some retro ska. Nothing better than Max Romeo to put you in the honeymoon mood.

I'd first met Dave years earlier, in Chelsea. I was dining royally – at Burger King – and he came up and thrust his latest garage anthem into my messy mitts. Turned out we had mates in common, not least of whom was Steve Whale, the guitarist from The Business. Steve is also a former member of my own band The Gonads, and one of the soundest people on the street punk scene. Over the next few years I kept bumping into Dave at places he shouldn't be - showbiz bashes, rock parties, even the National TV Awards. We became mates. At one stage he played my personal minder for a bizarre BBC3 TV show.

I tried to help him get a chat show with LWT. Dave wanted to use his connections to interview tealeaves, brasses, dippers, hustlers, unlicensed boxers, bouncers … the sort of people who would only normally be exposed on TV. LWT met us and treated us to lunch, but although they liked the idea you knew from the off that they would never deal with Dave. His self-created image was too much for them. They liked the cheap thrill of association, but shied away from actual promotion. It was their loss. It would have been a great show.

The more I got to know Dave, the more I liked him. He's a bright guy, full of ideas, drive and ingenuity. When TV knocked him back he just set up his own production company and made his own movie.

Hell to Pay used real villains as villains, real barmaids as barmaids, and real Page 3 girls, supplied by yours truly, to provide the eye candy. The cult film book Your Face Here called it "guerrilla film-making at it's best". It's good; as good as a no-budget semi-improved film could ever be. Plus it includes my death (and Cass Pennant's!) so it's a must-see for anyone who hates me and/or West Ham. Dave Legeno (now in the Harry Potter films) is terrific in it. The film features some of the most authentic fight scenes you'll ever see in a work of fiction. Some of it was even shot in my house. Fatty Lol, now the boss of Moonska Europe, helped put out the blinding soundtrack.

The main thing you need to know about Dave Courtney is that he's an eternal optimist with an eye for a pound note. I visited him in hospital after a vicious attempt on his life, and DC was sitting up in bed planning the book of the hit!

He's dangerous when he needs to be, but also genuine, loyal and generous. As a thank you he once turned up at my house on a Harley Davidson bearing aloft a sword as a gift, which turned a few heads in sunny Sidcup. He looked like some modern-day Knight of the Round Table (we share a love of the Arthurian legends). I in turn put him in touch with my New York associate Andre Schlesinger, private dick, musician, reverend (Church of Satan) and all-round good guy. And, as Andre found out, life with DC is never dull. He has the barbills and charge sheet to prove it.

Whether Dave will woo the Yanks is another matter, but if Hollywood ever makes a movie version of Kojak there's only one man for the job. Who loves ya, baby ...

Chapter Seven
Celebrity Squared

I'm probably not the first person that Barbara Windsor has snogged in front of a green room full of horrified BBC executives, but I bet no one enjoyed it as much as I did. And okay, she was 56 at the time, but it was Barbara Windsor, for God's sake, and I'd been a fan since I was thirteen.

I'd just come off camera from a live TV show, and, high on adrenalin, I found myself chatting to Bar. Booze was flowing, the conversation was flirty and funny, and suddenly, to the shock of her fellow EastEnders and other celebs, we kissed long and hard. What a carry on! After a while a BBC runner sidled up and told Bar that her car was waiting and our tonsil tennis came to an end before we'd got to the stage when the star famous for telling punters to "get aht of my pub" was telling me to get aht of my pants. If we'd drunk any more I would have probably proposed, which would have come in handy. Bar is so short I'd have to go down on one knee just to look her in the eye.

I've always believed that celebrity should be a by-product of talent, so how it came to me escapes me. In the name of celebrity I have been flung out of a plane at 12,000 feet on prime-time TV, had knives thrown at me by Freddie Starr, and been flown first-class to Los Angeles just so Noel Edmonds could mentally scar me by dragging himself up as Teri Hatcher (more about that later).

My parties are covered by *OK!* magazine, I've had to sign breasts, thighs and buttocks and I've notched up more TV and radio appearances than I can count, ranging from the worthy (*Newsnight*, *The South Bank Show*) to the shameful (*Pets Win Prizes*, *The Mint*). I've been gunged fifteen times and 'Gotcha-ed', stranded in a 'haunted' castle and hypnotised by Paul McKenna, who made me chat up a broomstick live on TV on *Children in Need*. He told me it was Claudia Schiffer, but it definitely looked more like Victoria Beckham. The next day potty Paul Devine left a brush outside my front door with a note saying it was my love child.

Once you start doing a lot of telly people begin to recognise you. Most people are friendly, but I did get insulted once. A bus driver pulled over by Sidcup Station, got out and shook my hand. "I've always wanted to meet Matthew Kelly," he said. Bastard. I did sign an autograph for him though: f.u.c. ...

I was in a working men's club in Pitsea the other year with Garry Johnson and this woman kept staring at me. After about fifteen minutes she came over and said, "You think you look like him but you ain't." Sorry? "You think you look like Garry Bushell but you ain't. I seen you signing on last week in Romford wearing motorcycle leathers." So not only was it not me, I was signing on and riding a motorbike! In the end I just agreed with her.

The worst one ever was in Tesco, when a woman came up and said, "You don't half look like Garry Bushell, no offence." I had someone start filming me shopping in Costco. "Why are you here?" she said. "Why are you buying sausages?" As Spike Milligan said, everybody's got to be somewhere.

Most people are amiable, however. I've had pints bought for me in pubs by strangers, and free cab rides from taxi drivers who agree with my views. But some are too friendly. I had a stalker once while I was working in Wapping. She'd seen me on the game show *You Bet!* and, bizarre as it sounds, she became obsessed with me, sending steamy letters, waiting at the gates for me and leaving suggestive notes under my windscreen outside Booty's bar in Narrow Street.

Filming in Blackpool in 1996, we brought a whole main road to a standstill, with wobbly Northern folk shouting, "Look, it's Garry fookin' Bushell!" (that appears to be my name up there). I went for a Chinese in Manchester with Bob Monkhouse, and a homeless guy pushed past the master comic to shake my hand. And in LA, while queuing up to board a plane, I had to sign autographs for people who had walked straight past Bill Wyman to get to me. It was mental. More recently, a People reader emailed me, saying that his wife wanted me to shag her and asked if I was up for it. I was horrified. What did he take me for? I mean, he didn't even send me her picture.

Incredibly, appearing on TV makes you a magnet for nutters, numpties and nubile women – even if you look like Matthew Wright. I have been propositioned by three famous soap actresses, two pop singers, two Page 3 girls, a glamour model, a couple of PRs and several talent show contenders, including a contortionist who wanted me to look up her antecedents. If I'd been halfway handsome I'd have been beating them off with a stick.

Often I just had to stop and pinch myself. I'd gone from seeing Ozzy Osbourne's sphincter winking at me during some drunken Halfin 2 a.m. photo session in the corridor of a posh hotel, to having a household name Page 3 girl showing me her breasts (good) and Joe Pasquale showing me his Jacobs backstage at the Circus Tavern (not so good).

Doing pantomime puts you right there in easy access of the public. Back in 1994 I was approached to appear in the Southend production of *Dick Whittington*, because the wife of the manager of Cliffs Pavilion was a fan of my column. My agent at the time was Stan Dallas, formerly of the Dallas Boys. Stan also managed Shane Richie, who called him The Colonel. It made sense. In my opinion Stan would have been far better working with fried chicken than he ever was handling turns.

The Colonel did the deal, the money was good, and the next thing I knew I was in the cast as 'The Ship's Captain' with funnyman Davro, *EastEnders* heart-throb Ross Kemp, Falcon from *Gladiators*, Rod Hull and that poxy Emu. Nobody gave me any direction. On the opening night, The Colonel came in the dressing room five minutes before I went on and said, "Remember, Garry, project!" I had no idea what he meant. Project? What was I doing, showing a film? That was the extent of my coaching.

For the first week or so I had the charisma of a cold chip, but I got better. I had to. I hate doing anything badly, but there wasn't much I could do about my dancing, which is diabolical. I danced like John Travolta in that movie ... the bit where he was machine-gunned in *Pulp Fiction*. The backstage crew used to watch me every night for a laugh. When I finally managed to perform the dance properly I came off to a standing ovation.

On the opening night I was having a drink with Garry Johnson when a rather large woman came up to us in the bar and said to me, "You know Grant, don't cha?" I told her I knew Ross who played Grant, but she just went into one. She was crying because Sharon Mitchell in *EastEnders* was betraying Ross's screen character. "That bitch," she said. "That cow ..." I was looking around for Jeremy Beadle, but she was for real.

Ross was a bit stand-offish at first, and a little bit 'actory'. One night he was method-acting King Rat and got so into character that he spat at the kids in the front row. He later denied it when the press followed up on parents' complaints. We got on well by the end, though. Ross was at the height of his soap fame and was fighting women off all day long. The following year he invited me down to Joey Banana's, a nightclub in Croydon, where he was doing a PA. It was full to the brim with birds trying to tear his clothes off. Inevitably, he pulled – he left me talking to the girl's flatmate while they made out for about fifty minutes. Although I don't know how much of that time was taken up with her just begging him to give her the old Grant Mitchell stare (which was very much like Nookie Bear's). A pair of girls came up to him once and one said, "I'm black, she's white, let's spend the night." How could he resist?

Rod Hull was the real nightmare during our run. I ended up having a fight with him on stage, too - a proper one. Rod used that bird to touch up the girls in the cast. One night the leading lady, Tracy Wilson, came to me in tears and I snapped. I got my own Emu-style puppet and hid it in the wings. Every night Rod had to knock me down twice, and he always did it as hard as he could. This particular show, just before he was due to poleaxe me for the second time, I went into the wings and came back with my puppet. Well, he hit me and I hit him. We were really going for it. We went offstage and he said, "Do you want some more?" I said, "Yeah," and we came back on like Itchy and Scratchy. The kids loved it. They thought it was part of the show. I'll tell you what: he never annoyed me again.

The headline act, Davro, was his usual funny, depressed, mixed-up self, storming it onstage and fretting about his career offstage. The impressionist was at a low ebb when I came out with one of my best ever adlibs. "Bobby," I said, "don't just sit there, do somebody."

Bob had a dog called Oscar, which he'd trained to lick itself on command. One night, during Tracy's big romantic ballad, Oscar trotted onstage, sat down and proceeded to lick his balls. The audience roared. We roared from the wings. Everyone thought it was hysterical - except the leading lady.

A lot of comics came down to see me at Southend to offer moral support, including Mickey Pugh, Dave Lee and Jimmy Jones. Good old Des O'Connor came along, too, although the only one who dicked a dumb-dumb was my mate Mark.

The People were trying to poach me from *The Sun* at the time, too. Kelvin MacKenzie was the mastermind behind the scenes, very kindly working a scam that got me a whopping rise. I was staying at Garry Johnson's house in Wickford when Kelvin called. Garry and I sound so alike on the phone that Kelvin refused to believe that he wasn't talking to me. He got agitated, and if Gal hadn't turned on the charm it could have blown the whole deal. As it was, on 2 February 1995 (the day Uncle Sam died), as a result of Kelvin's plot, my salary was more than doubled to £130K a year.

The problem with staying with Garry was that he had a young baby, and I was getting woken up in the early hours for the night feeds. So I moved in with Willie Thompson, the notorious cockney stag comedian in Benfleet instead. Looking for my bag, I looked in the wrong wardrobe one day and came across an array of uniforms – Nazi gear, nurses' outfits, a pilot's uniform. I'd stumbled on the Thompsons' love of dressing up for adult recreation. I made damn sure I wasn't there for Nazi night, so I can't tell you whether or not he actually invaded the hinterland.

The next panto I did was at Wimbledon in 1998 with Bradley Walsh, Britt Ekland and Kriss Akabusi. That was *Cinderella* and this time I had a more stellar support group in the audience. Ross Kemp, Billy Murray and Barbara Windsor all came along, either to cheer or to enjoy watching me screw up. I was never sure which. One day J.J. French, my old friend from Twisted Sister, turned up – I hadn't seen him for about fifteen years. I don't think panto rocked his world, but the dames must have made him feel at home. Reba McIntyre, the country singer, came down for a few drinks, too. She was fascinated by the whole panto tradition, because they have nothing like it in the States. Who else? Oh yeah, Elton John's gobby mate Gary Farrow came one night and started heckling. The silly git thought he was at a comedy club. And Dale Winton came twice. Tania, then my girlfriend and now my wife, was pregnant with Jenna, our first baby, and Dale begged us to let him be her godfather.

What's that? You say. 'Homophobe' Garry Bushell, friends with one of the gayest men in light entertainment? Absolutely. I first met Dale on an edition of ITV's *Celebrity Squares*, the day after I'd branded his show

Supermarket Sweep Number One in my list of the worst daytime TV shows. We had a bit of banter about it and got on really well. He's not the same as his TV persona. Dale's bright, funny and very up on all kinds of music. We were firm friends for many years, meeting up frequently on holiday in St Petersburg, Florida, and we stayed in touch until I left *The People* in 2007, when the phone calls dried up. I couldn't tell you whether it was because I'd now fallen off his networking radar, because I'd slaughtered his appalling cheapo *Sweep* remake or because I wrote that his face is lifted "like his shirt".

Actually, it may have been because I'd never ever been tempted by his sexual texts. Sorry, mate, sharing roll-mops with the still beautiful Britt Ekland in her dressing room was always going to be more of a turn-on than you offering to undo my jeans with your teeth.

It was Dale who'd conned me into going along to *An Audience With Freddie Starr*. "The producer's a friend," he said. "Nothing will happen to you." Yeah, right.

I'll never forget that night. I can't. I was traumatised by it. Freddie is nuts – and I mean that in a good way, and in a bad way. He's as predictable as a Third World dictator and just as dangerous. First he chucked maggots at us all, and then he dragged me up from the audience, strapped me to a wall, blindfolded me and seemed to be hurling knives at me. Janet Street-Porter was yelling, "Kill 'im!" One knife appeared to miss my head, and a balloon between my legs popped. It was terrifying. (Freddie also attempted to take my trousers off, but I kicked him away). And at the end of the show he left me up there while the celeb audience filed past. Thanks, Fred. It was ITV's highest rated *Audience With* … and is still shown today. The highlight for me was meeting Elvis Presley's backing singers, The Jordanaires, or, as I prefer to call them, Three Syrups & A Comb-over. ITV booked me for a revenge appearance on *Another Audience With Freddie* – I was meant to wheel him on in a straitjacket at the start of part two, but Fred was in a weird mood that night. To producer Nigel Lythgoe's helpless fury, he went off script and just did his club act. Freddie then booked me to do the straitjacket routine in a comedy video rushed release for the following Christmas.

It didn't all go my way. I was called in to meet the producers of *I'm a Celebrity … Get Me Out of Here!* twice, *Celebrity Big Brother* once, and C4 came along and filmed for two hours as a test for *Celebrity Wife Swap*. Each time, my agent was told the same thing: he's too nice. They wanted me to be chippy, aggressive and unreasonable. The agent told me to fake it, but I was never that desperate to be on telly. The closest I got was with the John Lydon run of *I'm a Celebrity*. They kept asking me whom on TV I couldn't stand, and I rattled off Ben Elton, Jo Brand, Mike Smith, 'Bore' George - the usual suspects. They wanted me to say Street-Porter, who'd already been booked; and although I have never liked her (see Feuds, later in this chapter) she'd fallen off my radar.

My first prime-time TV appearance was on a special edition of *Telly Addicts*, filmed in Birmingham back in late 1987. My old friend Heavy Metal Heather came to my hotel and spent most of the afternoon drinking wine and telling me about how she and some friends had contacted Hitler via a Ouija board. She also revealed that her groupie activities had robbed her of all feeling down below, and she preferred to use "trap two". This was an image I found hard to shake.

It probably wasn't the best way to prepare for a high-profile quiz show, but my team still won.

I usually took someone on the crazy side of normal along with me to TV studios to help keep the luvvies at bay. Usually it worked out okay. Millwall Roi came up to Leeds with me when I did the *James Whale Radio Show* (a TV series, despite the name) and the trendy telly folk were too terrified by the sight of him to come near. Colin from The Blood often accompanied me to ITV in the Midlands when I appeared on the bear-pit that was *Central Weekend Live*. And my old pal Mark Hanscombe, a publican from Charlton, was around for most of the nineties, before running off with a posh PR who worked for Butlins. Generally, they were well behaved, although Fatty Lol did traumatise the crew when I did *Riverside* by slapping his leather gloves into his hand like an angry brigadier and telling the producer and presenter Mark Ellen that REAL music was being kept out of the media. He went red with rage. The producer said nothing, but the look on his face said, "Fuck me, we've got one here ... that Garry Bushell knows all the nutters!"

My TV bookings went sky high from the early 1990s. Shortly after returning to *The Sun* from *The Star* I was spectacularly set up by Noel Edmonds, working in collusion with Andy Coulson, who by now was the paper's features editor. Carol enlisted my mate Paul to get me out of the house for five hours. This was like asking Pete Way to transport a bottle of Canadian Club safely. Paul's bright idea was to drive me down to Reculver, near Herne Bay, where we spent three hours drinking heavily in the King Ethelred pub. By the time we got back I was pickled. I tried to swap TV channels to watch the Barrymore show and was flustered when the picture wouldn't change – it was being controlled from the OB van that, unknown to me, was parked outside. Paul placated me by saying that if we kept calm the girls would let us go out drinking again later – which is how come I was sitting back reading the *Daily Mail* when Noel started talking directly to me, and suddenly my room was surreally flooded with Roly-Polys followed by beaming snapper Dave Hogan. If memory serves, Noel showed a picture of me as a chubby schoolboy and even played a blast of the Gonads song 'SE7 Dole Day'. I have never sobered up so fast in my life.

Of course, the classic Noel prank came five years later when Edmonds Gotcha-ed me in Los Angeles. Although I'm not sure quite how luring me to Hollywood via a first-class BA flight on the pretext of an exclusive interview with beautiful Teri Hatcher, the then 31-year-old star of TV's *Lois & Clark*, constituted much of a trick. Long story short, a bogus agent, who had been trying unsuccessfully to hit on me for cash, let me into Teri's hotel room. I could see her standing on the balcony. She looked shorter and dumpier than I had imagined. I stepped out behind her and said hello, and noticed there was a cameraman to my right. She must be filming a promo, I thought. There was another cameraman to my left. At this point Teri turned round and 'she' had a beard. I'd been expecting Lois Lane and instead I got Doris Pane - Edmonds in a dress.

However, not realising it was a set-up, I'd already arranged to meet up with the former Page 3 girl Christine Peake after my chat with Teri. I took Christine along for the post-recording dinner; she sat next to Noel and proceeded to give him grief for three hours. I'd say that made us even.

Later we went back to hers for a nightcap – her US flatmate Sue was obviously a discerning music lover - in her collection she had a Gonads CD!

Chris opened up my passport and read out my full name. "Garry Llewellyn Bushell," she said. "That's a mouthful."

Deadpan, I replied, "Can I have that in writing?"

It got me a laugh, if nothing else …

* * *

I've appeared in more than 2,000 TV shows over the years, but the three that meant the most to me were *The National Alf, Bushell on the Box* and *Gagging For It. Bushell on the Box* was a late-night ITV version of my column. It cost about tuppence a show, but we had a million viewers at midnight and it won its slot every week. One episode recorded a 68% viewing share. We filmed fifty - two series of twenty-five - mostly at my house in Eltham. I hosted it, wrote it and booked it, and loads of mates I'd made over the years rallied round. The guest list for that series included: Bob Monkhouse, Barbara Windsor, Bill Roache, Penn &

Teller, Noddy Holder, Ray Winstone, Lenny McLean, various Gladiators, Jim Davidson, Paul O'Grady, Joe Pasquale, Brian Conley, Vic and Bob, Bobby Davro, Dale Winton, Derek Martin, Roger Cook, Linda Nolan and Mad Frankie Fraser. Iron Maiden's Steve Harris left a message in the answerphone slot, as did Ross Kemp. The Blood, The Drifters and one of X-Ray Spex performed in my back garden.

The most outrageous interview revelations came not from Chubby Brown or Jimmy Jones but from Ivy Tilsley star Lynn Perry, who sat on my stairs and told me on camera how her husband no longer turned her on, so she had to use a lot of lube to shag him. Once, in her drunken haste, she'd scooped up some Deep Heat by mistake and rubbed it into his cock. The poor sod screamed his head off. It felt like he was poking a fire. Sadly, ITV censored the entire story.

We did outside broadcasts from Blackpool, Butlins and Montreux, Switzerland, where I was a judge at the Golden Rose awards. And I fell in love with my co-host, bubbly *Big Breakfast* babe Fleur Golding.

Unfortunately, Nigel Lythgoe didn't know this. In the summer of 1996 he invited me along to the final of the first series of *The Big Big Talent Show*, hosted by Jonathan Ross. I took Fleur. Ventriloquist Paul Zerdin began his winning act, picking on someone ugly in the audience – me. So that's why Nigel had been so keen to get me there! Then the camera cut to Fleur in a one-shot. The puppet said how beautiful she was, adding, "So what's she doing with ugly?" Cut to a two-shot, and cue an explosion worthy of the *Jerry Springer Show* when I got home.

Fleur was great, pretty, ditzy and funny – very much an English Goldie Hawn. We were never going to last, but you only have to watch back some of the shows to see the spark between us.

The strain of doing two jobs – writing the column and the Big Interview at the same time as writing and filming fifty shows – sent me a little potty. I was drinking heavily again, and shot up to over 14.5 stone. The pressure really hit home when Dad died on 8 October. I was at the

National TV Awards in a box with Beadle and Richard Desmond when I got the bad news. I still had to write and film that week's show, keeping my emotions hidden from the guests and the crew, so we could get the job done and I could demolish a bottle of ten-year-old malt in George's honour.

That had been the first time I'd met Richard Desmond and so I was surprised to get a handwritten note of condolences from him a day or two later. I had no idea of the part that Richard would play in a dramatic life change four years later.

* * *

The National Alf was a different show altogether. I made the film about patriotism and the English working class for Channel 4. Michael Collins, who went on to write the excellent book *The Likes of Us*, co-wrote the script, and I was really chuffed with it. It was the first serious documentary I'd been allowed to make for TV – and also the last. Ultra-liberal middle- or upper-class TV executives are terrified of my 'right-wing' reputation. Yes, because if you're working class and patriotic you must be dodgy, right? Wrong. I encountered similar problems with *Gagging For It*, a show I made on a shoestring for ITV in 1997. It was essentially an update of *The Comedians*, featuring sharp, funny turns such as Mike Pugh, Dave Lee and Johnnie Casson. The show had no promotion but it got a 27% share on a Friday night, up against the snooker, and *TFI Friday* – which we beat. But the network boss David 'Lemon Lips' Liddiment went ballistic and chewed off the ear of the poor guy who'd commissioned it.

Gag-telling blue-collar comedians had no place in Lemon Lips' shiny new ITV. The admen didn't like them, you see. Working-class people over forty didn't fit into their shiny new world. They were an affront to the false god of demographics. Yet turns like Mick Miller, Pughy, Casson and the rest can relate to mainstream audiences in a way that most fashionable, elitist, intellectual, establishment-approved comics never will. Dave Lee, who works tirelessly for charity, holds an annual variety show in Canterbury that sells out the 1,000-seater Marlowe Theatre within minutes of the tickets going on sale.

I had wonderful times on the road with great British comedians – and all of those stories will be told in the second book. The way the likes of Benny Hill and Les Dawson were treated by jobs-worth TV bosses is an absolute disgrace and one of the reasons I launched Campaign Corner in my column. Issues I have fought for over the years have included the Benny Hill Statue Fund (see the Epilogue) and the recognition of St George's Day – which back in the early nineties even Kelvin MacKenzie bizarrely claimed was "extreme" (eh?).

As for the televised variety shows and TV talent shows, it seems hard to believe that the popular talent formats that dominate the schedules today were once written off by the telly execs as helplessly old hat. I love talent shows. They have launched the careers of many national treasures (and Freddie Starr) over the years; although my own forays into appearing on them have tended to have a slightly tacky side.

For example, when I appeared as a judge on ITV's *Pot of Gold* I jokingly told a very attractive competitor, "I'm giving you seven, which by coincidence is my dressing room number." After the recording I was getting changed when there was a knock on the door. I opened it to see this vision of loveliness standing there. My jaw dropped. And then the vision was shoved aside and her mum barged in, chewing my ear about why her daughter hadn't won.

In 1995 I met Sam Chisholm, the boss of Sky TV, at his rented London home. He was a can-do kind of guy and I liked him. He reminded me of Mr Wolf, the character Harvey Keitel played in *Pulp Fiction* - a tough, no-nonsense troubleshooter. Sam wanted me to make a TV show I believed in. I immediately said, "I woke up this morning with a craving for nuts.

Let's do a talent show." The great man smiled, although on reflection it might have been wind, and we made the pilot in South London. It went well enough, and although it never went to series it did showcase a nutty band of herberts called Ken Dodd's Dad's Dog's Dead, who are still going today.

In the green room I got cornered by a statuesque brunette, who kept telling me how much her husband loved me. Yeah, thanks for that, love.

I got that a lot from women back then. "My dad/brother/husband loves you." If I'd been gay I would've had a field day. Also that year I brought out a talent-based Bushell on the Box board game for Bill Roache's games company Mambi.

These shows were fraught with peril. In 1997 I was resident judge on the entire second series of Jonathan Ross's *Big Big Talent Show*. One week there was a kids' river-dancing act. I said it was all passé, and twenty angry parents came on the warpath looking for me. If looks could kill the crew would have been picking shillelaghs out of my corpse for a fortnight.

We found some great turns – Charlotte Church made her first prime-time TV appearance on the series – and I'm still good friends with comics Andy Leach and Rikki Jay. The problem I had was the producer, Rob Clarke. He was a bright, creative guy, but he didn't realise that viewers actually want the judge to slag off the bad acts. He wanted me to like everybody and got angry if I didn't. When I rightly dismissed some naff camp singer for being just that, Clarke stopped the cameras and told me to take it back. I refused. The final got 10.5 million (singer Steve Brookstein, a future X Factor winner, was one of the finalists), but it lacked the must-see edge that unrestrained judging and lousier turns could have delivered. In contrast, *Britain's Got Talent* is too much about the judges, who haven't, and is top-heavy with dross. *New Faces* got the mixture right – they had judges who were both informed and outspoken, like Mickey Most and Tony Hatch, and also remembered to wheedle out most of the deranged and the deluded before the series started.

I did have one beautiful contender make an indecent proposal to me on the *Big Big Talent Show*, but I turned her down on the grounds that it wouldn't have been good for either of us if it ever got out.

I behaved much worse at Sky's *Search for a Star,* however. The extent of my involvement was minimal – I just encouraged acts like The Wise Guys, Frankie Flame and others to enter (most won their heats). I went up to the LWT studios on the South Bank when The Wise Guys played, and took Lesley. With Colin Blood involved, we inevitably got tanked up, and we ended up making love in the bushes outside the building in broad daylight. At one stage I looked up and Melvyn Bragg was hovering about a few feet from our heads. That was one South Bank show he mercifully was never aware of.

Melvyn later filmed a very funny spoof for my ITV show, where we claimed that I was an actor and that Bushell was just a comic creation. I never owned up about the bush incident, but I did have a couple of drinks with him and found him stimulating company for an Arsenal fan.

I've met thousands of genuine celebrities over the last twenty years, and have befriended a few of them. As a general rule, the more talented they are, the more down to earth and approachable they are. The fakes and the pretenders are the ones who give it the old, "Do you know who I am?" Bob Monkhouse was a wonderful man, warm, witty, caring, and generally on the level. Jeremy Beadle, despite the public perception, was bright, immensely likeable and a genuine campaigner for turns and talent snubbed by TV. Also, the much-maligned Jim Davidson always turned up to help me out when I put on charity shows – and his box at Charlton wasn't to be sniffed at either. All of their stories will be told in the next volume.

One 'celebrity' who I met on a couple of occasions was more of a let-down. His name was Anthony Blair, the Prime Minister, who would turn on the charm like a snake-oil salesman and tell you anything he thought you wanted to hear. Small example. Over dinner once I asked him what he was going to do about the TV licence fee. "Oh that?" he said with a smile. "That's going." That was in 2000 and, of course, it never went anywhere but up.

I can't pretend that all my TV shows have been quality, however. Once, Richard Desmond asked if I fancied making a documentary on lap dancers for his adult-oriented Television X fantasy channel. I filmed it at the Circus Tavern, but just before we started the producer said the plans had changed and instead of one hour-long doc we'd now be shooting a series of six ten-minute shows – most of which consisted of near-naked women thrusting their bits in my face. Still, it was a late-night porn pay channel, so how many people would watch it? Well, for starters, Rory McGrath, Ross Kemp, my 14-year-old niece (!), a pervy bloke who stopped me to talk about it in ASDA, and my local butcher. Great.

Garry Bushell Reveals All, a show that ran for three series on Granada's Men & Motors, was slightly more upmarket. It was like *Call My Bluff* with strippers, or, as I dubbed it, 'Call My Muff'. It involved me travelling to Manchester, shooting six half-hour shows in a day, and sharing a tiny dressing room with the likes of Jo Guest, Angelique Houston and Zoe Anderson. I'm quite shy, which made the situation awkward, but in the end I concluded, sod it, let 'em look.

Feuds

History books are riddled with feuds, mighty fall-outs that have altered lives and led to bloody reprisals. Think of Stalin v. Trotsky, Henry VIII v. The Pope, Ena Sharples v. Elsie Tanner …

My own battles have not been quite so dramatic, but feuds are an inevitable consequence of being a critic. Here are ten of my favourites:

1)   *Adam Ant*. I first saw Adam & The Ants play somewhere near the Elephant and Castle in early 1978 and enjoyed them. But their *Dirk*

Wears White Sox album was a stinker and I said so. Furious, Adam hit back at me and at the NME's Nick Kent in a song called 'Press Darlings', which included the lines: "If passion is a fashion/Bushell is the best-dressed man in town." This was released as the b-side of 'Kings of the Wild Frontier', which reached No. 2 in the charts in 1981. I was so cut up by this hurtful slur that I put the song on the jukebox of every pub I drank in.

2)   *Crass.* A similar thing happened with Crass. I gave them their first rock press coverage, but Penny Rimbaud was so stung by some obviously telling mild criticism and throwaway jokes about their middle-class background and hippy lifestyle that he hit back with the excellent song 'Hurry Up Garry (The Parsons Farted)', which had a pop at me and the great Tony Parsons. A few years later Rimbaud tried to set me up in a bizarre honeytrap. Honey Bane, the wild child punk singer, rang me up and asked to meet me, so I told her to come to the Cross Keys pub in Covent Garden. She came with a fella in a suit and tie who said he was an EMI executive, but who was actually Andy Palmer from Crass. I sat bemused while they staged a pretend row between themselves about EMI and their weapons-manufacturing wing. Palmer secretly recorded our conversation, with a view to releasing it. There were only two problems: I said nothing incriminating and I was with Skully, who saw through the ruse pretty much immediately, which is why I didn't write about it and they never released the tape.

3)   *James Whale.* I've always liked Whale, but back in the 1980s he had a Friday night TV series called *The James Whale Radio Show.* I'd get in from the pub and turn it on only to find, more often than not, Whale on screen pretending to be having a live ding-dong with me over the phone. I'd never even spoken to the big lug. So I responded by giving him a pasting in the column, and a war of words developed, culminating, I think, with me eventually appearing on the show. Later we worked together on *TalkSPORT.* He is a superb broadcaster, and clearly much

better on radio, where his hideous visage cannot scare the children and unsettle domestic pets.

4)   *The Exploited*. I was the first to review them, I came to Edinburgh to see them, and I made their debut release 'Army Life' single of the week in *Sounds*; then I got them a front cover, and put them on the first Oi album. Singer Wattie loved me until 1983, when I wrote a piece entitled 'Punk Is Dead' in *Sounds*. The article was clearly tongue in cheek – a wind-up inspired by my frustration at the collapse of the nascent street-punk scene. But Wattie, being thicker than a Scotsman's caber, took it literally and wrote a song called 'SingalongaBushell'. Naturally, I was delighted, although The Gonads did hit back with a thus-far unreleased gem called 'WankalongaWattie'.

5)   *Jo Brand*. Tedious woman. Has three jokes 'I'm fat, I like cakes and I hate men', yet because she's a frumpy middle-class feminist Jo is given endless TV time. We had some exchanges of insults. Hers were too feeble to be worth quoting. In 1996 the mischievous Piers Morgan thought it would be hilarious to pay Jo to review the first edition of my *Bushell on the Box* TV show. Eventually, in 2010, she did a five-minute slot on an ITV show and made me laugh. I was surprised but, then again, how bad would you have to be not to have a few minutes of funny gear after twenty-odd years as a comedienne? Disturbingly her sitcom, *Getting On*, is pretty good as well.

6)   *Ben Elton*. The ranting mockney hypocrite. No point trawling through his story – even his own kind of comics have now turned on the unfunny, sell-out bastard.

7)   *Wendy Richard*. A wonderful comic actress, who went from being the divine Miss Brahms in *Are You Being Served?* to the fearsome Pauline 'The Growler' Fowler on *EastEnders*. A few jibes about Pauline's rotten cardigans were enough to fuel more than a decade of hostility, with Wendy turning on me at awards ceremonies or glowering across at showbiz dinners. We were booked to do ITV's *You Bet!* together, with

Dale Winton, and Wend wouldn't even let me in the make-up room while she was there. It didn't help that just before we went on air Dale came up and whispered that he fancied me. If you watch the opening moments of that show, you see me hurtle out about twenty steps ahead of the two of them. But I did meet up with her a couple of times before she died, at her instigation, and we made our peace. Wend was very patriotic and a keen supporter of variety. It's a damn shame we ever fell out.

8)   *Janet Street-Porter.* Another mockney fraud; a hopeless trendy, infamous for making lousy TV shows. Janet, who looks and walks exactly like Muffin the Mule, started our feud while I was on the road with Sigue Sigue Sputnik. She didn't know me and we'd never spoken, but as soon as she heard that I was from the Bizarre column she emptied a glass of wine over my head. A shocking waste of wine. I hit back a while later by printing a picture of Janet's face and the back end of Hercules, the Steptoes' horse, and inviting readers to spot the difference. Few could. The mods put her in her place back in 1979 when she came down to film them at the Wellington pub in Waterloo. Crank, one of the Glory Boys, took one look at her teeth and said, "Why don't you get onto the council and get those railings seen to?"

9)   *Pam St Clement.* Fat Pat from EastEnders. I started this feud by saying of her fictional character, "A pig born that ugly would have demanded plastic surgery." Pam sued. What she never knew was that the colourful phrase was actually a quote from Peter Dean, who played her screen ex-husband Pete Beale.

10)   *Billy Bragg.* We had a running battle on the Mary Ann Hobbs radio show. It went on for weeks, with Bragg taking a traditional left-Labour stance and me arguing from an anti-State point of view. In the early nineties we both did ITV's *Central Weekend Live* debate show, and Bragg played the dirty trick of trying to link me with the neo-Nazi band Skrewdriver in the final moments, apologising with a grin as soon as we

were off-air. In 2006 we both appeared on a BBC4 show about the hymn 'Jerusalem'. The Beeb filmed me in a rather posh English garden, while filming Billy in front of the council estate that I used to live on – giving him the 'man of the people' look, while he actually lives in a lovely big house in Dorset. Bragg gets irate whenever anyone brings this up, so I'm certain to keep doing it. As it happens, he is one of the few socialists to realise that patriotism is a healthy emotion. That he also sings like a braying donkey is neither here nor there.

There have certainly been other feuds, but some (e.g. rock guitar ace Michael Schenker) are entirely forgotten, some were always overblown (I was never that bothered about Julian Clary and his single entendres), while some were never that serious in the first place. The first time I interviewed Les Dennis he seemed cold and very wary of me. I had no idea why. Eventually, Les reminded me that I'd once called him "Less Dennis", a term that had caught on. I'd also written, "Russ Abbott needs an operation to have Les removed from his back." I'd entirely forgotten all of it, but Les remembered every word. Sorry, mate. Les may be the world's worst impressionist, but he's actually a decent bloke.

The late Mike Reid was all right, too, but the Frank Butcher star was extremely touchy about his ears. Unfortunately, I fell out with him by noting that they were the size of satellite dishes and that he should get done for receiving. They really were elephant ears. Have a look! They were so big he could hear sign language.

Mike took jokes about himself very badly, which encouraged me to do more of them. In the end his agent, an Essex wide-boy called David Hahn, asked to meet me in my local. He had big news for me: Frank was to make another return (his last) to *EastEnders*. Hahn and Reidy had agreed terms with the producer, but Mike had one final condition – before he would commit to coming back to the show, he needed a guarantee from *me* that I would not write any more ear gags. A tough call, but in the end I decided that having Frank back in the Square with his "pilchards" and double-yoker remarks outweighed the small joy of joking about his lugholes. We shook on it, and Reid duly returned.

There have been others, of course. Brian 'Arthur' Smith. Zzzz. Radio presenter Chris Morris tried to set me up on a fake Radio One interview, which I realised was dodgy immediately from the unseen DJ's tone of voice. But it was Boy George who came up with one of the sharpest Bushell-bashing lines when he dubbed me "the Bernard Manning of pop". And if that's an insult, gawd knows what he'd call me as a compliment.

Also wonderful was the Viz cartoon creation, Bushell the Bear. Okay, it painted me as a grumpy bad guy, but so what? As someone once said, the world needs cartoon villains. Without Bluto, Popeye is just a vegetarian sailor with a speech impediment and a thing for skinny birds.

Chapter Eight
The Great Escape

When I left home in February 1998, I never expected it to be a news story. But within days I had paparazzi and news reporters outside my alleged 'love nest', and by the end of the month I'd made the splash of the *Daily Star*, which denounced me as a 'Telly Love Rat'. The funny part was that the front cover showed a picture of me together with a bigger one of Baby Spice, so the casual observer might have assumed that she had got lucky.

Less funny was the upset it all caused.

My divorce cost me half a million pounds and left me skint. And, although I don't regret it, I have no intention of saying anything bad about Carol. Our marriage had died a long time before, and by the end we had nothing in common except for three great kids. When I fell in love with Tania, my original plan was to leave home when Rob was 15 or 16. But she didn't want to be 'the other woman', a mistress, and six years was a long time to ask her to wait. I had to make a big decision: keep the pretence of the family together for Rob's sake or take a chance of happiness while it was there. I didn't take the decision to 'jog on' lightly, however. I spoke to everyone close to me first and took their advice before jumping ship, but the decision to leave was mine alone.

I'd met Tania the previous summer at a talent show down in Rochester, Kent. I'd gone with 'Fat Barry' *EastEnders* star Shaun Williamson. Tania was singing. She had a terrific new country voice and a great sense of humour. There was a spark between us, but she had a boyfriend and I was married, so I didn't think any more of it. But emotions are hard to control. We met up a few times, absolutely for business reasons; I put her in touch with Clyde Ward to produce a decent demo of her original songs, and we ended up going to a Watford nightclub where Shaun was doing a PA. That was the night we first kissed, and the glorious rush of falling head over heels in love followed. It happened so fast it overwhelmed us, to the extent that we hated being apart from each other.

I think it was The Gonads tour that made the difference. Tania came with us when we played our first ever US dates, supposedly to film the shows, and we had such a fantastic time that I didn't want to lose her. Two days after we got back, I moved in with her in her small Tunbridge Wells flat.

My marriage had been so non-existent that I was surprised at how badly Carol took it and shocked by how extremely she reacted. Within weeks she'd teamed up with the *Daily Star*, which merrily pictured her dumping my clothes outside the flat. There was a *Death Race 2000* moment when she drove behind me like a lunatic, and a litany of small petty crimes including, bizarrely, a bombardment of Princess Di trinkets from the Franklin Mint that ended with the police involved.

I remember thinking, Christ, what's she going to do next? The answer came a little later – a call from a gloating Piers Morgan, editor of the *Mirror* at that time. "I've just had your ex-missus in my office," he chuckled. "She's trying to sell a story on you. I'm not going to run it, I just want to hear the inside goss ... and make you squirm." Thanks Piers.

The Star wanted to turn me over badly. They sent a reporter to doorstep me. That day I'd received a big cheque for appearing on The Mrs Merton Show and I needed to go and pay it into the bank. Knowing how the press worked, I reckoned the reporter stationed outside would be a district man, and so I asked Mickey Pugh to phone up *The Star*'s news desk as a regular punter and tell them that he was in a pub ten minutes' drive away and that Jim Davidson had just walked in with two

Page 3 birds and was back on the booze. I watched the hack take the call and shoot off. I then slipped out, paid in the cheque and hit the town. Happy days!

When I was tipped off that *The Star* was about to run the story, I remarked to Tania that the only thing they didn't have was a picture of the two of us together. Right on cue, the doorbell rang. I looked out and saw a female reporter and a photographer on our doorstep. Right, I said, I'll leave first and draw their fire, then you nip down to the car and pick me up round the corner. I left very slowly, with a copy of *The Sun* under my arm, and strolled up to the corner of the road. It was ever so quiet. I glanced back, and they hadn't seen me. They were sitting in their car gassing. Tania came out, also unnoticed, picked me up and we drove to DFS at Sidcup to look at furniture for the house we were buying. We had an Indian and got back to Tunbridge Wells too late for them to be able to get the shot.

It didn't stop them splashing on the story the next day, however. And on it went. They published Carol's poem about our separation and the most unflattering papped picture possible of Tania. My immediate reaction was to contact Max Clifford to see if we could make any money out of all the hullabaloo. My pal Dee Ivens, the stunning Page 3 girl, had agreed to say that we'd been having an affair the previous year, and Max dreamt up the angle that in our sex games I made Dee pretend to be *EastEnders'* Kathy Beale and insisted that she called me Grant while I roughly ravished her. It was clearly ridiculous, but the old PR genius made a couple of calls and, within half an hour, the *Sunday Mirror* had offered £10,000 for the exclusive. My instinct was to take it, but Max said that it wasn't enough because we'd only trouser a couple of grand apiece. Other red tops made offers, too, but with the News International papers out of the running even Max couldn't push the bid past £10K, so that was that. A shame. Dee later married the terrific stand-up Terry Alderton; imagine the stick he would've copped from his fellow comics if they thought she'd had a Bushell in her box first …

My real ex was still causing problems. Carol went to one of the women's magazines, which published a laughably one-sided account of the break-up along with unpleasant remarks about my genitalia. It also claimed that I'd left her penniless, which I hadn't. Irritating though that was, the worst thing was that she wouldn't let me have proper access to Rob. I could see him once a week, I could take him down the Valley, but I couldn't bring him home. We'd end up in McDonald's on a Saturday with all the other sad dads, until in the end he was so upset about it that his nan intervened.

I did try to keep things civil, and when Carol asked if she could come to a show I was recording for ITV called *Gagging For It*, to keep the peace I agreed. She promised to behave. Before the show, though, she and her mate Janet came up to Tania in the bar and snarled, "You're dead later." But there was never any danger of that. Carol was with my daughter Julie and her brother Alan as calming influences. Tania was with my brother and Big Jim, her kick-boxing sister Kara, her jinxed friend Lucky Jane and, as additional security, Mick Pugh had invited along Kenny Tyler.

The show went without incident. Afterwards, I got my party out the back door and went to say goodbye to Julie and co. Carol asked if I'd be spending time with them. I said no because I was knackered – I'd been at work writing the column since 6 a.m., had rehearsed and filmed sketches all afternoon and it was now nearly 11 p.m. Carol followed me outside, moaning, with a glass of wine in her hand. She got close and threw the glass in my face. Everyone outside heard her shout, saw her chuck the glass, watched me cover my left eye, and heard the glass smash. It looked as though she'd glassed me. Now Kenny Tyler was a big bloke, at least 18 stone, but he moved like a rocket. He was straight out of the car. He lifted Carol up with one hand and threw her at the security men, barking, "Get this fucking woman inside now!" Knowing who he was, they obliged. It was a rotten ending to a long day. I didn't want to see my soon-to-be ex-missus manhandled, but what the hell were we supposed to do when faced by this sustained campaign of lunacy, threats and assault?

Everyone was now wide awake, so at Kenny's insistence we headed to a small local pub, which at his request stayed open until we'd drunk enough to sink a small fleet. In fairness, my brother Terry's first marriage break-up was worse. His ex tried to stab him with a pair of scissors and broke his hand with an iron. Garry Johnson and I found him bleeding in a gutter on the Ferrier Estate.

* * *

The divorce came through in 1999, soon after our daughter Jenna was born. Tarn and I got married in Las Vegas the following April. Fifty-seven people flew out for it, mostly family and friends. Mickey Pugh was best man. The showbiz guests included Christine Peake, Francine Lewis, Fleur Golding, *Generation Game* hostess Angelique Houston, comic Rikki Jay, and Glenn, my ex-Navy pal from Sidcup, who is also the now fashionable comedian Eric. My eldest kids, Julie and Danny, came – Robert wasn't allowed to; and so did my brother Terry and old pals like Si Spanner, the infamous Spider Mike, lovely saucepot Jackie Skinner, Billy Bishop, Arsenal Steve and Essex jeweller Dougie The Gold. We were married at Graceland Chapel; naturally, we hired an Elvis – he obviously based his look on the King's last few months of life, as he was nigh-on twenty stone. We'd only booked him to do two songs, but it was standing room only in the chapel and he belted out six numbers in the end - we couldn't stop him. I'd hired the Motown Cafe, then in New York, New York, for the reception. When we got there I wasn't sure about it, because it didn't look much – the terrace was just some tables and chairs outside on the Strip. But, as dusk settled and the neon kicked in, it was magical. Tania ended up leading a party onto the roller coaster that goes through the hotel – as well as her and her bridesmaids, sister Kara and Lucky Jane, all in their wedding costumes, there were Fleur, Francine Lewis, and Dougie The Gold, who lost half of his necklaces when it turned upside down.

Steve Lewis was taking pictures for *OK!* magazine and did a photo session with us the next morning. Because of the way that Angelique was dressed, the cops tried to move us on, saying, "You can't do porn shoots without a licence."

We met up with Ed Byrne while we were out there, too, and saw his show at the Imperial Palace, but nothing was as funny as my pal Chinese Tim on the flight over. Hideously drunk, Tim climbed on my armrest to allow a trolley dolly to pass, and then collapsed like a poleaxed ox, missing me and Tania's dad Vic and landing on top of the two strangers sitting next to us. At LAX Julie and Danny were holding baby Jenna, who was howling. A rattled security guy said, "Hey, the folks with the baby, come up now." Julie and Danny walked up, followed by me and Tania, because we had Jen on our passport; followed by her mum and dad, who'd never flown transatlantic before; followed by a clearly befuddled Chinese Tim. "Hey," said the exasperated security man, "how many fathers has this kid got?"

It got worse, though. When the Customs official asked Tim how much money he was bringing into the country, Tim replied, "That's my business." He was led off and strip-searched. A similar fate could have befallen Mickey Pugh on his last day there. Mick, who had never gambled before, walked into the Venetian and stuck a $100 bill on 0. The croupier said, "You'll wait a long time for that to come up," but come up it did. She then only gave Pughy half his winnings, claiming that he'd put the bill across 0 and double-0. He meekly accepted chips worth $1,750 instead of twice that. When I asked why he hadn't protested, Mick grinned broadly and informed me that his $100 bill had cost him

£6 from a bloke in Romford ...

As it was, there were only two minor dodgy incidents. First, my son Dan got so legless that he passed out on the toilet in his hotel room. Like father, like son ... Worried, Julie called security, who forced the door open. If they'd asked how old he was – 19 – I'd have been nicked. The other bad moment happened without either me or Tania knowing about it until months later. After the wedding Fleur had got rat-arsed at the bar in the Luxor and started telling people that I would have married her if she'd asked me. Terry tried to calm her down, but she insisted that she was going to phone our room, on our honeymoon night, to get me down to settle the argument. She only desisted when Terry's then wife Pat growled at her. Pat's dad had been in the SAS, and when she growled grown men took notice. For the record, it wasn't true.

One person who couldn't make the wedding was Wilf Pine, who left strict instructions to let him know where we were staying and when we had a couple of hours free. Wilf pulled strings with various Vegas pals and a classy chauffeur-driven limo arrived, laden with champagne, to whisk a small party of us down the Strip to Freemont Street and back at dusk. They wouldn't take a penny. I was a friend of a friend of theirs, and that was enough.

* * *

One of the great joys of falling for Tania was getting to know her family. In particular, I became great mates with her dad, Clint Eastwood lookalike Vic. I never thought I'd find another close friend at this stage in my life, but we got on like a housing estate on fire. Vic was ten years older than me, virtually to the day, but we went together like pie and mash or light and bitter. We thought alike about everything from the Goons to establishment politicians and we became great drinking buddies. He came everywhere with me. He was a strong, hard-working man who'd had a tough life. In 1999 Lady Luck dealt him what he jokingly called a bum hand - bowel cancer. Vic beat it and got the all clear in 2001, but sadly a year later he was diagnosed with secondary cancer. As soon as we knew, I flew him back out to Vegas for a lads' weekend. Four years later he was gone, and it felt as if my right arm had been cut off. Tania and I had spent the afternoon with him in a hospice on the day he died; we took the piss out of everything and he laughed solidly for a good ninety minutes. His last words to us were *"EastEnders* is shit." And he was right, as usual.

Half an hour later I was in the Rose & Crown in Burwash, East Sussex, drinking with Jeff from the Cockney Rejects, when Tania's Uncle Eric came in and broke the bad news. Minutes after we'd left him, Vic had gone. The only consolation was that he had died happy.

* * *

Vic, Tania's mum Marigold and her sister Kara all ended up in *OK!* a couple of times. The first was Jenna's christening, which was attended by the likes of Ross Kemp, who did the washing-up, Bradley Walsh, Billy Murray, Craig Fairbrass, Dave Lee, the usual flotilla of babes, and Rebekah Wade, the Amy Pond of journalism who would later edit *The Sun*. Dale Winton was godfather. In 2009 Kara did me the great honour of asking me to take her dad's place and give her away at her wedding.

Probably the best showbiz turnouts for one of my dos was my birthday bash on 9 May 1999 – the day before Jenna was born slightly earlier than expected. I billed it as the 'Oh no, he's 40 again' party, and held it at the Phoenix Apollo, which managed to gobble up the two grand that the mag stuck behind the bar in about half an hour flat. The turnout included Barbara Windsor, Jim Davidson, Sam Fox, Brian Conley, Richard Desmond, Paul Ross, Billy Murray, Ross Kemp, Richard Littlejohn, Bobby Davro, Joe Pasquale, Keith Chegwin, Jimmy Jones,

Mickey Pugh, Dave Lee, Dave Courtney, Cass Pennant, a few Page 3 girls, two of The Blood, some footballers and Antonia Moore, who took me outside for an unusual birthday present – a flash of her new £3,000 boobs.

OK! magazine have also kindly covered all of my book launches. Even the one Wilf Pine turned up for. Thanks, Richard.

I very nearly persuaded Richard Desmond to launch a new rock magazine. He was sold on the idea and paid a team to put a dummy issue together. The team was headed by Nick Ferrari - not the world's leading rock authority. It ended up looking like FHM and the project went down the khazi. I blame myself for not making time to oversee the dummy personally. The mag, I mean, not Ferrari.

Chapter Nine
Go Mad With The Gonads

January 1998, at first I thought the bouncer was having a bubble. As we arrived at the Clipper Club, Los Angeles, the meathead on the door said, "Have you got any weapons?" When I replied, "No, pal," he looked at me straight-faced and added, "Do you want any?" Then he leaned towards us and said quietly, "If you hear a gunshot tonight, don't panic, just drop to the floor." He wasn't joking. Drop to the floor? Don't worry, mate, if I hear a gunshot I'll be out of the door like Usain Bolt with a free pass to KFC …

That was the fastest gig we ever played.

It was almost inevitable that, after all of my trips to the USA with metal madmen and ragged-arsed rockers, I would finally take my own band, The Gonads, out there. Only there would be no stadiums for the second finest punk band ever to come out of Indus Road in Charlton. Our promoter, Dave Wood, an Anglophile Yank whose life-long idol was Arthur Daley, booked us into bars, clubs, and places that looked like asylums with optics.

The writing was on the wall from the off. We were picked up at Newark airport by Dave, his pal Mark Rainey (now the boss of TKO Records out there) and Tony, our ex-skinhead road manager (now a chef).

The first shock was the motel. Cheap is not the word. When we said we were staying for the whole night the receptionist's jaw hit the floor. He was clearly only used to people hiring rooms by the hour for crafty shags. Most US hotels are keen to tell you what they have in their rooms; some have jacuzzis or internet access. My one had pillows, and a carpet with more suspicious stains than a CSI crime scene. This non-smoking room smelt like Dot Cotton's index finger. To top it all, throughout the night we were woken up on the hour, every hour, by freight trains that passed about 100 feet from the joint. The trains were so long that it only seemed like minutes between one train going and the next one coming.

Then there was the locale. We were advised strongly to use the rough old bar on the corner and not to venture any further by foot. Being an awkward bastard, I did, and in less than a block I came across a chalk outline on the pavement. I span round, baby, right round, like a record, and made do with the bar.

Our first gig was that same night in Newark's Pipeline club. We were due on at midnight, but it was closer to 2 a.m. when we hit the stage – which was seven in the morning by our body clocks. Punk rock, mannn.

There were six of us: me, Clyde, Rockin' Dave, Kasanova Kev and our mod drummer, The Romulan, plus Tania, who was filming the tour for posterity, except unfortunately Clyde mislaid the footage.

The next night we played the Elvis Rooms in Portsmouth, New Hampshire. There was four foot of snow outside and the temperature was nine degrees below Anne Robinson. Incredibly, about sixty punters, mostly young, had made the gig on foot. Even more incredibly, Al Barr, of local band The Bruisers, took the stage before we went on to give me a big build-up. "This guy is the Godfather of Oi," he said. "Without Garry Bushell our scene would not exist."

This was humbling. It was also worrying. We might be out here for a laugh and a holiday, but the people coming to our gigs were deadly serious, which meant I had to raise my game, which in turn meant that by the time we played CBGBs in New York five dates into the tour I'd lost what little voice I possess. Obviously, this improved our sound no end and the audience, including Phil Rigaud from The Templars, lapped it up. Later, while I was exchanging views with some tedious fanzine bird with IRA sympathies, Rockin' Dave pulled a punk-loving stripper, who took him back to hers. She let him play with her snake ... and vice versa.

The tour highlight for me was San Francisco – where the Cocodrie Club audience knew the song lyrics better than I did. And one memorable small joy was hearing the Dropkick Murphys' single 'Bar Room Hero', which became the must-play song in the van. The low point was Boston, when Clyde waved at the 500-strong audience at the end of the set and three older blokes at the back Sieg-Heiled back. No thanks. (We met another Nazi backstage in LA. He'd had Hitler tattooed on the top of his left thigh, and said that every time he got a hard-on it would Sieg Heil. We said, we believe you, mate...)

Some of the audiences were pretty heavy; the poor old Romulan was so traumatised that he never came home. We lost him in Frisco. But the punters were generally friendly. We only encountered anti-English feeling in Boston when we were refused entry to an Irish bar because of our accents. Kev and Clyde were sitting in another Paddy pub having a quiet pint the next day when they came round with a hat collecting for "the boys back home". They refused, left their tainted beer and walked out, whistling 'No Surrender'.

On our last night in Frisco, Clyde and Dave were having a barney. Clyde was about to deck him, Kasanova Kev intervened and it all ended with Kev storming off into the notorious Mission area, then associated with immigrant gang violence. An ashen-faced Dave Wood warned that we'd never see him again. He returned safely a couple of hours later with a new, drunken Mexican best pal, who was wearing the new coat that Kev had bought a couple of hours earlier.

We get asked back every couple of years and will return – my ambition is to play the Punk Rock Bowling Convention in Vegas. I'm not bothered about making money from it; we just need to cover our costs.

What is the secret of The Gonads' universal appeal? Our music was once described as "timeless", which is why we got a new drummer. We sound like a fire in a monkey house; we are loud and raucous - the point where Motorhead end and migraines begin. They should play our stuff at Dover to repel bogus asylum seekers.

The Gonads grew out of the ashes of Pink Tent. We only ever played a handful of gigs back in 1977, and all of them were at the Lads of the Village pub in Charlton. Talk of a curry-house acoustic tour has always been tongue-in-cheek. We did attempt to busk for food in Indian restaurants. They tolerated it in Charlton Village, rewarding us with popadoms, but at Lewisham we were chased out of the restaurant by the chef, waving his chopping knife. Tsk. Everyone's a critic.

When Oi faced an unfair backlash in 1981, I re-formed the band to show solidarity with the other groups. Our comeback track was 'Tucker's Ruckers Ain't No Suckers' (on the album *Carry On* Oi), which just took the piss out of other bands' football hooligan obsessions. It was pretty much me and Jacqui Harthill – we were the first Oi band to have a female singer - backed by The Business. An EP, *Pure Punk For Row People*, followed, on Secret Records, and it made the Indie Chart, I suspect largely because of the jokey song 'I Lost My Love to a UK Sub', which is still requested at shows today. We were more inspired by cheeky monkey Sid James than by chronic junkie Sid Vicious. When we supported the UK Subs at the Garage, North London, in 2009, Subs singer Charlie Harper insisted that we include the song in the set.

In 1982 I sat at home on the Ferrier and wrote our second EP, *Peace Artists*, with new guitarist Steve Whale in about half an hour. We recorded it for Secret up in Kensington. In a moment of madness I'd invited Lenny Miller, an old drunk from the Lord Northbrook pub in Lee, to 'croon' his way through a song called 'S.L.A.G.' Lenny turned up tanked up, with assorted Lewisham herberts in tow, including Schitzy, Whopper, Steve Cooper and Little Pat. Mickey Fitz from The Business was there, and Matthew who sang with Case. Splodgenessabounds' former manager Dave Long and their former singer Baby Greensleeves arrived, both with dogs, which were soon running amok. Mickey Geggus was producing, although how he kept his temper escapes me. People were drunk, the dogs were barking, and at one stage Fitzy got bored and dragged a telly in to watch the football. Steve Strange (lead singer of Visage) was in the next studio dressed as a sailor, and when he complained about the racket he was told where to go in no uncertain terms. It was like Fred Karno's Circus.

Another single, 'Delilah', followed in 1983, for Razor Records, a collaboration with Max Splodge as The Brothers Gonad, which music experts describe as "fucking awful", although it did feature the punk granddaughter of tough guy actor Lionel Stander (Max from TV's *Hart to Hart*) on the cover.

The full story of The Gonads is probably best saved for another time. We carried on for a couple of years, recording a live double album, which included a pub singalong side, and generally having a laugh. The best-known songs from that time, other than 'UK Sub', are probably 'Jobs Not Jails' (a serious one) and 'The Joys of Oi', which set out my stall on the subject, managing to namecheck everything from Scouse Casual fanzine *The End* to Noddy Holder's vocals on *Slade Alive!*

Reviewer Spike Summer called the *Live & Loud* double album, "punk's answer to Exile On Main St.' (the Rolling Stones critically acclaimed 1972 album), while one *Sounds* freelance singled out the lyrics for praise, especially: "Beer was passed out, wine was passed out, and I just passed out on the floor/When the Old Bill came, I said Picasso's my name, and I had a brush with the law ..." (from 'The Lord My Harry'); and these from the Dallas oriented 'JR Ewing's Barmy Army': "Pam has lost her marbles, her husband and her kid/But that's only what she deserves, for fucking Andy Gibb."

The band became a very popular in-joke. The Cockney Rejects played with me on one track, 'TNT', and contributed to the *Total Noise* compilation EP, and The Blood with me on others. Even bands like Iron

Maiden, UFO and Def Leppard wanted to record with The Gonads. Ozzy Osbourne, too, but we never got it together. It never got past the late-night hotel bar stage.

Mark Brabbs from Tank did sing as Lord Waistrel (the aristocratic diarist I created for Sounds) on 'Reg and Ron'- our song about the Krays that appeared on one of the later Oi albums. That was a Gonads song written by me – I played guitar on it, too – but Lol was so worried about upsetting the underworld that it was credited to 'Lord Waistrel & The Cosh Boys'.

With Steve Kent from The Business, I created two studio-based bands – the Orgasm Guerrillas and the socialist Oi band Prole. The Business went on to record my first 'proper' rock song, 'Fire Down Under', which I wrote while on the road with Aussie rockers Rose Tattoo in the States.

I let my Gonads shrivel up in the mid-1980s and didn't record again until I demoed 'Lager Louts' and 'British Steel' with Colin Blood in 1990. Four years later I teamed up with Clyde and wrote the ska song 'Lottery Song', which was very nearly released as a single b/w 'Mystic Meg' by Andy Swallow's Labello Blanco. Why nearly? My own feeling is that Clyde's eccentric last-minute 'Cotton Eye Joe' style remix of the song may just have convinced them we were both nuts.

Clyde and I carried on, though, recording three studio albums together between 1998 and 2006. For my money, we wrote some of The Gonads' best-ever songs, especially 'Oi Mate', 'Gob' and 'Hey You'. But then he got bogged down with Right Said Fred and I very nearly broke up the band again. Two things dissuaded me. Firstly, I was contacted by Andre Schlessinger in New York, whose own socialist punk band The Press had been directly inspired by The Gonads. His enthusiasm for our stuff reignited my own. Secondly, I was asked to play at my friend Rebecca Pollard's wedding in Leeds, and when Clyde couldn't make it I formed a 'supergroup' instead, with Cockney Reject Mick Geggus on guitar, UFO's Pete Way on bass, Tony Van Frater (Red Alert, Rejects) on rhythm guitar and Paul 'RD' Haslin from Waysted on drums.

The whole weekend was the stuff of legend, not least because of such classic Pete Way quotes as: "Was Steve Marriott still alive when he played with you, Mick?" "I do have a newsagent's where you can stand and have a drink in the morning," and the frequently heard, "Can we get a few drinks on the Corporation, Gal?" Here is the tour report that ran on the website. Our Magical Mystery Tour began on 25 March. Although we were playing Leeds, we'd decided to rehearse in Newcastle. Read on:

10 a.m. Gal picks up Mick in Canning Town and Paul in Milton Keynes. They then drive across country to Birmingham to collect Pete, who informs us that a friend had given him three grams of cocaine for the journey but sadly it had 'evaporated'. "The wrapper kept talking to me," he says. "It was calling out 'Pete, Pete snort me.'" Once in the tour bus Pete treats us to his thoughts on TV, including the ugliness of Chris Evans and "I've got nothing against homosexuals but what we need is a poof-free TV channel." In a masterpiece of planning, the band drive on to Sunderland via the Lake District! Doing 90 on the M6, Pete wonders for the first time if it would be possible to turn off and find an offie for some vagrant strength lager, "Just to keep me topped up". A night on the tiles in Sunderland includes ten pints with Sticks (ex-Upstarts, ex-Rejects), Sticks's dad, and Nobby (Rejects drummer). Over a garlic pizza, the band's alter-egos emerge, with Mick as Mong Senor, Pete 'the High Priest of Mong' and Paul and Tony as Cardinals of Mong. Tone's house is colonised. The High Priest sleeps on the settee to take early morning calls from his other half, Rashida, stranded in the USA.

The next morning Tony's mum Brenda cooks a top quality fry-up and is awarded permanent Heroine-of-Oi status. We drive to Newcastle to rehearse for four hours. There are just a few problems. Pete pops out twice for vast quantities of extra-strong lager and Gal loses his voice. Mickey is well on top of the songs, though, and Tony and Paul click immediately. Pete, being a rock genius, comes up with a blinding re-arrangement of 'England's Glory'.

Everything is gelling brilliantly. During rehearsals we take calls from Dave Courtney in Miami who means to wish us well, but somehow "break a leg" doesn't sound the same in a Courtney growl. Phil Mogg from UFO phones too. "Don't tell him I've had a beer," Pete implores.

Gal gets his column faxed through plus a spread he'e written on Bobby Davro for the next day's People. The headline 'Bobby Davro's Sheer Hell' delights Pete, who reads out selected passages of Davro angst in hysterics. Then he decides to rename the band, Long Good Friday style. Gal is now Harold Shand, Mick is Razors, Tony is Parky, Paul is Charlie and Pete is Councillor Harris. Naturally all expenses are still "on the Corporation".

We drive to Leeds and assemble pre-gig in the Ibis hotel, joined by a Gonads away 'firm' of Nobby, Stuart Black, and chief Renee, Batttttty. Pete and Tony decide that Gal's throat problems would be improved by brandies and blue Bols. Suitably medicated, Gal leads the band on stage at nine p.m. Mickey and Tony are on top form, Paul is the best drummer we've ever worked with, and Gal's vocals were helped considerably by the Huddersfield Skins who as is now traditional knew the words better than he does. The half-hour set consisted of: 'Alconaut', 'I Lost My Love to a UK Sub', 'Go Mad With The Gonads', a seven-minute version of 'England's Glory' and 'Doctor Doctor' renamed 'Rebecca Pollard Please' in honour of the delightful bride who is also our webmistress. Due to an excess of medication Gal spent the song in the crowd, leaving vocals to Paul. Naturally the bride, who looked stunning, ignored our pleas. Other memories of the gig appear vague, though it was nice to meet Cucumber Girl. Paul wasn't too impressed by the Clockwork Orange boys. The cheery Scot, ahem, took one look at a kid decked out in full droog regalia and snarled: "He should go straight out a tenth floor window, that cunt." Back at the hotel we teamed up with Noel (Menace) and Steve Arrogant (Special Duties,) but the bums shut the bar early and we retired unhurt at 2 a.m., our ears ringing with Way-lead quotes from The Long Good Friday: "The smells that have been coming up from the galley all morning have been driving me potty", "I'm going into partnership with a German organisation, yeah, the

Krauts … the hardest organisation since Hitler stuck a swastika on his jockstrap", "The Mafia I've shit 'em", "Little acorns", "That's a right horrible ponce", "I'm not a politician I'm a businessman, I'm also a Londoner. Our country's not an island anymore, it's a leading European state", "These French geezers really know their stuff", "The Yanks love snobbery", "Mind my grief!", "There's a lot of dignity in that in't there, going out like a raspberry ripple", "Stick a rocket up their arseholes, they'll jump all right", "I want the name of your top grass", "What, Erroll the ponce from Brixton?", "This used to be a nice street this, decent families, no scum", "You seen anything of my Eric flying past your window about two hours ago", and "Is there no decency in this wicked world?"

The next morning we experience a short delay when the tour bus breaks down. The AA man tells Gal he is "surprised to see a celebrity of your calibre stranded in a Leeds car park." Indeed. The second delay is caused by a ten-minute detour to find a Spar for Pete's breakfast beer. The beauties of Leeds go down well with Paul: "You'd lay on top of her until the council came about the smell," he observes poetically.

Mick wonders how the Cockney Rejects book will go down with the Huddersfield contingent. Mick once battered a mouthy local, breaking his arm. Hours later he came back from Casualty and asked Mick to sign his plaster cast, saying, "I need a good leathering now and again."

The Gonads supergroup would never play again. But the sheer joy of the weekend recharged my batteries. I recruited Dale 'The Beast' Beeson as manager and we've been playing ever since, including festivals in Germany and Sweden. We've also recorded two more studio albums, co-writing songs with Tony Van Frater on the first (*Live Free, Die Free*) and Tony Feedback from The Upstarts on the latest (Glorious Bastards). The songs are getting better, the subject matter more varied, and we've rekindled a great following, including the Charlton Boys, Terry Hayes, Charlton Lisa and the ravishing Wattsie Watts, who graduated from flag girl to full-blown band member. The first full-blown member since the last German mini-tour …

One of the Noughties highlights for me was supporting the Rejects at the Circus Tavern, when we were joined on stage by our first flag girls – glamour models Vikki Thomas and Zoe Anderson. The low point was travelling to Germany overnight in a van in the middle of winter with five chain-smokers in January 2010.

Other memorable moments include our first appearance at the Rebellion festival in Blackpool. Paul Devine's son Dan, 17, was making his debut for us on drums. We walked on stage, I yelled, "Who wants it?" and a full pint of piss came flying at me. I ducked and it showered Dan and his drum kit. He hadn't even clicked 1,2,3,4. The rest of us were in stitches. We were back at the Queen's Hotel that night, where we drank into the early hours with the great Northern comics Mick Miller and Johnnie Casson. The Queen's is run by my good friend Pat Mancini and it's a magnet for Blackpool turns – there will be much more about this marvellous showbiz establishment in volume two.

Another regular source of hilarity was our bassist Andy 'Scoops' Gonad. There have been tight people in Oi before, of course – Mickey Fitz used to drink bitter rather than lager because it was 2p a pint cheaper. But Scoops made him look like an amateur. This guy would starve to death on a pay-to-leave bus. When he played Boston with the East End Badoes, the lanky tightwad almost got run over when he spotted a caff on the other side of a busy main road selling coffee six cents cheaper than it was where his mates were drinking. At work he was caught fiddling the drinks machine with a coin on a piece of wire. While at Blackpool, Scoops stayed at the most decrepit flea-ridden 'hotel' in town. It looked like a before scene on C4's *How Clean Is Your House?*. Eye-witnesses testified that "you wouldn't house a homeless dog there". He then had the cheek to invite friends to the hotel bar, where he neatly manoeuvred them into paying for the beer with his catchphrase: "Am I

buying this or are you?"

Scoops really came into his own when we headlined Sweden's Rassle Punk festival at Emmaboda in 2009 – he brought no foreign currency with him at all. When asked why, he explained that if he had brought some, once he'd broken into it he'd spend it all. Of course, he didn't mind breaking into ours ... (Andy tried the same trick with Superyob, who just added up every meal and drink they bought for him and deducted it from his earnings after the gigs.)

We went back to Blackpool in 2008, opening for Bad Manners at the Merrie England bar. Local legend Joey Blower compèred, with special guest Max Splodge on top form. Not surprisingly, the day ran about as smooth as Patti Smith's legs. Here's how it all went:

Nov 29: We hit Blackpool, driving through a pea-souper fog so thick we were running over noodles. You can barely see a yard in front of you, which considering the state of bassist Andy's hat is just as well. As soon as we arrive at the Queen's Hotel, I get press-ganged into an appearance at a charity gig at the Grand with the likes of showbiz legends Joe Longthorne, Buddy Lee and Johnnie Casson. After that it's over to the Merrie England bar to be insulted by comic Joey Blower and meet up with our Blackpool flag girl and headwear expert Kerry McLeod and pals. Sad to report, drummer Paul MacGonad proceeds to get more smashed than Ollie Reid in a free bar on his 21sth birthday. As the clock strikes 3 a.m., like a coiled cobra MacGonad inflates his hood and strikes. Various folk on the receiving end of his wrath include the delightful Kerry, Kerry's hat and our manager the Beast. Was it just the booze, or was MacGonad allegedly spending the previous three hours chatting up a lesbian, a factor behind his mood? We don't know the answer, we merely present the facts.

Nov 30: I'm woken up by the Beast's snoring at 6.30 a.m. The Beast is in the next room. We struggle through a full English breakfast and make our way back to the North Pier for the 10.30 a.m. soundcheck. We're using Bad Manners backline. Bad Manners don't show up until 12.30 p.m. There is no soundcheck. At 11 a.m. we receive a text from our guest singer, punky goddess Kiria, explaining that she can't make it after a series of disasters that frankly wouldn't look out of place in a black and white *Perils of Pauline* film. This woman is so unlucky she could catch an STD from a wet dream. People on *EastEnders* hear about her life and say, "Poor cow, we wouldn't want to be her ..." Anyway, we recruit feisty local Tracy as stand-in, but she has never heard the songs and it shows. We're due on at 1 p.m. but end up going on at two. We must be playing well, cos at 2.15 our flag girls Kerry and Ash are outside having a fag and miss the cue for 'England's Glory'. Thanks to the girls from the audience who stand in for them at the last minute. I get some revenge digs in on comic Joey by saying, "Joey Blower, that's not just his name, it's also his hobby," but I suffer for it later. I'm so hung-over, I bugger up the words to 'UK Sub', a song I've been singing for over 25 years. Doh! We're shit but it goes down all right with an audience including a firm of Seasiders, Preston hooligans and Mark Chester of Stoke's Naughty Forty mob. The shock of the afternoon comes when two girls tell me how our generous bassist has been buying them drinks at the bar. Scoops is generous in the way that an MP is truthful. He hadn't bought them anything, he'd just charged their shorts to the bands' free tab. At 6.30 p.m. we finally prise a sozzled MacGonad away and leave for London. The Beast turns off the M6 at junction 20 to miss heavy traffic. MacGonad is incensed. "Get ye the fuck back on the M6, man," he growls. "It's clear ahead." The Beast complies. Clear? It was about as clear as the amazon.com warehouse. It was 10 p.m. by the time we made junction 19. Paul neither knew nor cared. He'd passed out on top of the merchandise. Happy days.

* * *

Going back on the road has done nothing to improve my still deteriorating hearing. I came off the stage in Hartlepool, my ears still ringing, and a fella got me in a corner and started trying to tell me something in a very thick North East accent. I thought he was criticising the gig, so I invited him to come backstage and have a beer. He was actually a dealer, and as soon as we were in the dressing room he produced a gift – five grams of cocaine. If we'd asked for his sister, he'd have probably got her down as well.

Oddly, The Gonads have accumulated many famous fans along the way. Benny Hill was tickled by 'Sandra Bigg (Really Big)'. Kelvin MacKenzie was frequently seen around the Bizarre desk hollering snatches of 'Hitler Was An 'Omo'. Johnny Vaughan shocked me by quoting the incredibly dumb lyrics of 'Sandra' – "I'd like to fuck you, Sandra, but I'm bursting for a shite." Joe Strummer described our song 'TNT' as sounding "like Charlie Harper meets Van Halen" (high praise indeed!) Ross Kemp said he was partly touched "and partly horrified by 'Grant Mitchell'". While Paul Ross raised some eyebrows by playing our 1997 single 'Oi Nutter' on his ITV show, and comic Mickey Pugh is such a fan that he has written a film script called *Curry On Up The Gonads*.

The latest band line-up includes RD on drums, Nacho Jase from Waysted on guitar and Mick Maverick on bass. After 33 years of being an absolute shambles, in three gigs these guys have turned us into a tightly organised punk rock machine. Success eludes us but the legend continues.

Gonads Fact: our weirdest ever song was 'Stop That Drumming', featuring the strained vocals of 'potty' Paul Devine, the notorious round-dodger and all-round bad egg. After recording the song, Devine conned his way onto some ITV special on UFOs hosted by Chris Tarrant. He was filmed on the show sitting in shadows and claiming that he'd been kidnapped by aliens and kept in a five-cornered room.

Devine also single-handedly sparked the 1980s radio phone-in backlash against Jimmy Tarbuck, which Tarby to this day blames for his long absence from our screens.

PS. In May 2010 we played a riotous punk festival in Saxony, Germany. Here is our blog entry for the trip:

May 30. Thank you Germany! Danke schön! The Torgau Total Oi festival was a hoot; even if it did end with a wild-eyed R.D. MacGonad decking a punter... The DRINKING began at 6.30am on Friday morning. The LAUGHS started when Gal's bag was searched by customs and his stage dildo was held aloft by a shocked security lady ("I always thought that Garry Bushell was a pervert," observed a passing pensioner). The FUN climaxed when German flag girl Nicole decided the Union Jack should best be displayed while topless. The MADNESS reached a peak after the show when a Spanish skinhead dropped his strides and underwear backstage to show his "respect" for Gal... Yes, you read that right, he flashed his cheeky little chorizo, not once but several times in "honour" of Mr. Gonad. The honour was then reciprocated by MacGonad and two of the lads from Scottish band Hateful just as the promoter walked in and drew entirely the wrong conclusion about how we like to party. Gott in Himmel!

It would be wrong to say our rhythm section was blitzed by the time we went on stage. They were as sober as any judge would be if said Barnaby Rudge had started his day with a few breakfast Stellas at Stansted airport, then moved on to a Turkish kebab house in Torgau for some afternoon liveners and continued in earnest back at the hotel with a session on Meister Jäger's 70-proof liquorice restorative ("Good for the voice" - RD) before getting back on the lagers for a couple of hours pre-show. The festival itself was fine. Great atmosphere, a good audience, decent people organising it...it was just a shame about the on-stage sound monitors which didn't seem to work at all.

The show was delayed for ten minutes while RD growled at the sound man and denounced the stage manager as an absent fool. In the second half of the set, however, the drummer's anger found a new focus in the shape of a sozzle German skin who, in between singing along to the songs, was calling us "Schiesser" and allegedly glaring at RD. The first we knew about the fast-developing problem was a friendly exchange of drum-sticks - two were hurled forcefully at the guy's head. And when one was returned it was fired back with a side-order of venom. At the end of the set, as Gal and Jase debated about whether or not to defy the stage hands and do the encore the audience was clamouring for, we noticed that RD was no longer with us. He'd vanished into the crowd and given the skin a pasting. Some bands might be horrified by such behaviour. We merely promoted RD to his new role as Gonads Complaints Department. The Gonads! We're back and now we're hard! Harder than the rest! Who wants it, you Muppets (etc etc).

In the dressing room, RD explained his behaviour to anyone who'd listen, saying repeatedly "I dinnae give it, but I dinnae take it either." Within an hour or so he advanced the argument to suggest that the band should reimburse him for the drumsticks he'd thrown; it was a suggestion we chose to ignore. Even this wasn't the end, however. The promoters were filming a documentary of the event, which RD promptly took over, handling all the interviews with natural aplomb ("RD MacGonad, News At Ten, sober."). We felt it best we left after that.

Gal, the Beast and Jase found an open bar, full of friendly bilingual Cock Sparrer fans and drank with them till about 1.45am; Mick and RD joined us and stayed on in there until 3.30am... When our driver turned up to take us back to the airport at 5am, MacGonad furiously denounced him as an effing bastard who'd woke him up an hour earlier then he'd said he would (in reality RD had simply forgotten to adjust his watch to German time). In the subsequent scramble Mick lost his mobile and RD threatened to "come back and take over this excuse for a country"; both men then passed out on the plane.

So much happened, we haven't got the time or the energy to detail the many small joys of the trip. Thanks to Hechti, Ecke, Krummel and the Contra crew, especially our driver who may well have been Charlie

Harper's 62-year-old love child. Thanks also to our new friend Katia who joined us for 'Infected' and was suitably surprised by the dildo, and the very lovely Nicole whose topless appearance for 'British Steel' inspired a standing ovation (even amongst blokes who were sitting down). Good to meet the guys from Denmark's The Guv'nors and Catalonia's Secret Army, although we wished our new Spanish pal had kept his privates secret too. Cheers to Control and Hateful for the crack. We haven't even mentioned Mick's true tales of his time in the Royal Green Jackets, or the self-styled table football champion who Gal beat 10 - Nil (although he was a) drunk and b) Scottish). Aye. What a give away! Happy daze! •

* AS well as having his stage dildo examined, Gal also had his deodorant confiscated by airport security. He moaned: "They take our water, our shaving foam, our deodorant... everything terrorists never use, we can't have." And quoth Paul: "You're not allowed deodorants but you could kill the pilot with the cheese-burgers they sell on board. Gae away and fuck."

A few weeks later R.D. MacGonad left the band to pursue a different musical direction. He has been replaced by South Coast Steve. The madman has gone, the madness goes on...

Chapter Ten
Aliens Ate My Sun

On 11 June 2001 I got a call from Dale Winton at about 8.15 a.m. "Darling boy," he said, "have you seen the Daily Star?" I hadn't. "You should," he said mysteriously.

The Star were serialising my crime novel, *The Face*. It was their splash – their main front-page story. The headline read: 'The book *The Sun* banned'. Oh dear.

I just had time to get home from buying it when the phone rang again. It was Sun editor David Yelland's secretary. "Can you come in and see David?" she asked. Certainly I could, and I did, but I wasn't sure what I was going to say to him. I had every reason to be furious with Yelland over the book. Earlier that year, in January, I had been offered a huge sum to take my Bushell on the Box column and my weekly showbiz interview feature to the *Daily Star*. The sum was £250,000 a year. That was more money than my dad had earned in his lifetime.

Out of loyalty I went in to see my editor. I hadn't wanted to leave the paper, but who'd turn down this kind of salary? It was like winning the lottery. David Yelland had been understanding. He didn't want to lose me, he said, and although he couldn't match their offer he came close. He knew I was writing a novel, due out in May, and I told him the *Star* had also promised to promote it heavily. David smiled and said, "All three of my columnists, you, Richard Littlejohn and Jane Moore, have novels out this year and I will treat you all equally." We shook hands on it and the deal was done. I stayed.

My mistake was not to get it in writing.

A few months later, in April, I threw a launch party for *The Face* at the Phoenix Apollo restaurant in Stratford, East London. The turnout was incredible: Barbara Windsor, Jim Davidson, Piers Morgan, Billy Murray, Bradley Walsh, Gail Porter, Paul Ross, plus various Page 3 girls, boxers, comedians, Richard Littlejohn, Jane Moore, Dave Courtney, the Lambrianou brothers and various other underworld faces who would prefer that their names weren't mentioned. There were people from my old *Sounds* days, Steve Whale and Fatty Lol, plus the likes of Andy Swallow and Cass Pennant - a veritable rogues' gallery of duckers and divers. David Yelland and other senior *Sun* executives came too; he hadn't liked seeing Piers there, but later he sent me a note and an email congratulating me on the turnout.

In the following weeks Yelland's attitude shifted, however. He went back on his word. I could plug the book in my column, he said, but *The Sun* would not be promoting it. The only surprise was that this surprised me.

Fair enough, though. I could live with disappointment. But then one day at work I glanced at the page proofs for the next day's paper – Richard's book was being serialised. Now I was pissed off. I was owed a week's holiday and I took it immediately.

My publisher, John Blake, was pissed off too. His reaction was different. He asked the *Daily Star* if they fancied serialising my book instead.

All this was going round my head on the way in to the Wapping plant. I was going to bring up all of this and let David know how I felt about his broken promises. If it came to it, I decided, I would also tell him to poke his job. But it didn't come to that. When I walked into Yelland's office, he told me not to say anything but just go home.

I worked from home.

He'd called me in to send me back.

Pathetic.

He also had my byline removed from the next day's What To Watch section on the TV page. He kept the words but snipped off my name, which was even more pathetic.

On the way back home, I called up two lawyers I knew well, Henri Brandman and Gary Jacobs, to ask where I stood about the serialisation and what I could do. The simple answer was sweet FA.

The *Daily Star* had a field day, finding *Sun* readers who backed me – a whole pub in Aveley, Essex, boycotted the paper because of it. And *The Guardian* of all people took my side, referring to me as *The Sun*'s prince over the water. I found a lawyer, Stuart Jacobs, and went through The Sun's internal appeals procedure. I'm forbidden legally from revealing anything about this horrible, draining process, but for a taste of how it felt read *The Trial* by Franz Kafka.

The charges were absurd. The paper said I was guilty of gross misconduct, which makes it sound like I'd flashed at the canteen ladies. All I'd done was write a book.

Let's consider the evidence.

The Sun management said I should have known in advance that when I sold the book to a publisher - John Blake - he in turn would give the serialisation rights to the *Star*, who in turn would publish it alongside digs about *The Sun* ... So basically I should have been Mystic Meg.

This may strike you as being about as fair as Frank Bruno's arse, but that was exactly their case for sacking me.

Yet the *Star* were only able to serialise the book because David Yelland broke his word and refused to promote it. If he'd done what he'd promised, even half-heartedly, it wouldn't have been of any interest to them. So why did he break his word?

David claimed later that he'd objected to a passage where my fictional gangsters have a pop at GMTV's Lorraine Kelly, referring to her as "the Paisley pig". (I have since apologised about this, as I understand she comes from Arbroath.) It's hard to believe that this is the truth, however, as Yelland was shown that passage in the book at the launch by chortling Sony Music boss Gary Farrow (who considered Kelly a rival to Jane Moore, his other half) but didn't change his mind about promoting it until ten days later. And if we take him at his word, what does it say about him? That the editor of a national newspaper was so dim he believed that every line of dialogue in a work of fiction must reflect the opinion of the author. These are ruthless villains with nasty views; I no more share their thoughts than I spend my spare time pulling off bank jobs. Perhaps David also believed that Harry Potter really can do magic; he certainly has the look of a man well accustomed to polishing his own wand.

I went through the internal appeals procedure, believing the truth would out, but it was farcical.

It seemed fairly obvious to me, however, that they had already made their decision and were just trying retrospectively to construct a case to justify it. In the end most of the charges that were levelled against me were thrown out, so all they could sack me for was, as I said, not knowing in advance that the book would be serialised elsewhere if they happened to change their mind about plugging it. I must have mislaid my crystal ball that week. How in the name of sweet reason could I be guilty of "gross misconduct" for signing a contract eleven months before I was sacked when:

a) *The Sun*'s top executives knew I was writing the book for Blake and actively encouraged me to do so? Rebekah Wade's husband at the time, Ross Kemp, had even expressed an interest in playing my detective character Harry Tyler in a mooted TV spin-off!

b) I had signed hundreds of similar contracts with TV companies and book publishers before? And

c) There was a list of News International employees as long as Dion Dublin's dick who had done pretty much the same deal with Blake without getting the tin tack?

It was a case built on straw.

Three years later, in June 2004, Yelland gave an interview to *The Guardian*, in which he admitted that I was sacked because he was "uncomfortable" with me and "when an editor is uncomfortable with a columnist one of you has to go". In other words, his entire case against me was as manufactured as Jordan's boobs and he just used the *Star* serialisation as an excuse to hang me with. And he knew it was sod all to do with me, as John Blake had written him a 'mea culpa' letter accepting full responsibility for the serialisation and confirming that I'd had been an innocent party. I had been as stitched up as a box of Underworld Knickers.

I was amazed that the *Star* devoted so much space to *The Face*; I honestly hadn't expected anyone to serialise the book. It's far too rude for a family newspaper. That's why I had only asked Yelland to promote it. I was also unaware of any animosity between us, although other execs told me later that he seemed strangely jealous because I was on TV a fair bit. He would sometimes wander into my office and say that his mum had seen me on telly – it was the only thing he ever spoke to me about. He resented me being a household name.

It's probably wrong to get personal about him; even if he is a screwed-up weirdo who looks like he's wandered in from Roswell and makes Gordon Brown look like a people person. Later he revealed that he was secretly uncomfortable at being at *The Sun* full stop, and not so secretly battling alcoholism at the time. He was definitely the wrong guy for the job. He turned the paper into a schizophrenic, Blair-worshipping mess; it was losing sales hand over fist until they slashed the cover price to 10p. He was installed to be a management 'yes man', because the previous editor, Stuart 'The Human Sponge' Higgins, fought his corner when the execs were wrong.

The bottom line is that Yelland knew economics but he didn't know showbiz, and he never understood Sun readers. One of his first decisions when he took over was to scrap the serialisation of Lenny McLean's book

The Guv'nor, claiming that no one knew who Lenny was. The book went on to sell a million copies.

As to why I was sacked, I couldn't tell you. Dave Courtney reckoned it was because I'd written about him and plugged his *Hell to Pay* movie in my column. I think that's fanciful. I think the answer is simpler: partly it was because I was seen as a remnant of the old *Sun* who couldn't fit easily into the paper's cheesy new relationship with New Labour; and partly they were now paying me too much money. And if those were the charges I would gladly hold up my hands to them. I detested New Labour, whom I saw as a bunch of phonies, and I hated the way the newspaper management made the paper do U-turns to support the disastrous Dome and slippery Mandelson. It's not the business of any newspaper to be the government's lapdog, and it made us a laughing stock. I said this at work, but never in public. And, as it happens, they *were* paying me too much – but it was them who kept upping my salary. The only difference money had made to my lifestyle was that I took the family to Florida instead of Spain or Butlins.

Back in 2001 I had the hump about it all, naturally enough, but loads of people rallied round and they were far angrier than I was. I had to stop a gang of mates from going up to picket Wapping. Courtney offered to "blow the bloody doors off" – an offer I politely refused. Everyone I knew stopped buying *The Sun* and friends in the business were very supportive. Ally Ross sympathised and then asked if he could use my Barrymore jokes. The late great Bob Monkhouse even took to ringing up the news desk in a thick Scottish accent every Wednesday to ask where Bushell on the Box had gone.

It was never going to make a difference, but I appreciated their solidarity.

On the surface I was laughing about it all. Roy Hudd invited me to address his music hall society in the West End and I told them that my way of coping with the hot summer was to pop along to the *Sun* plant –

just for the cold shoulder. The psychological impact went deeper, though. It mucked my head up for a couple of years. I was hurt and disoriented. I felt betrayed. Even now, I think it was a poor way to treat someone after sixteen years of loyal service, especially after the crap I took on the paper's behalf. I had slogged my guts out for them over the years, and to get the boot without Yelland even asking me to give him my side of the story was a real kick in the cobblers. But that's the *Sun* management for you.

There are desert coyotes with more principles, and skunks with more pleasing aromas.

* * *

The next twist in the tale also surprised me more than it should have done. *The Daily Star* still wanted me, they said, but - surprise, surprise - their budget had changed. Forget the quarter of a million, I could start tomorrow for £70K. Maybe I should have taken the deal; it was still decent money, of course, but not when compared with my salary at the Currant Bun. Like a Man United groupie I was being double-shafted. This called for emergency measures. I even spoke to Piers Morgan at the *Mirror,* who toyed with the idea of running Bushell on the Box on a Wednesday, but his execs talked him out of it and he hired Jim Shelley from *The Guardian* instead. (And the way their sales are going, you might conclude that if you hire *Guardian* writers you get *Guardian* circulation figures ...) I had talks with six Fleet Street editors in all, and a very pleasant night out in Manchester with the hilarious *Sunday Sport* editor Tony Livesey, which ended with my elfin model friend Zoe Anderson walking out of our hotel into the street stark bollock naked for reasons none of us can remember. We'd had a lot to drink. After all that, the *Sport* couldn't afford me, and it might have proved a step too downmarket even for me. Of the serious offers, Neil 'Wolf-Man' Wallis of *The People* impressed me the most. He had a lot of drive and a great news sense, he paid well, he bought a decent lunch and he gave me tremendous backing. *The Sun* were always censoring the jokes by the end of my time there. Neil didn't.

Unfortunately, he didn't have any promotion budget either, so he had no way of letting Sun readers know where the column was – for years I had people coming up to me saying, "I haven't seen you in the paper for a while."

I met up with the producers of *The Big Breakfast* that summer, too, at their invitation. They were fans of my old *Bushell on the Box* show and wanted to recreate it as a weekly item on the Channel 4 morning show, which meant me going in and bantering with witty Richard Bacon, sexy Amanda Byram and cheeky chap Man City fan Mike 'Squeaky' McLean. They didn't care about the *Sun* situation and I spent a great nine months on the show, even though it did mean getting up for work at the time I used to roll in from a gig.

In 2002 I settled out of court with *The Sun*, and then something very funny happened. A poll of their own readers included the question: who is your favourite Sun writer? And my name topped the poll. A fitting end to the bell-end Yelland saga. By January 2003 he was gone.

Back in 2002 Neil Wallis quit *The People*, fed up with Trinity Mirror's refusal to invest in the paper. The new boss, Mark Thompson, was widely regarded as a creep, and after five years at the paper I'd had enough, too. I briefly toyed with the idea of giving up TV criticism and devoting myself to books and film scripts, but I missed the weekly deadline, so at Paul Ross's suggestion I met up with Gareth Morgan and Mickey Booker, editor and deputy editor of the *Daily Star Sunday*. Bushell on the Box has appeared in its lively pages consecutively ever since. At the time of writing, I'm on column number 160. And the great thing about this paper is that the gags aren't censored.

PS: In 2010 David Yelland claimed in interviews that he'd been pissed most of the time while editing *The Sun*. This backfired because a) it infuriated Murdoch, who in his own words had treated Yelland "like a son", and b) no journalists believed it. For starters, if he had been as drunk as he claimed he was (wearing a shirt and tie over a shirt and tie – is that even possible?) it would have been common knowledge. Yes, Yelland did like a drink and outraged many a hackette with his inappropriate night-time behaviour at parties, but the suggestion that he was pie-eyed all day was cobblers cooked up to help publicise his book. Mind you, if he had been plastered it would have explained why he was so crap at editing.

Yelland also claimed that he was out of the office on the day *The Sun* prepared its infamous Gay Mafia story. (Is a Gay Mafia running the country?) He was very much in the office, because he asked me to write a humorous commentary on the story, and then congratulated me on the jokes after I had done so.

Epilogue
Forever England –
the Noughties & Beyond

Losing the job on *The Sun* shook me up more than I ever let on. I think I lost my marbles for about eighteen months. It felt like an unexpected bereavement, or as if I'd been the innocent party in a marriage split I hadn't seen coming. Most of the time I felt empty, useless and tired – all symptoms of depression. Nothing seemed to matter much anymore. I didn't want to leave the house. I wouldn't answer the phone. I could easily have given up the column, and more, if Tania, Rob, Jenna and later Ciara, who was born the following February, hadn't given me something to fight for.

The experience changed me, initially in a bad way. I became ratty and difficult to be with. But long term it was probably for the best. Once I'd got over all of the shock and the negativity, I became hungry again and eager to fight for things that mattered. The shake-up made me do things I would never have done if I'd stayed in that safe little niche. I stood for parliament, put on live shows again, wrote more books, and threw myself into the *People* column, trying to raise the quality of the writing week on week. But when Neil Wallis gave up editing the paper to take a lesser role at the *News of the World* I knew the writing was on the wall. Trinity Mirror management starved *The People* of a promotional budget – I only remember seeing one TV ad for it in all the time I was there. Their only strategy was to let the paper die a death of a thousand cuts. At one stage I attempted to raise the capital to buy out the paper and turn it into a real people's paper, with populist sympathies. Several meetings were held and investors were interested, but when we investigated further there was a massive black hole at the heart of the plan – a vast pension problem – and the scheme had to be abandoned. After five years the paper's creepy editor Mark Thomas asked me to take a pay cut and I told him where to poke it.

I took a month off to write a film script based on the Cockney Rejects with Mick Geggus, and then brought the column back in the *Daily Star Sunday* – for a lot less money than Richard had offered me in 2001, but hey ho.

The best telly work I did post-*Sun* was on C4's *Big Breakfast* morning show, which was a real laugh despite the early start, and I reprised the role of resident telly critic later for Nuts TV.

I also carried on campaigning for things I believed in: like England and the English, who have become a forgotten people in our own land. I was writing about St George's Day back in the early 1990s. And so when I put on that St George's Day gig at the Circus Tavern back in 2006 it was like every part of my life coming together. We had the Cockney Rejects, Neville Staple from The Specials, Brian Conley, Page 3 girls, Secret Affair, Rick Wakeman, Mickey Pugh, Motty's Sheepskin, Mike Osman, John Barden from *EastEnders*, Right Said Fred, Secret Affair, The Artful Dodger, Hilary O'Neill, and Max Splodge … a mad bill; it shouldn't have worked, but it did. We raised more than £5,000 for the Benny Hill Statue appeal. It was one of the best nights of my life … but C4 came down to film it and managed to cut out the black acts on the bill and any black faces in the audience – because they wanted to paint anyone who supported St George's Day events as racists and Little Englanders.

It was shown as part of a documentary called *100% English*. They asked me to do a genealogical DNA test for it. The 'shock' reveal was their claim that I am eight per cent African. Their expert said the "probable" explanation was a single black ancestor six generations back on my dad's mother's side. Were we the Bushell-Men of the Kalahari? I'd be delighted if it were true. But it isn't. Their science was flawed, and their conclusions were at best misleading and at worst deceitful.

In the original email from production company Wall To Wall, it said quite clearly: "It is important to stress that these tests are ... *incapable of identifying any personal family data.*" (My emphasis). There were two ancestry tests, one going back 10,000 years, the other 20,000 years – when the UK was covered in ice and no one lived here. From that perspective, every one of us is 'foreign'. The tests also have a 28 per cent margin of error for European DNA, and the same DNA has been shown to produce radically different results. To mean anything they'd have to test me, my parents and my grandparents. Without that kind of genealogical investigation they couldn't possibly make such claims about an ancestor 200 years ago – as well they knew. But logic and science went out of the window for a staged TV moment, which didn't work on me because I wasn't shocked or bothered.

Suspect science and a hidden agenda produced the kind of sneering exercise that C4 were after. Presenter Andrew Graham-Dixon interviewed me at length twice, but none of the things I said about English history, English social achievements (unions, parliament, and habeas corpus) or the English cause made the cut, because all they wanted were Alf Garnett-type quotes. They built up a straw man and then demolished it.

It was a pointless exercise, clearly politically inspired. And you could apply exactly the same tests to the French or Italians and get very similar results, yet no one questions their right to nationhood. Only the English liberal-Left beat themselves up about patriotism ...

I stood for parliament twice – not because I have any ambition to be a politician, but to use my small degree of fame to help draw attention to the unfairness created by the Barnett formula and the West Lothian question (all explained on my website). The English have become second-class citizens in the UK; our taxes are used to subsidise better health care and education for the Scots. It's blatantly unfair to English voters. Scotland and Wales have their own Parliament and Assembly, but they are still over-represented in the House of Commons. Scottish and Welsh MPs preside over English matters. English MPs have no reciprocal right. The Barnett formula gives about one-third extra spending to Scotland for EQUAL need. The set-up is out of kilter, and the only constitutionally workable solution is the creation of an English parliament. But, of course, that wouldn't mean a light while real political power is being siphoned off by Brussels ... and if you want to read more of that sort of thing, take a look at *The World According to Garry Bushell*.

I have carried on writing books throughout the last decade. These include *Two-Faced*, the follow-up to *The Face*, *Cockney Reject* – Jeff Turner's authorised autobiography, and *Hoolies*, which tells the story of Britain's youth cults, with special reference to the cult revival that followed punk. I've written two short horror stories for Comet Press, a New York publishing house, and I'm just putting the finishing touches to Jimmy Jones's biography too. Sometime I'll get around to writing the third part of the Harry Tyler/Face trilogy.

TV producers don't come knocking as often as they used to, but the stuff I get offered tends to be more challenging – shows like *The Enemy Within* and *The Execution of Gary Glitter*. Four years ago, Classic Pictures shot a DVD of *Bushell on the Box*, including the sketches that ITV banned, such as the tongue-in-cheek 'How to Cure a Lesbian', starring the excellent Dave Legeno who went on to play Fenrir Greyback in the Harry Potter movies. I admit now that I wrote the bedroom sketch scenes for me and sexy impressionist Francine Lewis merely to satisfy a private *fantasy*. In bed Fran joked, "You're ever so well endowed." I said, "You're pulling my leg, love."

Several small channels are keen on recommissioning the show, and that may still happen. It currently lives on as an occasional web-cast, and I've been doing a pod-cast for Total Rock Radio for the past four years, showcasing unsigned or small-label bands. It's meant to be good-humoured, but one show featured a row between two of my old mates, left-wing ex-punk Rhoda Dakar from the Specials and mod legend Dave Cairns of Secret Affair. Rhoda had the hump when she met us in the Grapes and Dave was reading *The Sun*. "I only read *Liberation*," she said, sneeringly and not a little pretentiously. On the show she turned on Dave over the 1979 Affair song, which stated, "We hate the punk elite," and he held his own. It was glorious stuff. I like Rhoda, but she is utterly nuts. She almost wrecked a pilot I was filming at my home because Dave Courtney was there and she claimed he encouraged knife crime. Dave actually campaigns against it.

Dave's mate Steve Whale still meets up for a regular curry night. A few years ago he brought Lars Frederiksen from Rancid to have a beer with me in a Sidcup pub. Lars seemed a bit quiet and drank coffee while we rabbited on. Later, in the car, he welled up about how much my articles in *Sounds* had meant to him when he was a kid. If it weren't for *Sounds*, he said, he'd be dead. I didn't know what to say. I was flattered, of course, but also humbled. The guy is brilliant, a modern punk legend; I was chuffed to have connected with him in any way.

As well as my own band, I am now managing Leah McCaffrey and New York's Maninblack – an aggressive, radical, Oi-influenced outfit mixing hi-tech synth and lo-fi Streetpunk whose debut EP comes out on Contra Records later this year. I'm helping out as an unpaid consultant on a great new female-fronted Streetpunk band called The Blades, whom Steve Whale is producing. And I've started work on my first solo album, which will be largely ska, with guest stars including lovely, bubbly Jennie Matthias from the Belle Stars and former Bad Manners star Nick Welsh, also known as King Hammond.

Bizarrely, as I write, my attention has been drawn to *Shotgun Harley,* a parody of 1980s police TV shows. It features a two-fisted, womanising cop, and is 'written by and starring Gary Bushell'. This turns out to be the nom de stage of real-life Canadian comedy actor Jason Jones, who appears on US TV's *The Daily Show*. It's irony gone mad. I've been caught up in a postmodern identity spiral.

I have stuck a toe into the waters of stand-up over the years. I started with an eight-minute spot at Stringfellow's in October 1995, which *Private Eye* sarcastically referred to as "Footlightsy". And some of my material is featured on the *Bushell on the Box* DVD. But those stories are best left for the next book.

In 2009 I also ventured into the world of after-dinner speaking, but not in the conventional sense. Oh no. That would have been too easy/sensible. Instead, I teamed up with Jeff Turner of the Cockney Rejects and Mickey Pugh in an 'Audience With' set-up at East Ham Working Men's Club. Not too surprisingly, the audience consisted largely of hardcore West Ham hooligans who weren't that interested in my Ritchie Blackmore stories – I think they thought he played for Palace. One or two of them looked as if they'd be hard pressed to spell Oxo backwards. Jeff was electric though, a natural orator. His stories worked a treat – who would ever have thought that one day the Battle of Birmingham would ever be seen as the good old days?

Jeff's spot went down like a UKIP plane and we were looking forward to the final section, where we both sat on stage and took questions from the audience. Disaster ensued.

A fella at the bar asked which decade had been better for music, the seventies or the sixties. Jeff said the seventies. It was an innocent question, and Jeff's answer was uncontroversial given that he'd been six in 1970. But an old Canning Town drunk took angry exception to it. The bloke was 58, and approximately as sober as The Blood on a beano. He came towards the stage jabbing a finger at Jeff. I tried to calm him down, firstly by agreeing that the sixties had been better because of Tamla and ska, but he wouldn't shut up. "Maybe you mean the 1860s, mate," I said, trying to defuse the situation. But the guy kept coming. I glanced at Jeff and I could see in his eyes that he'd had enough. As the nuisance ranted and raved from the audience, Jeff got out of his chair, leaned forward and smacked him one on the chin. It wasn't a hard punch, but it was enough to send him reeling backwards. Immediately, the four blokes he was with stood up, at which point the twenty-strong Geggus clan also stood up – and stormed towards them, with Mickey at the head. It looked like a barroom brawl was about to break out. Mercifully, the guys with 'Trappy' sat straight back down again. "Quick, Mick," I whispered to Pughy. "Move to the raffle." And that was it. Our first and last after-dinner speaking experience. I'm not doing another one without body armour.

And so there you have it. My story. You can still see the column every week in the *Daily Star Sunday*, or on my website, garry-bushell.co.uk, which has a comprehensive list of all my books, as well as a more political blog. You can see The Gonads live or buy the records from the-gonads.co.uk. The madness will carry on as long as I do.

My ambition is still the same as it always was: to bump into Pamela Anderson – very, very slowly.

PS: Channel 4's interest in my family did give me the impetus to shake the tree and see what nuts fell down. On my mum's side, Nin's dad John Jonathan Wager had worked at the lino works in Greenwich, and her Poplar-born mum May Thomas, had been in service. Nin's granddad Samuel was a labourer from Welling, and her paternal grandmother was Irish. Johnny Barker's dad Fred was a painter and decorator from Hackney, and his mum Mary Edwards was a parlourmaid from Cwmaman, South Wales, whose brothers were all miners.

On George's side, his dad Fred was a milkman and a house painter from Dartford. Fred's mum Emily had been in service, and his dad Alfred had loads of jobs including milkman, railway porter and harbour man. Emily's mum Jane Hawkins was a maid, and her dad Tom May was a painter at Chatham dockyard. His maternal granddad Harry May had been a labourer, his uncle, also called Harry May, had died in France during the First World War. It's interesting gear, but it's still a mighty long way from Africa.

Coming in
Bushell On The Rampage II

The Punk Years: The Clash, The Ruts, Skids, Splodge, Dead Kennedys.

The Ska Years: Madness, The Specials, The Selecter, Bad Manners, Judge Dread.

The Comedy Years: Jim Davidson, Freddie Starr, Howard Stern, Benny Hill, Harry Hill, The Pub Landlord, Bernard Manning, Frank Carson, Rob Newman, Bob Monkhouse, Frank Skinner, Bradley Walsh and the Funny Old Bastards.

The Showbiz Years: Engelbert, Brian Conley, Bruce Forsyth, Michael Crawford, The Nolan Sisters, Shane Richie, Davro, Pasquale, Gary Beadle, the great Butlins Festival of The Sixties.

More Rock 'n' Roll Years: Iron Maiden, Def Leppard, Thin Lizzy, Gary Moore in Japan, Twisted Sister, Rose Tattoo, Sigue Sigue Sputnik.

The Radio Years: Virgin, TalkSPORT and Total Rock.

Also by Garry Bushell

Dance Craze – The 2-Tone Story (1981); *Iron Maiden: Running Free - the Official Story of Iron Maiden*, with Ross Halfin (Zomba Books, 1984); *Twisted Sister: The First Official Book*, with Mark Weiss (Cherry Lane Music, 1985); *Ozzy Osbourne: Diary of a Madman*, with Mick Wall (Zomba Books, 1986); *The Best of Garry's Goofs* (Amalgamated Book Services, 1992); *The Face* (Blake Publishing, 2001); *King of Telly – The Best of Bushell on the Box* (BlooZoo, 2002); *Two-Faced* (Blake Publishing, 2003); *Cockney Reject,* with Jeff Turner (Blake Publishing, 2005); *The World According to Garry Bushell* (Metro Books, 2008); *1,001 Reasons Why EastEnders Is Pony!* (Pennant Books, 2009); *"I Had a Good Eight Inches Last Night": The Book of Outrageous TV Gaffes* (Pennant Books, 2009); *Hoolies: True Stories of Britain's Biggest Street Battles* (John Blake Publishing, 2010), *Now This Is A Very True Story* (John Blake Publishing, 2010).

www.apexpublishing.co.uk